THE LANGUAGE OF LITERATURE
General Editor: N. F. Blake
Professor of English Language and Lingui
University of Sheffield

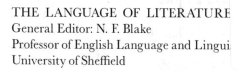

THE LANGUAGE OF LITERATURE

General Editor: N. F. Blake
Professor of English Language and Linguistics
University of Sheffield

Published titles

An Introduction to the Language of Literature	N. F. Blake
The Language of Old and Middle English Poetry	G. A. Lester
The Language of Shakespeare	N. F. Blake
The Language of Chaucer	David Burnley
The Language of Wordsworth and Coleridge	Frances Austin
The Language of Irish Literature	Loreto Todd
The Language of D. H. Lawrence	Allan Ingram
The Language of Thomas Hardy	Raymond Chapman
The Language of James Joyce	Katie Wales
The Language of Drama	David Birch
The Lnaguage of Jane Austen	Myra Stokes
The Language of George Orwell	Roger Fowler
The Language of Twentieth Century Poetry	Leslie Jeffries

Series Standing Order

If you would like to receive future titles in this series as they are
published, you can make use of our standing order facility. To place a
standing order please contact your bookseller or, in case of difficulty,
write to us at the address below with your name and address and the
name of the series. Please state with which title you wish to begin your
standing order. (If you live outside the United Kingdon we may not
have the rights for your area, in which case we will forward your order
to the publisher concerned.)

Customer Services Department, Macmillan Distribution Ltd
Houndmills, Basingstoke, Hampshire, RG21 6XS, England.

THE LANGUAGE OF OLD AND MIDDLE ENGLISH POETRY

G. A. LESTER

MACMILLAN

First published 1996 by
MACMILLAN PRESS LTD
Houndsmill, Basingstoke, Hampshire, RG21 6XS
and London
Companies and representatives
throughout the world

ISBN 0-333-48846-6 hardcover
ISBN 0-333-48847-4 paperback

A catalogue record for this book is available
from the British Library

10   9   8   7   6   5   4   3   2   1
05   04   03   02   01   00   99   98   97   96

Typeset in Great Britain by
Aarontype Limited, Easton, Bristol

Printed in Malaysia

Contents

Acknowledgements		vii
1	Introduction	1
2	The Social Context	11
3	The Literary and Linguistic Context	26
4	Old English Poetic Diction	47
5	Old English Verse: Structure and Organisation	67
6	Middle English Poetic Diction	88
7	Middle English Verse: Structure and Organisation	107
8	Linguistic Varieties	131
9	Examples of Analysis: *Beowulf* and *Sir Gawain and the Green Knight*	148
Notes		166
Bibliography and List of Works Cited		170
Index		176

Acknowledgements

A small book on so large a subject as the language of Old and Middle English poetry may seem an ambitious and even foolhardy undertaking. However, as I explain in the Introduction, there is something to be gained from this broad approach. It is inevitable that I have had to draw heavily on the work and ideas of others, particularly authors, former teachers, colleagues and students. Had I not experienced their scholarship, interest and enthusiasm, over a number of years, I could not have written a book such as this, which, in view of the breadth of its subject matter and the narrowness of its page limit, is inevitably a synthesis of my own ideas and what I consider valuable in what I have read and heard. Where I have used specific published material I have acknowledged the debt, but generally I have tried to keep references to a minimum, at the same time providing sufficient information to suggest approaches to more detailed study for the non-specialists and general readers for whom this book is principally intended. Without doubt there will be errors, omissions and over-simplifications, for which I take absolute responsibility, as is customary, while hoping that the rest of the material will be enough to stimulate insights and new trains of thought into medieval English poetry.

SHEFFIELD   G. A. LESTER

1 Introduction

English, like any living language, is constantly changing, so the terms 'Old English', 'Middle English' and 'Modern English' are little more than convenient labels for dividing the continuum into manageable parts. Language change, of course, does not proceed at a steady and regular pace, and at times there are major developments, some of them resulting from important social changes, which encourage us to think in terms of different phases.

One such phase is associated with the Anglo-Saxons, whose earliest surviving written records date from about the year 700. The vernacular language they spoke and wrote, which we now refer to as 'Old English', came to an end largely as a result of the Norman Conquest of England in 1066. The change, naturally, was not immediate, but written evidence suggests that by the year 1100 (or 1150 at the latest) a new phase, involving substantial changes, had been established. Middle English in its turn was subject to very great pressures in the fifteenth century. These stemmed less from a single political event than from a variety of factors, including the far-reaching sound change known as the Great Vowel Shift, the rise in the importance of London with the consequent feeling that London English was somehow a standard to be aspired to, and the spread of printing, which, at the literary level, helped consolidate the increasing uniformity of English. After about 1500, therefore, the language is said to be in its early 'modern' stage, although anyone acquainted with, say, an original, unmodernised text of Shakespeare will know how unlike present-day English the language then was.

It is relevant also to mention the term 'medieval', an adjective from the Latin *Medium Aevum*, which means 'the Middle Age'. In

1

its original sense this term relates to the period from the end of Classical Antiquity to the beginning of the Italian Renaissance, and encompasses therefore both Old English and Middle English. This is the sense in which the term will be used in this book, despite the fact that it is often now understood as referring only to the post-Conquest period.

The Anglo-Saxons who constituted the earliest English people were of Germanic origin and settled in Britain after the withdrawal of the Romans in the fifth century. The migration was protracted and piecemeal, and the name 'Anglo-Saxon' was not used of any tribal group on the mainland of Europe. The earliest settlements were of small tribal or family units, so a general name was not at first relevant and did not become widely used until the ninth century. The term 'Anglo-Saxon' was first used to distinguish the English Saxons from the Old Saxons of the Germanic homelands. Alfred the Great (d.899), himself a Saxon, referred to his language as *Englisc*, i.e. 'Angle-ish', and his people as *Angelcynn*, 'the Angle-race', so it appears that the distinction between Angles and Saxons was even at that time regarded as unimportant.

Old and Middle English language is widely studied, both for its own sake, as illustrative of the early history of English, and as the key which unlocks the literature of the times. Linguistic studies of individual works are common, and indeed a section on the language usually forms part of the standard introduction of editions of medieval texts. In addition, there are several excellent books on the history of the English language in general, some of which are mentioned in the Bibliography. This book will therefore not attempt to go over the same ground, but will be more concerned with those aspects which most affect poetry, particularly the lexis (vocabulary), semantics (the meaning of words) and syntax (structural matters such as varied clause elements and their effect on style, narrative pace, cohesion etc.), rather than phonology (sounds) and morphology (the internal structure of words, such as their 'stems' and inflexional suffixes), which are excluded except where relevant. A linguistic overview of a whole genre, still less one as broad as medieval English poetry, is rarely attempted, and may seem to be an unrealistic aim for this book. But a broad survey can be as enlightening as a minute analysis, and can highlight the continuity within Old and Middle English as well as the differences and changes of direction. Above all, a general study is a sensible starting point for those who may wish to go on to look at the language of medieval English poetry more closely.

This book is aimed, therefore, at the general reader and beginning student. It assumes prior knowledge neither of Old and Middle English language nor of the literature, nor does it presuppose anything more than a basic understanding of traditional linguistic concepts and terminology. Anything else will be explained.

Two contextualising chapters (2 and 3) come at the start. The first deals with the social context, including the origins of Anglo-Saxon England, paganism and Christianity, the Scandinavian settlement and its effects, relationships with France, the influence of the church, social classes, daily life, the court and the countryside, literacy, and the medieval world-view. The second looks at the literary and linguistic context, including dialects, Scandinavian and French influence, the rise, suppression and re-emergence of English as a language of literature, poetry in society, literacy and the making of manuscripts. It also reviews briefly the Old and Middle English literature which now survives.

Four fundamental chapters (4 to 7) then follow. The first is on Old English poetic diction, and deals mainly with lexis and some related matters of semantics. The next concerns the organisation of Old English verse, and deals mostly with syntax and figures of rhetoric. The remaining two cover similar ground in the context of Middle English, except that Chapter 7 additionally considers the fundamental differences between rhyme and alliteration.

There is a separate chapter (8) on linguistic varieties of medieval English, including regional and other varieties, the effects of the rise of a written linguistic standard, colloquial and aureate language, formality and informality, registers, and some of the effects of translation into English from French, Latin and other languages. And in the final chapter (9), following the normal practice of books of this series, passages from Old and Middle English poems are selected for specimen analysis.

One important matter needs to be borne in mind at this introductory stage. All the works we shall be discussing, except for a few from the very end of our period, survive in manuscript rather than in print. This has implications which we would be well advised to consider at the outset.

If we wish today to learn the publication details of a book, all we usually have to do is turn to the reverse of the title page. There we usually find the name and address of the publisher, information as to who holds the copyright, when the book was published, and whether and when it has been reprinted or issued as a revised edition. There may be cataloguing data summarising biographical information about the author and specifying the subject classification for use in libraries. And there will probably be an International Standard Book Number (ISBN), enabling it to be precisely identified. The printer may be specified, and even the size and style of the typeface. The implication will be that the author has provided the typescript (today often on computer disk) and that he or she has received at least one set of proofs, corrected them, and given approval for printing to proceed. The publisher will have arranged a standard binding, and may have consulted the author about the design of the cover or dust-jacket. In all, the published book can be assumed to represent the author's approved work right down to the last comma and full stop.

Nothing could be further from the circumstances of the publication of medieval English works in manuscript. The author was frequently anonymous, as were the scribes and other artisans involved in reproducing the text. He or she may not have intended the work ever to be written down, and in some cases may not even have been able to read and write. The date of publication is rarely known. Once a work went into circulation it was commonly regarded as something which was, as it were, in the public domain and could be modified at will. It might be copied, curtailed or expanded. The language might be altered, by design or by accident. And the work might be bound, either by itself or as part of an anthology, or left unbound in the small parchment or paper booklets which were the basic units with which the scribes worked. In short, the text which appears in a modern printed edition may be far removed from what the author intended.

For most of the period book production in England was organised on a local basis and the bulk of the work was done in the scriptoria of monasteries. From the fourteenth century there are signs of commercial speculation, and it was at this time that publishing centres, such as Westminster, started to assume importance. It was here in 1476 that Caxton set up his press and that many of the other early printers had their premises. The history of book production in England, however, is not a straightforward progression towards centralisation, for as early as the ninth century King

Alfred had issued translations of key works from Latin into English for dissemination via the monasteries. These, and another centrally regulated work, the *Anglo-Saxon Chronicle*, were predominantly in prose, and the signs are that poetry was dealt with more randomly.

Random factors have also determined the texts which have survived to the present, and the further back we go the greater the number of hazards. Even if a work happened to get written down it was subject to many dangers, among them damage through neglect (e.g. by damp) or through deliberate destruction (e.g. at the Reformation). Destruction by fire was a constant danger, a fate which almost overtook the manuscript of the great Anglo-Saxon poem *Beowulf* in 1731, which was rescued only in the nick of time and not before the flames had eaten away at the text. As books became old and the English language changed, there was a likelihood that they would become less appreciated as they were less well understood. Old books were therefore sometimes cut up for use in the bindings of newer books. One of the four great manuscripts of Anglo-Saxon poetry, the Exeter Book, was used for a while as a cutting board. The result of all these accidents and acts of destruction is that those which survive cannot be regarded as representative of the English books in existence and use in the medieval period.

In any case, we should not forget that works in English were very much in the minority in medieval England. Most were in Latin, which was an international language, the use of which was therefore more likely to secure a wide readership. Other reasons why Latin was assumed to be the natural language for books include the long tradition of scholarship in that language, the fact that Latin was the language of the medieval church (which also controlled education) and that Latin, being a dead language, was not subject to the dialectal variation and diachronic change which undermined the status and usefulness of the vernacular languages. Although writings in Old English were far more extensive than other contemporary vernacular literatures, output was minute in comparison with that of Latin. The situation was similar with regard to Middle English, except that it was complicated by the introduction of French, which was of considerably higher status than English. Rich and influential people in England patronised works in French, usually in the Anglo-Norman dialect, and a flourishing literature developed. Latin continued to flourish, and is the language of by far the greatest number of works produced in England in the period 1100–1500, followed by French and then – far behind – English.

King Alfred's translations from Latin into English were part of an educational policy by means of which he hoped that talented young men might be identified who could go on to learn Latin and take religious orders. So even at that time the ability to read and write in English was viewed mainly as a stage towards something better. However, a strong tradition of copying works in English developed in the Anglo-Saxon monasteries, and it was here that the 30,000 or so lines of extant Old English verse were probably written down. Since Alfred and most of the later Anglo-Saxon kings belonged to the dynasty of Wessex, it was a form of the West Saxon dialect which was used in these works. Words from other dialects which are found in the poetry suggest either that non-West Saxons have been involved in composing or copying it, or that a special 'poetic' variety of English (sometimes called a literary *koiné;*, i.e. 'a common language') had developed which transcended dialectal boundaries. This variety of Old English, as we shall see, was highly artificial, and its continuance depended on the unbroken support of the monastic establishment and the existence of rich and influential Anglo-Saxon patrons.

After the Norman Conquest all this came to an end. The English were removed from positions of power in government, in the church, and in other spheres of society. With the disappearance of English patrons, the composition and reproduction of English works came to an abrupt end, with the exception that the copying of religious prose works, which was an established monastic duty, continued into the Middle English period and eventually contributed to a new prose tradition. In Chapter 3 we shall discuss further the emergence of English as a literary language in the thirteenth and fourteenth centuries, but an important linguistic consequence needs to be mentioned here. There was after the Conquest neither an agreed literary variety nor a general 'standard' form of English. Consequently Middle English poetry was written down in a wide range of different regional dialects, a situation which only begins to change with the emergence of preferred forms of literary English towards the end of the fourteenth century.

Since an English text did not have the same authoritative status and permanence as a Latin text, scribes and copyists considered themselves at liberty to make changes. If they were reproducing a work from an old manuscript, for instance, they would be likely to modernise the language, which in its written form was not then as stable as it is today. Similarly, should the dialect of the exemplar be one with which the transcriber did not feel comfortable, or which he thought would not suit his patron, he would substitute familiar words and forms. Alterations of this sort can sometimes be detected or suspected where a rhyme is defective. An example occurs in the thirteenth-century interlude *De Clerico et Puella*, where in the couplet

And myn *Auy Mary*	*Ave Maria*	
(For my scynnes hic am sory)	*sins I am sorry*	(73–4)

the rhyme can be restored if the (presumably original) dialect form *sary* is substituted for *sory.* This would be in line with the form of other words in the interlude (such as *hame* 'home', which rhymes with *dame*) in which the vowel is said to be 'unrounded'. Rounding of long *a* at this time was a feature of more southerly dialects, not of the North-East Midland dialect of this text, so it seems likely that *sory* has been introduced by a copyist who was more familiar with the rounded form and who gave no thought to the damage its introduction would do to the rhyme.

Nor is it only within manuscripts that modification occurred. Books were scarce and many people could not read them, so those who memorised and recited poems also played a part in the process of change. The three surviving manuscripts of the early fourteenth-century romance *Sir Orfeo* illustrate the point:

King Orfeo knewe wele bi þan	*by then*
His steward was a trewe man	
And loued him as he auȝt to do,	*ought*
And stont vp, and seyt þus: 'Lo!'	*stands; says thus*

(Auchinleck MS, lines 553–6)

The kyng beheld þe stewerd þan	
And seyd he was a trew man	
And louyd hym as he auȝte to do,	
And sterte vp, and seyd: 'Lo!'	*started*

(Ashmole MS, lines 546–9)

Þe kyng behelde þe steward þan
And wyst he was a trewe man.
To hym he seyde, without lesyng: *without a lie*
'Syr,' he seyde, 'Yam Orpheo þe kyng.'

                              (Harley MS, lines 492–5)

The many omissions, contractions and transpositions of the Harley version, especially in the last hundred lines of the poem, have led to the suggestion that the text in that manuscript may have been taken down from the memory of a minstrel (Bliss 1966, xvi). The weak rhyming tag *without lesyng* (without a lie), for instance, could be an attempt to patch up a misremembered couplet.[1] Whatever the explanation, if either the Harley or the Ashmole manuscript had survived alone, we would have a very different appreciation of the poem than we have from the far superior version in the Auchinleck manuscript.

The date of the Auchinleck manuscript is about 1330, Harley early fifteenth-century, and Ashmole after 1488. However, it is not always the case that the earliest manuscript contains the best version. In any case, many medieval poems and manuscripts are difficult to date. Furthermore, we should also be clear what we mean by 'date', since the date of the original work will differ from the date(s) of subsequent versions and from the date(s) of the manuscript(s). Nor should we assume that differing versions are necessarily the result of outside interference, for authors themselves sometimes spent many years reworking their material. The long fourteenth-century poem *Piers Plowman*, which survives in three distinct versions, is a clear example. All sorts of internal and external pieces of evidence sometimes have to be drawn upon before a tentative date can be ascribed. As we go further towards the beginning of English literature the situation becomes more difficult, and most Old English poems can be dated only approximately. Present-day readers should beware of the firm dates which are sometimes assumed in older critical works on the subject, for recent studies have suggested that linguistic dating criteria are more open to doubt than was formerly believed. *Beowulf*, for example, is now dated by some as early as the eighth century and by others as late as the eleventh.

The present-day reader of Old and Middle English poetry needs to remember that what he or she sees on the page has already gone through a sort of 'filtering' process by the editor, who will have made certain assumptions which will inevitably direct the reader's response. A large number of medieval English poems – the entire corpus, in fact, in Old English – are without original titles, their present ones having been given by editors. The modern titles of the Middle English lyrics even today vary from one edition to another. The nature and integrity of a work may be in doubt, even if the manuscript is not defective. It was the usual practice in Old English collections to use extra spacing between poems, with large capitals to mark the beginning and perhaps the word *finit* or *amen* to mark the end. But even basic indications such as these are sometimes not found, as with the Old English poetic *Riddles*, about which there is disagreement as to the exact number in the collection. Other poems were never completed, such as Chaucer's *Canterbury Tales*, which the author had been working on for at least fifteen years before his death in 1400. At this time the draft version probably consisted of a collection of completed and half-written poems, false starts, outlines and notes, which a succession of editors have subsequently grouped into ten or twelve fragments or sections. It is easy to forget that the ordering of these sections is a matter of editorial conjecture, and that hypotheses about the dynamics of the pilgrim group, such as the suggestion that some tales are told in response to others, may therefore be seriously flawed.

Even where the issues are less contentious, the reader's response is constantly being predetermined by the editorial process. Old English verse, for example, was written in the manuscripts in continuous lines like prose, and has to be arranged in lines according to predetermined metrical principles. In manuscripts of both periods the lack of a standardised spelling system confuses the situation, and editors have to make decisions as to the extent to which they should modernise, as well as how far they should go in identifying and correcting mistakes. Punctuation is also sporadic and often seems to be arbitrary, as are capitalisation and word-division. The certainty that the present-day reader expects in such matters is alien to the medieval way of thinking. And in any case such certainty may not be appropriate to times when poetry was intended less for the few who could read than for the many who might be expected to listen to poems being read aloud or recited from memory. In such circumstances the ambivalence and richness of meaning, which our punctuation system often eradicates, may well have increased the pleasure and quality of the listeners' response.

Readers of this chapter may be thinking 'What does it matter?' and I can best answer this by quoting the words of Dorothy White-lock from her book *The Audience of 'Beowulf'*:

> There may be persons who are content to study the impression that the poem makes now, concerning them-selves only with what has survived the changes in our civilization and methods of thought, and caring little that ignorance of what the author counted on his audi-ence knowing robs many of his remarks of their point. The poet has perhaps conveyed something of perma-nent value that is above the accidents of time and place and has survived the ravages of the centuries. I think he has. It is not for me to discuss the legitimacy of such an approach, but it is not such persons that I am addressing. For my own part, I should like to know what effect the poet was consciously striving to produce on the men of his own time; I want to see if by studying these men we can get any nearer to that knowledge.
>
> (Whitelock 1951, 2–3)

Many medieval poems, and the majority from the Old English period, are poems without a context. They exist now in isolation from the society which produced them. The presuppositions which a present-day reader brings to a piece of Old or Middle Eng-lish verse will colour that person's appreciation of it. It is right that this should be so, but not to the exclusion of historical considera-tions. Understanding the language of Old and Middle English poetry is, therefore, not just a matter of 'translating' medieval works into a digestible form. The language was itself the subtlest expression of the whole culture. To understand all its complexities is an impossible task, but to make the attempt immeasurably increases the pleasure and value of a reader's experience.

2   The Social Context

The origins of the Anglo-Saxons cannot be precisely identified, but a number of the tribes from which they were formed came from northern Germany and part of present-day Denmark. The Venerable Bede, the great eighth-century historian of the English, describes the first settlers as Angles, Saxons and Jutes. The Angles, he understood, settled in Britain north of the River Thames far into what is now Scotland, the Saxons took land south of the Thames and also on the north side of the river Estuary (whence the county name 'Essex', i.e. 'East Saxons'), and the Jutes, he claimed, occupied Kent, the Isle of Wight and the mainland opposite the island. The evidence of place names and archaeology shows that this is an oversimplification, for there were others, such as Frisians and Swedes. This complex mix of peoples developed a distinctive and homogeneous language and culture, which none the less reflected strong links with the rest of the Germanic world.

From these small beginnings the history of Anglo-Saxon England is one of gradual consolidation and shifting fortunes. As time passed the original small social units became welded more tightly together, eventually into kingdoms, of which one or another achieved supremacy at varying times, though it is never relevant to think in terms of 'nationhood'. At first the people of Kent were the most prosperous, probably because they were well placed to engage in trade with the mainland of Europe. Their pagan graves contain gold and garnet jewellery, precious weapons and fine domestic objects, which cannot be matched anywhere else in England in the fifth and sixth centuries. The East Anglian kingdom was rich and powerful in the seventh century, and from the ship-burial at Sutton Hoo near Ipswich we have the regalia and property of one of its kings, which are breathtakingly magnificent. In the later seventh and early eighth centuries, after the introduction of Christianity, power shifted to the Northumbrian kingdom, which became a centre of learning unrivalled in Europe, from which fine illuminated manuscripts, churches and sculptured stone monuments survive to this day. Ascendancy passed in the later eighth century to the Midland kingdom of Mercia, whose king Offa proudly claimed to be 'King of the whole of Britain'. But Northumbrian and Mercian power was undermined by the invasions of the Vikings, most of whom were Danish. Only Wessex managed to hold out against them. King Alfred, who ruled from 871 to 899, organised military resistance, and he and his successors won back land seized by the Danes and consolidated their hold by setting up a series of 'boroughs', or strongholds, throughout the land, a number of which have now grown into substantial towns. Because of West Saxon dominance in politics and society, most of the institutions of government came to be organised and controlled by them. Most of the surviving written records from Anglo-Saxon England are therefore West Saxon in origin, and consequently written in the West Saxon dialect.

No written records would have been made in the first place had it not been for the conversion of the Anglo-Saxons to Christianity, for this brought not only the knowledge of reading, writing and the making of books but also, in the monasteries, conditions of peace and stability in which scholarship could flourish. We know very little about the pagan beliefs of the Anglo-Saxons when they arrived in Britain, for later Christian writers generally thought these matters too shocking to describe. The early settlers probably engaged in fertility cults, as we know some of their continental ancestors had done. The pre-Christian calendar included some interesting names, such as 'Month of Cakes' (February), 'Month of Sacrifices' (November), and 'Yule' (December and January), while March and April were named after two goddesses, *Hreda* and *Eostre* (the source of our 'Easter'). Four of the names of the old deities – *Tiw, Woden, Thunor* and *Frig* – are known because they survive in place names and in the names of days of the week. They are obviously related to the Scandinavian *Tyr, Othin, Thor* and *Frigg*, but it would be wrong to assume that the beliefs about them in fifth- and sixth-century England were similar to those which were written down in the Norse *Eddas* and sagas about six hundred years later. Other evidence of religious activity comes from place names such as Harrow (a sanctuary) and Weedon (a shrine), and more can be gleaned from the Anglo-Saxon charms, in some of which a residue of pagan ritual is to be found, mingled with Christian belief and practice. The best archaeological evidence about the early religion is from pagan graves, especially those in which the body was interred along with grave goods, such as weapons or domestic objects, which imply a belief in some sort of afterlife. In recent years excavations at Sutton Hoo have produced suggestions of human sacrifice, and at Yeavering in Northumbria evidence has come to light of a building which was probably a pagan temple.

In 597 a Christian mission from Rome, led by Augustine, landed in Kent, where within a year Ethelbert, the Kentish king, received baptism. The conversion of the heathen English was under way, but it was a long time before it was complete, and there were many lapses. A Christian mission from Kent to Northumbria met with initial success, and the Northumbrian King Edwin was converted in 627. His death in battle five years later brought a reversion to paganism in his kingdom. When Christianity was reintroduced in the north it was by missionaries from the Scottish island of Iona, who founded their first monastery in 635 on the island of Lindisfarne off the north-east coast. These men followed the practices of the Celtic church, which differed from those of Rome in matters of ecclesiastical organisation and in the computation of the date of Easter. For a while the differences between the Roman and Celtic factions were a source of difficulty, but they were settled at a synod held at Whitby, Yorkshire, in 663, when it was agreed that the Roman practice was part of a tradition stretching back to St Peter and should therefore prevail. In the secure years following the synod Christian Northumbria reached the summit of its power and productivity. But the conversion from paganism proceeded at an uneven rate, and Sussex did not embrace the new faith until 681.

Conversion in most cases began at the top of the social scale. One of the means by which ordinary people might be taught the faith was through the parish priests, but finding suitable educated people for the priesthood was a constant problem. An approach which was in many ways more fruitful was the founding of monasteries. Kings and noblemen often granted land and money for this purpose, and some monastic houses in the course of time grew to be influential as centres of learning, among them Lindisfarne, Monkwearmouth and Jarrow (Bede's monastery) in the seventh and eighth centuries, and Winchester and Canterbury in the tenth and eleventh. Winchester and Canterbury owe much of their reputation to the strong movement in the tenth century to reform monastic communities on Benedictine principles, as a result of which they strengthened their links abroad, especially with monasteries in France, and became pre-eminent as centres of book production.

As to living conditions in secular society, domestic buildings ranged from sunken-floored huts to impressive halls, and were invariably built of wood with roofs of thatch or shingle. The prefer-ence for wood is reflected in the Old English word for 'to build', which is *getimbrian* (cf.'timber'). Archaeological evidence is scanty, usually consisting only of post-holes or trenches, but literary refer-ences to buildings sometimes bring the picture to life. Much of the poem *Beowulf*, for instance, is set in a royal hall, where the king and his retainers feast, drink and enjoy convivial warrior society until the ravages of the troll Grendel put a stop to it all. However, the society depicted in the literature is aristocratic and idealised, and bears little relation to the life which most of the population endured in the villages and towns. Daily life was hard. Ordinary people were concerned to know how to keep sickness at bay, where the next meal was coming from, how to balance their own agricul-tural needs with service to their lords, and where to obtain redress if a neighbour's ox broke down a hedge and strayed into a sown field or a garden. In these matters the Anglo-Saxon legal codes or the charms and medical recipes are more informative than the poetry or the literary prose.

Theirs was a subsistence economy based largely upon farming, which was organised on the 'open-field' system, whereby the land each person cultivated was not a compact holding but was scat-tered about in a number of places and worked in rotation, with the whole community collaborating over the choice of crops for the year. Farm animals were managed rather differently from today. For instance, oxen were the most common draught animals and domesticated pigs roamed woodland grubbing up acorns, while wild boars abounded in the extensive tracts of forest and provided sport as well as meat. Craftspeople such as potters, leatherworkers, smiths and woodworkers supplied both the rural and the urban economy. Women might occupy positions of influence and own and run extensive estates, but they also had traditional domestic roles, including spinning, weaving and embroidery, in the last of which Anglo-Saxon women excelled and had a high reputation throughout Europe.

We have virtually no evidence as to the social structures of pre-Christian times, but four social classes are normally distinguished in written records: kings, nobles, free peasants and slaves. The king was supreme in his kingdom, but might be subject to a more powerful neighbour. The West Saxon Athelstan, who ruled from 924 to 939, has the best claim to be considered first king of all England following his great victory over a combined force of Scots and Norsemen at an unidentified place named *Brunanburh* in 937. A king was elected by a council of great lords, but his right was considered especially strong if he could claim to trace his ancestry back to the founder of the kingdom or even, in pagan times, to one of the gods. A nobleman was distinguished from a peasant freeman both by birth and by the property he owned, usually measured in units of land called 'hides'. Some of his power might arise from an important service on behalf of the king, for instance as *ealdorman*, or governor, of a shire or as one of the king's thanes, or servants. The backbone of society was the free peasant, or churl. He inherited and owned land, had status in law, participated in the local 'folk moot' and could travel wherever he wished. Finally, at the lowest social level was the unfree man, the serf, who was regarded in law simply as property, and could therefore be bought, sold and bequeathed. A person could be born to serfdom or become enslaved through bad luck or misdemeanour. The Vikings and other enemies sometimes seized whole families to sell into slavery abroad, and in hard times a household might sell some of its members to escape starvation. Conversely, serfs might be freed as an act of charity in a person's will, though in those difficult times life might be little better for them after emancipation.

A person's social standing had important implications concerning his or her rights under the law. At this time greater weight was attached to a person's oath than to establishing the facts of an alleged crime, and the value of an oath depended upon a person's rank in society. If a king's thane, for example, were accused of murder, he could clear himself by finding twelve other king's thanes who were willing to swear on his behalf. The usual measure of a man's 'value' in law was his *wergild*, literally 'man-price'. This was originally devised as a means of mitigating the wasteful effects of feuding by allowing compensation at a fixed price to be paid for a death or injury. Classes of *wergild* varied according to place and time, but the most typical were 1200, 600 and 200 shillings, while King Alfred's laws go so far as to stipulate a fixed scale for lesser injuries, such as 30 shillings for an ear struck off, 60 for a nose and 20 for a big toe.

The three fundamental public obligations shared by all freemen were mending bridges, repairing fortresses and serving in, or contributing towards, the local militia. This was a violent society, in which the likelihood of war was ever present. By far the greatest outside threat with which the Anglo-Saxons had to contend came from the Vikings, who burst upon the scene in the late eighth century and found easy plunder in the unprotected villages and exposed monasteries. Their attacks took place over two and a half centuries, and were not all a matter of rape and pillage. They involved Danes, Norwegians and a variety of others, with differing motives and in different alliances with each other and with the native population, and they moved from an initial phase of piratical raids to a long period when land-taking was the primary goal, and then to a later stage when the aim was political conquest and when for a short time in the eleventh century England was governed by Danish kings.

It was the Danes who, of all the Scandinavians, had the greatest effect upon England. But although their military activities furnish the most graphic images, in the long run it was probably their settlements which had the most lasting influence. In 850 the Danish armies, which previously had gone home for the winter months, decided to remain in England. The *Anglo-Saxon Chronicle*, a graphic contemporary account of events, records that in 875 the Danish leader Halfdan 'shared out the lands of Northumbria, and they were engaged in ploughing and in making a living for themselves'. Soon afterwards Mercia and East Anglia were occupied by them, and in 886 Alfred was obliged to agree an area of Danish jurisdiction in the whole of eastern England north of the River Thames and east of the Roman road called Watling Street. This area, later known as the Danelaw, was won back by subsequent West Saxon kings, but not before the Danes had established their influence at every level of society. Place name evidence suggests that much of their settlement was peaceable; for instance, names in -*thorp* (a secondary settlement, an outlying farm) imply that they did not always seize established farms and villages. Their influence is signalled today not only by place names but also by distinctive agrarian patterns and by administrative divisions such as Ridings and Wapentakes, which are not found elsewhere in England. They have left archaeological evidence of their daily lives in centres such as the midland 'Five Boroughs' of Derby, Leicester, Lincoln, Nottingham and Stamford, and also especially in York. When they first came to England they were a pagan people, and it was a constant worry that they would lead the Anglo-Saxons back to heathen ways. But in time they were converted, and sculptured stone crosses are monuments to their acceptance of the new faith.

The first Scandinavian king of England was Swein, who succeeded in 1014 after a period of weak rule by Ethelred 'the Unready', whom he drove into exile. But Swein died only a few weeks later, and after a period of further struggle his son Cnut assumed the throne in 1016. Cnut proved to be a competent ruler and a supporter of the church, but was unable to establish a secure line of succession. The throne therefore soon reverted to Edward the Confessor, the last of the West Saxon kings. During the reign of Cnut Edward had lived in exile in Normandy, where he enjoyed the hospitality of Duke William. William's later claim to the throne of England rested on a promise which is supposed to have been made at this time. But on Edward's death the throne was taken by the nobleman Harold Godwineson, and William immediately made preparations for invasion. The Battle of Hastings in 1066 is one of the best known events in English history. It brought military success for William, but not before the outcome had been in the balance for much of the day. Narrow though the victory was, its effects were immediate and far-reaching.

William moved swiftly to consolidate his gains. Estates throughout England were handed out to those who had supported him, a move which led to the establishment of a complicated feudal system which was to affect every element of society. Although William saw himself as the rightful successor of Edward the Confessor and pledged to continue ancient customs and laws, he replaced men of influence in church and state with Normans. His efficient rule is exemplified by the compilation in 1086 of the vast survey of the whole country known as Domesday Book, which furnished him with an accurate account of the taxable resources of his subjects, right down to the number of plough teams and the value of local woods, mills and fisheries. Royal power was disseminated by means of writs (formerly issued in English, but now in Latin), which were usually addressed to the *shire-reeves*, or sheriffs, who had them read out and interpreted to the people. The court still moved about the country with the king, but the establishment of the treasury and exchequer in Winchester and Westminster was a sign of the process of centralisation which was to increase as London continued to grow in importance.

Domestic politics under the Normans (1066–1154) and Plantagenets (1154–1485) were extremely complicated. Memorable among them for a variety of reasons were: the anarchy under the last Norman king, Stephen, details of which are given in the last entries of one version of the *Anglo-Saxon Chronicle*; the murder of Thomas Becket in 1170 at the instigation of Henry II; the struggle for power between the kings and their magnates, especially the signing of Magna Carta by King John in 1215; the inexorable growth in the power of parliament, especially during the long reign of Edward III; the deposition of Richard II in 1399 by Henry IV; the Wars of the Roses (1455–85) between the Lancastrian successors of Henry and the adherents of Richard of York; and the victory by Henry Tudor, later Henry VII, at Bosworth in 1485, which traditionally has been taken as marking the end of the medieval period in England.

The wider political scene was dominated by fluctuations in the relationship with France. The continuing lack of English national identity is reflected in the fact that most of the early kings of post-Conquest England either could not or would not speak English. Henry I could allegedly speak it, and Henry II could apparently understand it, though he had to speak it through an interpreter; but the unrivalled language of the court was a regional and social variety known as Anglo-Norman. A landmark in relations with France was the loss of Normandy. When he was crowned in 1154 the English king Henry II ruled a great swathe of land stretching from the Scottish border right down the west of France as far as the Pyrenees. But under his descendants Richard I and John these dominions were severely reduced. The loss of Normandy in 1204 was of particular significance because it severed the material and emotional links which many of the English barons still had with their relations and with their ancestral lands in France. It brought a more insular outlook, which grew in the succeeding century into a consciousness of separate identity. When, therefore, Edward III and Henry V resumed the conquest of France, they were able to take advantage of a sense of national pride, despite the fact that their claims were hereditary. The so called 'Hundred Years War' of 1337 to 1453 between England and France was really a series of sieges, skirmishes and pitched battles in which England took on the lumbering, feudal might of France. It began with success for the English but ended with disaster for them. It brought famous English victories such as Crécy (1346) and Agincourt (1415), but also ignominious defeats as the French rallied around Joan of Arc, who was executed in 1431. By this time a third force had become involved, the powerful Duchy of Burgundy, whose Dukes held extensive land in eastern and northern France and in the Low Countries. In the fifteenth century the influence of Burgundy spread throughout the courts of Europe, and nowhere was this more strongly felt than at the court of Edward IV, where Burgundian fashions were imitated in all aspects of art, literature, manners and ceremonial.

It is a common view that there is a relationship between the pomp and ceremony with which the nobility and knights increasingly surrounded themselves and the decline in their importance as mounted soldiers on the field of battle, especially with the gradual increase in the use of gunpowder. Cannon became known in Europe in the early fourteenth century, and Edward III and Henry V used them extensively to bombard French towns into surrender. Even before the introduction of firearms the effectiveness of the crossbow and longbow had made it necessary for the armour of horse and man to be increased in thickness and weight, so that heavy cavalry came to be useful only under ideal conditions. The change is mirrored in the conventions of the tournaments, which in the thirteenth century were most likely to take the form of the mêlée, or mock battle, in which participants fought in bands of perhaps fifty or a hundred within a prescribed area. By the fourteenth century individual combat had become the norm, in the form of a mounted joust or a foot-combat. By the later fifteenth, under influence from Burgundy, fanciful elements began to appear, with a knight under an assumed name enacting a scene from romance in the pretended defence of a lady. This is a far cry from the real military service expected by William the Conqueror, in reward for which he distributed among his supporters the rich estates which were eventually to provide the resources for such extravagance.

Elaborations such as these were accompanied by changes in the theory and ethics of knighthood which we usually refer to as 'chivalry'. Once meaning simply 'the collective body of mounted and armed fighting men', the term came to refer to the knightly system of feudal times with its attendant religious, moral and social code and practices. The rise of Islam in the Mediterranean regions and the Holy Land offered the knights of medieval Christendom a collective outlet for the pursuit both of their military ambitions and their chivalric ideals. Richard I's crusading zeal led to his almost permanent absence from England, and his romantic reputation as 'the Lionheart' belies his meagre achievement.

The 'chivalry' of such knights encompassed 'courtesy', which meant generosity and consideration in dealing with others of similar rank, for in this hierarchical society good qualities and a noble demeanour were associated with the court as inevitably as unrefined, literally 'villainous', qualities were with the unfree labourers, or *villeins*. Life for the villein, or serf, remained hard throughout the Middle Ages. He was bound to the soil, so much so that he and his dependants were sold with an estate when it changed hands. He could not move home or withdraw his labour, but had to work unpaid for his lord for a specified number of days each year, providing his own oxen for the plough. When he died his best beast (and perhaps his only one) could be seized in payment of *heriot*, an ancient tax which originated in lieu of the return of weapons loaned by a lord to his men. On the other hand, he held land of his own and was free to work on it on those days of the year when his lord had no claim. And he had his share in the village meadow, pasture, woodland and waste. But life was not all work, and he and his family probably entertained themselves in traditional ways, enjoying on the village green the communal celebrations of Twelfth Night, May Day, Midsummer and Lammas (Harvest Thanksgiving). There would have been much drinking of ale, as well perhaps as such things as wrestling, putting-the-shot, archery, cock-fighting, bear-baiting, and the like. And on Shrove Tuesday there may have been 'football', though the name is not recorded until 1409 and the game would have been very different from that which we now know (probably more like the general scrimmage which still takes place annually at Ashbourne in Derbyshire and Corfe Castle in Dorset).

The last centuries of the Middle Ages saw an increase in the influence of people of middle rank. The process was a slow one, for the main power struggle of post-Conquest years was between the king and the great barons. But an underlying stimulus to change was already in place in the shape of the Norman system of primogeniture, whereby the eldest son inherited the family property while the others either slipped into relative poverty or found careers in the church or chanced their fortunes further afield. With good management and the help of carefully arranged marriages, the prosperity of a modestly well-off family could be consolidated and enhanced over the generations, and we begin to see the emergence of a figure not far removed from the English country gentleman of later times. Towns and trade were another means of advancement. In particular the wool trade brought vast profits, as can be seen today in the elegant churches of the Cotswolds and East Anglia, in which brass memorial effigies of merchants stand proudly under elaborate canopies with their feet on woolsacks, displaying their wealth for all to see. As towns grew and prospered their social and financial organisation became more complex, especially with the development of the trade guilds, which were fraternities into which groups of professionals and craftsmen (such as merchants, bakers and tanners) formed themselves for mutual assistance and for the exclusion of rivals. There was not yet a sense of nationwide 'middle-class' identity, nor were there yet parliamentary means for such people to enforce their collective demands, but they were an influential section of society, and the production of the Mystery Play cycles by the guilds in the fourteenth and fifteenth centuries shows how well they were capable of organising themselves.

A great leveller, which affected all ranks, was the plague, or rather the succession of plagues and epidemics which swept the country and against which medieval medical knowledge and superstitious remedies offered little defence. Worst of all was the Black Death of 1349, when perhaps more than one third of the population perished. The social effects were enormous, not only to those who suffered direct physical harm. The market value of labour rose sky-high, and villeins found that they could now demand and receive comparatively generous wages and even promises of freedom. Those whose masters would not pay wandered off to seek others that would. In the unsettled years that ensued landlords made a vain attempt to put the clock back by legislation. The Statute of Labourers of 1351 directed that wages should revert to the rates existing before the Black Death, and that prices should be 'reasonable', on pain of whipping or branding for the labourer or a fine for the lord. Not surprisingly, these measures did not work, and the disintegration of the old hierarchy went on apace. Repressive counter-measures brought huge discontent, which found expression in the Peasants' Revolt of 1381, when a band of Kentish labourers under Wat Tyler marched on London and threatened to overthrow the very seat of government, until their leader was killed and his followers mercilessly put down.

The political and social turmoil which accompanied the Wars of the Roses made the fifteenth century one of the most lawless of times. An interesting way of discovering what life was like over a number of generations is to look at the letters and papers of the Pastons, a Norfolk family whose correspondence is one of the main sources of information about social life in the fifteenth century both in the provinces and at court. The letters tell of the rise in the fortunes of the Pastons, of their acquisition of land and other property, and of the constant litigation with which they were involved in order to keep hold of it. Some members of the family, particularly John II (there were three of that name), spent much of their time at court, where they hoped to win the support of men of influence. Others stayed on their Norfolk estates, where on one occasion at Caister Castle they had to resist an armed siege and eventually to surrender the property. From these original documents we learn far more about the concerns of everyday life – about bringing up the children, love and marriage, education and books, the management of servants and land, transport and communications, health and recreation – than the best history books can tell us.

In this age of authorities there was no greater authority than the Roman Catholic Church. The control it exercised can be traced back to the very introduction of Christianity into England. It grew to become a powerful religious, political, economic, social, educational, moral and legal force, sometimes in harmony with the secular authorities, sometimes at odds. Many people were in clerical occupations of some sort. Those who had taken orders were either 'secular' or 'regular'. The secular clergy (from Latin *saecularis*, 'of the world') fulfilled a role similar to that of present-day clergymen in caring for people's souls. The regular clergy (from Latin *regularis*, 'governed by rule'), were those who had taken vows of communal life, such as monks and nuns. For many centuries the church controlled all levels of the country's education system, and for most of the period it was assumed that the main purpose of education was to prepare a man or woman for religious life. Even when universities came into existence in the late twelfth century, as communities of scholars who banded together out of mutual self-interest, their ethos was strongly clerical. The three oldest universities are Bologna, Paris and Oxford, although it was only later, when they came to be given some sort of official recognition, that definite dates in their development can be determined. In England the two medieval universities, Oxford and Cambridge, provided at first neither for the very poor (who were too much engaged in scraping a living together) nor for the very rich (for whom private tutors in the baronial courts offered a preferred all-round education), but for a middle class of men who aspired to careers in the church and the professions. Whether these people's aspirations were lay or clerical, they most likely had to take orders if they hoped for advancement, so in Middle English the term *clerk* means many things from 'student' to 'cleric' and 'scholar'. The church also owned vast estates and capital, and could demand taxes and dues of its own. It was influential at court, in parliament, and in all levels of the civil service. It provided care for the sick and poor. It had its own law courts, at which those offenders claiming 'benefit of clergy' were tried according to canon law (which was considered to be more lenient than civil law). It enforced regular weekly attendance at church, where the services were conducted in Latin and the scriptures were expounded from the pulpit. Through its priests it administered the sacraments, such as Baptism, Communion, Marriage, Penance and the Last Rites, all of which were tremendously important to a society of believers. In short, its influence in every sphere of life can hardly be overestimated.

Not surprisingly, in view of all these conditions, the medieval world-view differed fundamentally from our own. In Anglo-

Saxon times, when security and happiness depended on mutual support within small social groups, there was a strong and reciprocated sense of loyalty to lord and kin. This loyalty was both a practicality and a fundamental ideal, and it is frequently a theme of the literature. Along with it went a strong sense of fatalism, which, although it may have originated in pre-Christian patterns of thought, did not necessarily run counter to Christian principles. In an age in which death and disaster were held at bay only with difficulty it is not surprising that there should have been a deep feeling of the transience of worldly things, which in Christian literature is naturally linked to the promise of salvation and eternal life in God. Then again, the hierarchical structure of medieval society, early and late, no doubt contributed to the widely held belief that everything had its proper place. This seems to have been most strongly felt in post-Conquest years, when the heavenly and natural world, social institutions, the human body, and even inanimate objects were thought to be logically and interdependently organised. The earth was thought to be a sphere at the centre of nine other concentric spheres, the first seven of which each held one of the planets, surrounded in the eighth by the fixed stars and finally the 'prime mover', an invisible sphere which was the source of all motion. Within this universe everything was organised into a hierarchical 'chain of being', from God and the angels downwards. Within each category were further categories, both practical and theoretical. Sin, for example, was divided into the Seven Deadly Sins of Pride, Envy, Wrath, Sloth, Lechery, Gluttony and Covetousness, of which Pride, Envy and Wrath were considered 'Sins of the Devil', Sloth, Lechery and Gluttony 'Sins of the Flesh', and Covetousness (which meant believing in material rather than spiritual things) the 'Sin of the World'. Each of these sins had subdivisions, such as Pride, which encompassed Untruth, Despite, Presumption, Ambition, Vainglory, Hypocrisy and Wicked Power, and there were even further subclassifications of these. There were also related Virtues, which were organised into a similar scheme and were considered to be the 'remedies', or antidotes, to the sins.

In short, this was an ordered, if not always orderly, society, in which established beliefs counted for much and new ideas were often treated with suspicion. Patterns of thought were vastly different from those of today and some established beliefs were frankly preposterous. But we should at all costs avoid any temptation to feel superior. Literary masterpieces like *Beowulf*, *Piers Plowman* and *Sir Gawain and the Green Knight* should remind us of the need for humility. Likewise, every medieval poem, however mean, offers something to be learned or some enjoyment to be gained – pleasures which are hugely enhanced when the contemporary context is taken into consideration.

3 The Literary and Linguistic Context

The English language in Anglo-Saxon times was made up of a number of dialects which were more distinct one from another than the dialects of present-day English. Dialects come about when speech communities with a common language become geographically or socially separated, so that each of the parts develops differently. It would be impossible to say exactly how many dialects there were. Even if we had adequate written evidence for all areas, which we have not, there would be no means of understanding the complexities of spoken Old English, such as comprehension between dialect groups, and so on. However, from surviving records, four main ones are usually distinguished: West Saxon, Kentish, Mercian and Northumbrian, corresponding approximately to the four major kingdoms.

Scandinavian influence, especially the settlement of large numbers of Danes and Norwegians in the north and east of England, was a complicating factor. The effects of their languages can be appreciated from the fact that East and West Mercian developed into substantially different dialects of Middle English. Today, areas of Scandinavian influence, such as Lincolnshire and the Lake District, can be detected most easily from place names ending in *-by* (village), *-thwaite* (clearing, meadow) and *-toft*, (house-site, homestead), and from those with Scandinavian personal names as their first element. Words and patterns of speech in the present-day dialects of these areas can often be traced back to Old Danish or Old Norse. But Scandinavian settlement also affected the language more generally, and it has left its mark on what is now regarded as Standard English. Few people realise when they use such everyday words as *call, egg, fellow, hit, husband, ill, low, odd, root, skin, sky, take, they, their, them, ugly, want* and *wrong* that they are in the debt of the Scandinavian settlers of medieval times from whom these words were borrowed.

We know most about the West Saxon dialect of Old English because the vast majority of surviving literature and documents is written in it. This is because West Saxon became the standard literary and administrative language in late Anglo-Saxon times. But the variety of English which has gained acceptance today does not stem from this source, for West Saxon fell out of favour after the Norman Conquest when for a time no English dialect had particular prestige. Then, in the fourteenth century and into the fifteenth, as London acquired commercial, political and social pre-eminence, the language in use in the capital, which by that time had absorbed many central and East Midland characteristics, gradually became accepted as the standard written form of English, and so subsequently developed, though with many modifications, to become the basis of the written English of today.

Pre-Christian Anglo-Saxons were not entirely illiterate. A small number of them knew 'runic' writing, the use of an alphabet of predominantly straight-line letters, for inscriptions on stone, bone, wood and metal. Nearly all surviving runic inscriptions, however, are post-Conversion. The number and shape of the letters varied from place to place and time to time. In Scandinavia in the eighth century systems of only sixteen letters were used, whereas in ninth-century Northumbria the number was as many as thirty-three. Runes had names which were meaningful words, such as *feoh* (wealth) and *eðel* (native land), and occasionally these were used by Anglo-Saxon scribes as a sort of shorthand in their manuscripts. The poet Cynewulf wove his name in runes into the text of some of his poems so that readers and listeners might pray for his soul. Christian missionaries introduced the Roman alphabet which superseded the runic. It was in a form developed in Ireland and conveyed to England through the missionaries in the north. The fundamental differences between this and our own alphabet are that *k*, *q* and *z* were rarely used, and *j*, *v* and *w* not at all. The digraph *æ* was a vowel, called by its runic name 'ash', and stood for a sound between *a* and *e*. Two symbols were used to express *th*, a 'crossed *d*' or *eth* (ð), and the borrowed rune called *thorn* (þ).

Another borrowed rune called *wynn* (joy) was used for *w*, but this is usually modernised in present-day printed texts because of its confusing similarity to þ.

The earliest handwriting is known as 'uncial' and 'half uncial', the rounded bookhand used for the Latin text of copies of the Gospels, which were the earliest books in England. A script which developed later and is used in most books of the period is a minuscule (lower-case) script known as 'insular' or 'Anglo-Saxon minuscule'. Towards the end of the Anglo-Saxon period, particularly for Latin texts, an elegant French-inspired hand called 'Carolingian minuscule' came into use. With Christianity there also came knowledge of the complex technology of bookmaking. Only a small number of Anglo-Saxon books have survived the centuries of neglect, damage and deliberate destruction, but those which remain show that much artistry and skill went into them. To begin with, vellum or parchment had to be prepared from the skins of calves, sheep or goats. The skins were put through various processes of soaking in lime-water, depilating, washing, 'fleshing' (removing surplus flesh or fat), stretching and shaving-down to the required thickness. The sheets were gathered into booklets, usually of sixteen pages, and then trimmed, care being taken to have the 'hair' side of the vellum, which was slightly darker, facing another hair side, and two 'flesh' sides likewise. Margin and guide lines were made by pricking through several pages at regular intervals and ruling between the marks. Ink was made by one of two methods, involving either a mixture of soot, gum and water, or gallic acid, iron sulphate and gum. The writing instrument was a quill or reed-pen, which the scribe kept sharpened with his pen-knife. Fine illuminated manuscripts involved a whole range of additional processes. Designs had to be planned, outlines inked in, and pigments prepared and applied with a durable medium which would not discolour with age. Then there was the binding, an art in itself, even when it did not involve the setting of gems and precious metalwork with which the most sumptuous books were adorned.

It was natural, since these arts were introduced by the church, that they should be developed and perfected in Christian institutions such as the monasteries. Not only bookmaking, but the whole range of formal education quickly became the province of the church. Schools were set up to prepare young men for the priesthood by providing organised instruction in interpreting the scriptures, the sciences which regulated the ecclesiastical calendar, religious music and the metrical rules of religious poetry. Novices were entrusted to the monasteries at an early age. Only here and in the schools did those gifted in learning have access to libraries and the chance of contact with other scholars.

A development important for the subsequent history of English was the impetus given to vernacular (as opposed to Latin) writings by King Alfred in the ninth century. Alfred's plan, implemented through the church, was revolutionary in its organisation and scope.

> It seems better to me, if it seems so to you [he wrote to his bishops], that we...should translate certain books which are most necessary for all men to know, into the language that we can all understand, and also arrange it, as with God's help we very easily can if we have peace, so that all the youth of free men now among the English people, who have the means to be able to devote themselves to it, may be set to study for as long as they are of no other use, until the time they are able to read English writing well; afterwards one may teach further in the Latin language those whom one wishes to teach further and wishes to promote to holy orders.
>
> (Swanton 1975, 31–2)

Though Alfred's later years were not blessed with the necessary peace, the ideal of a centrally inspired scheme of education for any young freeborn man wishing to receive it was, for its day, remarkably enlightened.

The Anglo-Saxons had a flourishing literature in both poetry and prose, of which the poetic tradition was the more ancient. The earliest poems of pagan times were not written down, but passed on orally. These dealt with subjects which had been popular and traditional amongst the ancestors of the English, and some of them probably told of myths, legends and historical events, such as the conquest of Britain. In Christian times some of the old poems were written down, much changed, no doubt, from the time when they were first current, but the vast majority were never committed to writing and have passed out of memory. Nor was it only the old poems, for new ones were sometimes composed in the head and circulated by word of mouth. Only a fraction of those that were set down has survived to the present day, the majority being found in four manuscripts dating from the late tenth or early eleventh centuries. In all, approximately 30,000 lines remain. Just how much chance is involved in the survival of Old English manuscripts is shown by the fact that in 1860, at Copenhagen, two fragments of a poem about a hero called *Waldere* were found in use as part of the binding of a book. It is only by extreme good fortune that the story of Waldere can be reconstructed from a tenth-century Latin poem on the subject, written by a monk in Switzerland. Medieval records are full of tantalising allusions to stories, like that of Waldere, which are now lost for ever.

Old English poetry was predominantly alliterative, that is, it was based on the patterning together of words which had the same initial sound. Alliteration was widely used throughout the Germanic world, for it is specially suited to languages, like those of the Germanic group, in which the initial syllables of words are strongly stressed. End-rhyme did not become a common feature of English verse until after the Norman Conquest, when its popularity owed much to the influence of French verse. The basic unit of alliterative verse was the half-line (sometimes rather confusingly referred to as a 'verse'), which was separated from its corresponding half by a natural pause known as the *caesura*. The two halves were linked together by means of alliteration, which always fell on the strongly stressed syllables ('lifts'), the unstressed syllables in between (together called the 'drop') being variable in number. In the following example from *The Battle of Maldon* the lifts (/) and the caesura (//) in each line have been marked, and the alliterating sounds are printed in bold type:

     /   /   /   /
Wodon þa **w**æl-wulfas // for **w**ætere ne murnon,

  /   /   /   /
wıcinga **w**erod, // **w**est ofer Pantan,

    / /   /   /
ofer **sc**ır wæter // **sc**yldas wegon,

  /   /   /   /
lıdmen to **l**ande // **l**ınde bæron.   (96–9)

(The slaughter-wolves advanced, to the water they paid no heed,
the troop of Vikings, west over the River Panta [Blackwater],
over the clear water they carried their shields,
seamen to the land bore their bucklers.)

The translation loses most of the alliteration, but the rhythmical structure of this type of verse should be familiar from nursery rhymes like

/   /   /   /
Peter Peter Pumpkin Eater
/   /   /   /
had a wife but couldn't keep her.
/   /   /   /
So he put her in a pumpkin shell,
/   /   /   /
and there he kept her very well.

In Old English verse every consonant alliterates with itself, except that the sound-groups represented by *sc*, *sp*, and *st* were each thought of as separate and distinct, so a word such as *speru* could alliterate with *sprang* but not with *sang*. Vowels and diphthongs, however, could alliterate with one another indiscriminately, as *isig* with *ut-fus* and *ealdor*. The main alliterating syllable, which determined the alliteration for the whole line, was the one which occurred after the caesura and was known as the 'headstave'. Convention demanded that this must alliterate with one of the lifts in the first half-line (e.g. line 98 in *Maldon*) or with them both (e.g. lines 96–7, 99), but not with the last lift in the line. Where alliteration occurs on the last lift it is either a mistake or an extra embellishment (e.g. line 98 in *Maldon*, where the alliterative pattern *sc/w/ sc/w* occurs, which is sometimes referred to as 'crossed alliteration'; in this case the main, structural alliteration is on *sc* and the *w* alliteration is an extra, decorative feature).

Old English metre is a complicated matter to explain in detail, and has in itself been the subject of many studies (e.g. Bliss 1958; Bliss 1962). All that needs to be said here is that the half-lines have been found to fall, on the basis of the interrelationship of stress and alliteration, into five basic patterns, or 'types'. In the following illustration, which utilises examples from Modern English as well as genuine Old English half-lines, the only feature not yet mentioned is a secondary level of stress (\) which falls somewhere between that of a fully stressed and an unstressed syllable. Each lift is marked (/), as before, and each drop, whether of one syllable or more, by (×). Final -e is pronounced as a separate syllable. Since the Old English examples do not show the whole of the long line, the alliteration does not show up in every case (i.e. not in B and C), but it should, of course, be understood as falling on one or both of the lifts:

		Old English	Modern English
Type A	/×/×	/ ×/ × gar to guþe	/ ×/ × spear to battle
Type B	×/×/	× / × / ofer yða gewealc	× / × / over billows' surge
Type C	×//×	× / / × ac he gefeng hraðe	× / / × but he seized quickly
Type D	//\×	/ / \ × bat ban-locan	/ / \ × bit bone-locker [the body]
Type E	/\×/	/ \ ×/ longsumne lof	/ \ × / long-standing praise

Within each of these classifications subtypes may be found. Sometimes the rhythms produced by varying combinations of types affect the progress of the verse. For example, a heavy predominance of A-types may move a piece of narrative quickly forward while the varied rhythms of a more mixed range of types may slow it up (see Raw 1978, 97–122; Scragg 1991, 60–3).

Works were sometimes declaimed or recited to the accompaniment of harp or lyre, though we do not know what form the music took. They might, therefore, as appropriately be termed 'songs' as 'poems', and *singan* (to sing) is a verb often used to describe the delivery. *Beowulf* describes several scenes associating poetry with music-making and conviviality, including the party in the mead-hall to celebrate Beowulf's defeat of Grendel, the troll who for years has been oppressing the Danish court:

> þær wæs sang ond sweg   samod ætgædere
> fore Healfdenes   hilde-wisan,
> gomen-wudu greted,   gid oft wrecen,
> ðonne heal-gamen   Hroþgares scop
> æfter medo-bence   mænan scolde.   (1063–7)

*(There was singing and music together before Healfdene's battle-
leader; the harp was plucked and a lay often recited, when Hrothgar's
minstrel had to entertain the company in the hall along the mead-
bench.)*

Earlier (lines 867–74) Beowulf's victory is celebrated by a retainer
of the king who composes extempore a song or poem about the
exploit in words which were *soðe gebunden*, which perhaps means
'correctly linked in metre'. Beowulf himself seems to suggest that
poetry-making was an occupation fit for kings, for he describes
how Hrothgar, lord of the Danes, recited 'true and tragic' tales
from the distant past, accompanying himself on the harp (2105–14).
The small six-stringed round lyre discovered in the seventh-cen-
tury royal ship-burial at Sutton Hoo may be the type of instru-
ment that was used.

Surviving poetry can be roughly categorised as heroic, reli-
gious, elegiac and gnomic, although few poems belong rigidly to
one category only. By chance it happens that one heroic poem,
called *Beowulf,* survives in its entirety. Its 3182 lines tell a fantastic
folktale set in a vaguely historical context. It was composed some-
time between the eighth and the eleventh centuries (recent reap-
praisal has undermined confidence in a firm date) and, in a
heavily ornamented style, it relates the deeds of Beowulf, a cham-
pion of the southern Swedish tribe of the Geats, on the basis of
which it explores the ethics and ideals of the warrior culture.
Heroic treatment was also given to other stories of old, such as
the *Fight at Finnsburg,* and to real, contemporary battles, notably
the great victory of King Athelstan at an unidentified place
named Brunanburh in 937 and the defeat of Anglo-Saxon levies
at Maldon by the Danes in 991.

Surviving Christian poetry is much more extensive than secular
heroic. The main subjects are Old Testament paraphrases and nar-
ratives, poetic homilies, poems on the lives of Christ, the apostles
and saints, and moral allegories. Whatever the true origins of
Christian poetry in English, a tradition told by Bede ascribes it to
an old man called Cædmon, a herdsman at the monastery of
Whitby under the rule of the Abbess Hild (d.680). Cædmon had
never learnt the art of song and, when the harp was passed around
after the communal feast, he would slip away, ashamed, as his turn
came near. On one occasion, when he had crept out and settled

himself down in the cattle shed which housed the animals in his charge, someone appeared to him in his sleep, commanding him to sing about the Creation. Cædmon began to sing, in praise of God the Creator, verses which he had never heard before. Once awake he remembered all he had sung in his sleep and added more words in the same style. He became a monk at Whitby and continued to exercise his divine gift of poetry. Part of the *Hymn* which Cædmon received in his dream has survived and is perhaps in its Northumbrian version (given here) the earliest extant poem in English:

> Nu scylun hergan   hefaen-ricaes uard,
> metudæs maecti   end his mod-gidanc,
> uerc uuldur-fadur,   sue he uundra gihuaes,
> eci dryctin,   or astelidæ.
> He aerist scop   aelda [*or* eordu] barnum
> heben til hrofe,   haleg scepen;
> tha middun-geard   mon-cynnæs uard,
> eci dryctin,   æfter tiadæ
> firum foldu,   frea allmectig.
> (*Now we must praise the keeper of the heavenly kingdom,*
> *the might of the Creator and the thoughts of his mind,*
> *the work of the glorious Father as He, of every wonder,*
> *the eternal Lord, established the beginning.*
> *He first made for the children of men [or of the earth].*
> *heaven as a roof, the holy Creator.*
> *Then a middle-enclosure the Guardian of mankind,*
> *the eternal Lord , afterwards made,*
> *the earth for mankind, the Lord almighty.*)

The complete poem would have been longer than this, for Cædmon added more on awakening, but on the basis of these lines alone it is difficult to see why so simple a poem was considered remarkable. Probably it was because it was believed to have been divinely inspired, and perhaps also because here, for the first time, Christian subject matter was expressed in traditional alliterative verse.

A small group of poems known as elegies falls between the Christian and heroic traditions. Among the best of these are *The Wanderer, The Seafarer* and *Deor's Lament.* The theme of the elegies is the transitory nature of human life. They tell longingly of past conviviality in the meadhall, of treasure-giving and music and friendship, which they contrast with present exile, bereavement, poverty, cold and hardship at sea. In these poems God's mercy and divine Providence are glorified as the sole remedy for harsh misfortunes, but some heroic ideals such as stoicism and good reputation are also put forward, to the extent that some commentators claim to be able to detect 'pagan' elements or even a 'pre-Christian creed' (Mitchell and Robinson 1992, 269). The contrary opinion is that

> the Germanic heritage, when it emerges in Anglo-Saxon poetry, emerges re-shaped, absorbed, chastened, in a form quite distinct from survivals elsewhere of the pagan, heroic, Germanic past.
>
> (Pearsall 1977, 1)

Certainly, no pagan mythology is implicit in the elegies, nor an alien or unfamiliar world-view. Like all Anglo-Saxon poems, they are thoroughly Christian in outlook, and readers looking for echoes of a pagan past will find evidence very thin on the ground.

The last group of poems can for convenience be called 'gnomic', consisting, as they do, of wise and sententious sayings. Foremost among them are two sets of *Maxims*, which express moral precepts and commonplace facts. A collection of *Proverbs*, *The Fates of Men* (a catalogue of good and evil fortune), *The Arts of Men* (which surveys more cheerfully the talents with which people are endowed and reflects on God's bounty), *The Runic Poem* (an alphabet of verses), *The Dialogue of Salomon and Saturn* (a battle of wits between representatives of Christianity and paganism) and an interesting collection of charms and riddles complete this rather miscellaneous group.

Prose literature is not the concern of this book and therefore requires only brief mention. Some of its roots may be in a saga tradition, but the earliest written prose was in Latin. Chronicles, histories, saints' lives and epistles were among the most common genres, and the great exponents were Aldhelm (d.709), Bede (d.735) and Alcuin (d.804). The earliest writings in English, surviving only in later copies, are the laws of King Ethelbert of Kent (d.616), and most other early vernacular prose is similarly documentary and utilitarian. The earliest prose that might be said to possess literary merit was instigated by King Alfred, both in the translations from Latin that he had made and in the *Anglo-Saxon Chronicle*, which, in the form in which we know it, was probably begun under his influence. The works he chose for translation were Gregory's *Cura Pastoralis*, 'Pastoral Care', which set out guidelines for the higher clergy; Orosius's *History*, the standard historical geography book of the time; Bede's *Ecclesiastical History*, the classic account of the Christianisation of England; Boethius's *Consolation of Philosophy*, one of the most popular of all books in the Middle Ages; and St Augustine of Hippo's *Soliloquies*, a meditative work concerned with the eternal life of the soul. Thereafter these works were extensively copied and recopied. Though Alfred's translations were full and lively and the original prose frequently vigorous and moving, their style is underdeveloped in comparison to works by the later exponents Wulfstan (d.1023) and Ælfric (d.*c*.1012). Wulfstan, who became archbishop of York in 1002, was active in the field of law and administration, but is most remembered for his thundering sermons denouncing the slide into sin and despair which accompanied the renewed Scandinavian attacks of the early eleventh century. Ælfric is known as a teacher in Latin and English, most famous for his homilies, saints' lives, and biblical translations. As a grammarian he was keenly interested in many aspects of language and his writings are usually regarded as representing Old English prose at its finest and most mature. Both Wulfstan and Ælfric introduced verse rhythms and alliteration into their prose, and extensive passages (particularly in Ælfric's work) are sometimes indistinguishable from verse.

The victory of Duke William at Hastings in 1066 brought about substantial political and social changes which had an immediate effect on the output of literature and a rather more delayed effect upon the English language. The social change which had the most profound immediate influence was the speedy removal from all positions of power in church and state of English-speaking nobles and church leaders, and the substitution of a French governing class whose language and traditions were, for the most part, quite alien. The change was not entirely without precedent, for the last Saxon king, Edward the Confessor, had been brought up in exile at the Norman court, and after his accession in 1042 he rewarded many of his Norman friends by appointing them to positions of influence. A sign of this is the early appearance of French loan-words, more than a dozen of which are recorded in eleventh-century English writings, including *bacun* (bacon), *capun* (capon), *gingifer* (ginger) *castel* (castle) and *prisun* (prison). But this was as nothing compared to the huge scale of French influence and the sheer speed and completeness of the removal of the English upper class once the Conquest had been achieved and consolidated.

For two centuries French was spoken by the aristocracy in most spheres. At court and among the legal profession it was pre-eminent until well into the fifteenth century. Latin remained unchallenged as the language of scholarship and religion throughout Europe. English, of course, continued to be spoken, but was considered to be the language of the uncultivated. It was not a proper medium for literature, and aspiring English authors could expect no patronage and no material rewards for their writings. The only place in which the copying of classic English texts continued was the monasteries, where the tradition of reproducing key prose texts was too strong to be snuffed out. Copies of established authors such as Ælfric, therefore, continued to be made, as did versions of the *Anglo-Saxon Chronicle*.

The term 'French' as used in these contexts needs some qualification. At first those who spoke French were the victorious Normans and their families, most of whom spoke the Norman dialect of French. But this phase was brief, for at a time when geography was less important than feudal ties, it was inevitable that England would within a generation or two be brought into contact with other areas of France. The gradual rise in the importance of Paris brought prestige to its regional dialect, and the French spoken in England began to look increasingly provincial. The dialectal distinction can be traced in present-day English by contrasting words derived from Norman French such as *canal*, *catch* and *warden* with their counterparts from Central French, *channel*, *chase* and *guardian*. Meanwhile, developments were taking place within England itself. Gradually, through intermarriage and other contacts, some sections of English-speaking society, especially from the aspiring middle ranks, learned French for social or economic reasons. As the *Chronicle of Robert of Gloucester* (7542) points out about the year 1300 'unless a man knows French he is not thought of very highly'. Equally, many French-speakers found it convenient to learn English in order to carry out their daily business and to communicate with English-speaking people. In time, therefore, the sharp edge of distinction between French and English became blurred, so much so that a hybrid, known as Anglo-Norman, emerged and for a while, in the twelfth and thirteenth centuries, enjoyed status as the language of the court in England and even of a fairly extensive literature. There are, for example, religious and historical writings, romances, and some excellent drama written in it. Anglo-Norman, therefore, was a channel of literary influence in addition to having an effect upon the development of the English language, particularly in expanding the poetic vocabulary, as described in Chapter 6.

Unlike the French, the Scandinavians at first had no literary tradition of their own, and to them English was a language with a written culture which they could not emulate. The spoken language, however, was very much affected by them from the time of their earliest settlements in the ninth century, but this is not seen until the Middle English period, when Scandinavian words began to find their way into documents and literary texts. Not that the influence is confined to loan words. The areas of northern and east-midland England, where Danish and Norwegian settlement was heaviest, were at the forefront of linguistic change, and much of this can be attributed to their presence there. Their languages belonged to the Germanic group, as did English, and the fact that they were so closely related meant that many of the structures and much of the vocabulary would have been relatively familiar, even across the language boundaries. The main barrier to understanding would have been the inflexional endings, those grammatical suffixes which convey such distinctions as number, gender, case, person, and tense, and this factor may have helped weaken the importance of inflexions and encourage a greater reliance on syntax. The weakening and loss of inflexions, which is known as 'inflexional levelling', is a process inherent in all the Germanic languages, so the Scandinavians cannot be entirely responsible, but their intermixture with the English no doubt greatly accelerated the process.

The resurgence of English began in the thirteenth century and is in part associated with the loss of Normandy in 1204, after which there were increasing pressures, and eventually a legal requirement, for landowners to hold land in one country or another, but not both. This helped to separate those nobles residing in England from the influence of France. There is a rising confidence in English into the fourteenth century, and authors increasingly turn to it as a means of reaching a wider audience. In the words of William of Nassington (*c*.1325):

In English tonge I schal ȝow telle,   *write for you*
ȝif ȝe wyth me so longe wil dwelle.   *remain*
No Latyn wil I speke no waste,
But English, þat men vse mast,   *most*
Þat can eche man vnderstande,   *that everyone knows how to*
Þat is born in Ingelande;
For þat langage is most chewyd,   *in evidence*
Os wel among lered os lewyd.   *as much; educated as uneducated*
Latyn, as I trowe, can nane   *no one knows*
But þo, þat haueth it in scole tane,   *except those that have taken it*
And somme can Frensche and no Latyn,
Þat vsed han cowrt and dwellen þerein;
                  who have experience of court
And somme can of Latyn a party,
Þat can of Frensche but febly;   *who know hardly any*
And somme vnderstonde wel Englysch,
Þat can noþer Latyn nor Frankys.   *neither*
Boþe lered and lewed, olde and ȝonge,
Alle vnderstonden English tonge.

                        (*Speculum Vitae*, 61–78)

The rise of English at the expense of French continued as the fourteenth century went on. John Trevisa, in a note in his translation of Higden's *Polychronicon* in the 1380s, claimed that the prestige of French had waned to such an extent that it was no longer used in the schools and that gentlemen who wished their children to learn French were having to send them abroad.

English, then, gradually became accepted as a language of literature. But the variety, or rather *varieties*, used were very different from the Old English literary language. The Old English literary language had become highly stylised and artificial over its period of use and was remote from the language of speech. It depended upon conventions which, once broken, could not be restarted. A new beginning was therefore made using forms of the language which were closer to the spoken language and which reflected the many changes which had taken place in the intervening period.

Middle English literature, therefore, exists in a confusing variety of regional dialects, for until the later part of the fourteenth century no one of them enjoyed countrywide prestige. The apparently wider variation in dialect, as compared to the situation in Old English, is in part the result of the survival of a greater number and variety of manuscripts. There was also individualism in the methods of scribes, which may suggest greater variation than that which really existed. We rarely find consistency in the spelling of Middle English texts, and consequently when we compare the spelling of several writers of the same period we may mistake for differences of dialect those features which are merely experimental attempts by the scribes at the best way of representing the same sound.

Broad distinctions of dialect are usually made for Middle English, based on the divisions discernible in Old English. Thus Old English Northumbrian is thought of as giving rise to Northern English and Scottish, Mercian to East Midland and West Midland, West Saxon to South Western and Central Southern, and Kentish to South Eastern Middle English. Political, social and economic factors played a part in these developments. For instance, Mercian developed differently in the east than in the west, because the former became part of the Danelaw and fell under stronger Scandinavian influence. These traditional divisions into broad areas of dialect are, of course, very crude. This fact has been demonstrated by the publication of *A Linguistic Atlas of Late Mediaeval English* (McIntosh et al. 1986), in which detailed distribution maps, showing varying phonological, morphological and lexical features, present a much more intricate picture of complex, overlapping regional and local forms. Then again, many of the differences between Middle English texts are attributable to changes that occurred as a result of the passage of time, rather than because of preferred regional forms. The weakening and loss of inflexional endings, for instance, are part of a general tendency in English and had begun even before the first written records in Old English came to be made. They continued throughout the Middle English period, albeit at different rates in different regions, so that the same text recopied in the same locality after a lapse of time would look very different in its early and late versions, given the fact that it was normal practice for scribes to update the language as they went along.

There were local standards, certainly, to which writers in one dialect or another were drawn. One variety which acquired inter-regional currency as a literary standard from the late fourteenth to the late fifteenth century was based on spoken dialects of the central midlands, and was used by a range of authors as varied as Wyclif (from Yorkshire) and Pecock (from Wales). But a more important development in the long term was the gradual increase of London in social and economic importance to the extent that people began to look upon the London variety of English as something of a countrywide norm in the written sphere. This development was particularly encouraged by the adoption of English in the fifteenth century for use in the written business of administration. Previously government business had been conducted largely in Latin and French, but after about 1430 large numbers of administrative documents were issued in what has become known as 'Chancery Standard'. So when Caxton came to use a literary version of this London standard for his printed editions from the mid 1470s (despite some uncertainty, he tells us, over individual words), its establishment was assured.

The main linguistic differences in Middle English, as compared to Old, are: firstly, phonological changes, which give the vocabulary a more familiar appearance for the present-day reader; secondly, a marked simplification of the inflexional endings, especially in the nominal phrase; thirdly (and consequently), an increased reliance on prepositions and on word order as a means of conveying the sense; and, fourthly, an expanded vocabulary, based partly on new combinations of native elements but more distinctively on extensive borrowings from Latin, French and the languages of the Scandinavian settlers.

Middle English writings in both verse and prose are so varied that it is difficult to classify and summarise them. In one sphere established scribal practices continued for almost a century after the Conquest and provide valuable evidence as to what was happening with the language in the period of change from Old English to Middle. This was the copying and continuation of the *Anglo-Saxon Chronicle*, which at Peterborough Abbey went on until as late as 1154. Thereafter historical prose in English lapsed until late in the fourteenth century when John Trevisa produced a translation of Ranulf Higden's Latin *Polychronicon*, a 'Chronicle of Many Ages'. Another popular prose chronicle began about 1400, when an anonymous writer translated into English a version of the Anglo-Norman *Brut*, a history of England going back to its foundation by the legendary Brutus, great-grandson of Aeneas of Troy; with various continuations over the next 60 years, this became (judging from the number of manuscripts) the most popular secular work in Middle English. English chronicles in the interim had been in verse, the most notable examples being Laȝamon's *Brut* (*c.*1200), the *Chronicle of Robert of Gloucester* (*c.*1300), Robert Mannyng's *Rhyming Chronicle* (1338), and John Barbour's vigorous *Actes and Life of the most Victorious Conquerour, Robert Bruce King of Scotland* (1375).

Laȝamon, in particular, is of great value for the history of the language and as representing an interesting stage in the development of prosody, utilising as he does a mixture of rhyme and alliteration which looks both forward and back. The continuing power of alliteration is also seen in the prose texts of the 'Katherine Group' – the lives of Saints Katherine, Juliana, Margaret, and a work in praise of chastity known as *Hali Meiðhad*. In using alliteration as an embellishment of religious prose the writers were continuing the tradition of Ælfric. Together with two non-alliterative texts, *Ancrene Wisse* (Guidebook for Anchoresses) and *Sawles Warde* (Guardian of the Soul), they constitute a compact group of prose texts of instruction for women, all in the West Midland dialect of the late twelfth century.

A fine poem, also of about this date, is *The Owl and the Nightingale*, a witty debate in short couplets between birds representing two differing points of view – and perhaps, therefore, two different sections of society. Debates and dialogues were popular literary forms. Examples in alliterative verse are the dialogue between *Wynnere and Wastoure* (representing thrift versus spending) and *The Parlement* [i.e.'discussion'] *of the Thre Ages*, which treats the perennial theme of youth and age. These are among the earliest surviving poems of the so-called fourteenth-century 'Alliterative Revival' (a remarkable resurgence of a distinctive group of fine poets who utilised alliteration, rather than end-rhyme, in a way which is comparable to that of Old English verse), and share features with later poems of the same school, especially in their use of allegorical figures within a dream framework. William Langland's famous political and social satire *Piers Plowman* (1365–90) has both of these features, as has the elegant spiritual allegory *Pearl*, a poem found only in the manuscript containing *Sir Gawain and the Green Knight*. In fact, all four of the poems in the manuscript (its sole contents) are unique, the other two being *Patience* (which commends the virtue after which it is named by retelling the story of Jonah) and *Purity*. All four are of approximately the same date (*c*.1370–90) and may be by the same author.

Romance is one of the best represented genres of Middle English, and no classification entirely makes sense of the varied subject matter. Some of the earliest romances deal with legendary English and Germanic heroes, such as *King Horn* (*c*.1225), *Havelok* (*c*.1250–75), *Guy of Warwick* (early fourteenth century) and *Athelston* (*c*.1350). The romance of *Richard Coer de Lyon* (late thirteenth century) makes use of a real hero, Richard I, King of England. Romances about the legendary King Arthur and his court are particularly numerous, and include tales of Arthur's youth, such as *Arthour and Merlin* (*c*.1250–1300), and, above all, of his death, including the alliterative *Morte Arthure* (*c*.1350–1400) and the stanzaic *Morte Arthur* (*c*.1400). Of Arthur's knights it was not (as in France) Lancelot who held centre stage but Gawain, especially in the finest of all English romances, the alliterative *Sir Gawain and the Green Knight*. More distant settings are the courts of Charlemagne and Alexander the Great and the cities of Troy and Thebes, while the story of *Floris and Blancheflur* (*c*.1250) is partly located in the Saracen east. The small group of Breton Lays, which includes both translations and imitations of material from Brittany, includes the delightful tale of *Sir Orfeo*, a retelling of the legend of *Orpheus and Euridice* translated from a French source early in the fourteenth century. All the above are romances in verse. Prose romances only become widely popular in England in the fifteenth century, the finest and best known being the works of Sir Thomas Malory which go under the name *Morte Darthur*, which is adapted from the title mentioned by Caxton in the colophon of his edition of 1485.

The strong strain of contemplative writing represented in the Katherine Group re-emerges in the mystical works and spiritual autobiographies of the fourteenth and fifteenth centuries. An important figure here is the mystic Richard Rolle (d.1349), hermit of Hampole in Yorkshire, whose popularity is attested by the numerous extant manuscripts of works by him and by his imitators. Most of his devotional and instructional writings, which were intended mainly for women, are in prose, the long poem known as *The Pricke of Conscience* now being thought not to be by him. Also well represented among surviving manuscripts are other mystical and devotional prose works, notably the anonymous *Cloud of Unknowing* (late fourteenth century), *The Scale* [i.e.'ladder']*of Perfection* by Walter Hilton (d.1396), and Nicholas Love's *Myrrour of the Blessed Lyf of Jesu Christ* (early fifteenth century). Related works are the spiritual autobiographies by Dame Julian of Norwich (d.*c.*1416) and Margery Kempe (b.*c.*1373) of King's Lynn in Norfolk, but we can assume from the lack of surviving multiple copies that these two did not enjoy anything like the same contemporary popularity.

Sermons and homilies (i.e. religious discourses containing illustrative stories) tend to be preserved in collections or series. An early series in verse is *The Ormulum,* written probably about 1180 in the North-East Midlands, possibly Lincolnshire, by an Augustinian canon named Orm. It is a collection of dull metrical homilies comprising about 20,000 lines, of which the literary merit is far outweighed by the linguistic interest. This interest stems principally from the fact that the manuscript is in Orm's own hand and preserves his idiosyncratic but consistent system of spelling, which furnishes valuable information about English sounds at this period. It also contains the first occurrence of many Scandinavian loan words. A later work (in prose), also dull but notable for its linguistic interest, is Michael of Northgate's *Ayenbite of Inwyt* (Prick of Conscience). This, too, is in the author's own hand, and is dated 1340 and located in Canterbury, a combination of contextual information rarely found. From later in the fourteenth century are those collections of sermons and other prose tracts associated with the Yorkshireman John Wyclif (d.1384) and his followers which are usually described as 'Lollard', a disparaging contemporary term for reformers within the Catholic church who advocated the translation of the Bible into English. A translation, in fact, survives, in two versions, but for many years it was a punishable offence to be found using it. A light and entertaining treatment of moral issues is found in verse in the thirteenth-century *Bestiary* (descriptions of animals and their supposed characteristics, allegorically interpreted), humorous fables such as that of *The Fox and the Wolf* (before 1300) and collections of exemplary tales, like Robert Mannyng's *Handlyng Synne,* begun in 1303 and directed specifically at ordinary, uneducated people, and John Gower's more learned *Confessio Amantis* (Confessions of a Lover, 1390).

Gower was a contemporary of Chaucer, by whom he was admired. Many poets, in turn, admired Chaucer and attempted to imitate him. The two most famous of the 'English Chaucerians' are Thomas Hoccleve (*c*. 1370–*c*. 1450) and John Lydgate (*c*. 1370–*c*. 1450), a monk of Bury St Edmunds, whose voluminous works enjoyed much contemporary popularity. The best known of their slightly later counterparts, the 'Scottish Chaucerians', are King James I of Scotland (1394–1437), Robert Henryson (d.*c*.1505), William Dunbar (b.*c*.1460), and Gavin Douglas (*c*.1475–1522). Their works, partly because they are in the English dialect of the Scottish lowlands, show a distinctiveness and vigour which is sometimes lacking in the verse of the English Chaucerians.

Informative, encyclopaedic writing is another genre of Middle English. In verse it is best represented by the anonymous northern poem *Cursor Mundi*, a long paraphrase in couplets of biblical history, dating from about 1300. John Trevisa's prose translation of the Latin *De Proprietatibus Rerum* (On the Nature of Things) by Bartholomaeus Anglicus is more in line with what we understand today by the term 'encyclopaedia'. An informative and entertaining collection of travellers' tales, cast as a guidebook for pilgrims to the Holy Land, is *The Travels of Sir John Mandeville*. This popular book was written in French, perhaps *c*.1366–7, and translated into English shortly before 1400.

From the middle of the twelfth century until the close of the period we encounter an increasing number of songs and lyrics on a wide variety of subjects, secular and religious. The secular, especially in the early years, are often very haphazardly preserved, some being no more than a verse or two jotted down in the margin or on the flyleaf of a manuscript. But the religious lyrics are usually better preserved, and survive in greater numbers and often in more than one copy. An exceptional collection of mixed secular and religious subjects, known as the *Harley Lyrics*, is found in a West Midland manuscript of *c*.1314–25. Anonymous until the fourteenth century, when some of the authors begin to be known, the lyrics take many forms, some being popular songs meant for singing or dancing while others are scholarly and literary. Some are original compositions, while others are translations from Latin or French, and some are some deeply devotional while others are saucy and scurrilous.

Finally, there is the drama. What survives is almost entirely religious, the principal types being the Mystery and the Morality plays. The Mysteries were civic dramas depicting biblical history from the Creation to the Last Judgement. They were organised in cycles of short plays, each one performed by a different group, usually a trade or craft guild, at some fixed time of the year, commonly on the feast of Corpus Christi. Such cycles survive from York, Chester, Wakefield (almost certainly the home of the *Towneley Plays*), and an unidentified place known as N-Town. The Moralities took a figure representative of humankind, such as 'Everyman', and depicted him being tempted by various allegorical personifications of evil or worldliness, the object being to show that God's mercy is always available to the sinner who is truly repentant. Other types of play are less well represented, including plays based on the lives of saints, such as Paul and Mary Magdalene. It is strange that there is so little evidence of a secular dramatic tradition. The fragmentary interlude *De Clerico et Puella* and a comic poem called *Dame Sirith*, which is partially adapted for performance, are virtually all that survives. Both date from *c.*1300 and are based on a comic theme featuring a young man's efforts to woo a woman and the trick he uses to win her.

4   Old English Poetic Diction

A basic structural principle of alliterative verse is the association of alliteration and meaning, the semantically most important words being linked and focused upon by the likeness of their initial sounds and by the metrical stress that falls upon them. For this reason we find that the poetry of the Anglo-Saxons gives special prominence to the nominal phrase. Analysis of the syllabic patterns of Old English verse in relation to the grammatical and semantic importance of individual words led the great pioneer of Old English metrics, Eduard Sievers, to realise that there is an inherent tendency to give a high place in stressing to nouns, adjectives, infinitives, participles, and certain lexically important adverbs, a lower place to finite verbs and simple adverbs (such as adverbs of degree), and the lowest place of all to pronouns, conjunctions, prepositions, articles, prefixes and suffixes. Nouns are therefore commonly found in the formally stressed (lift) positions and most often participate in the alliteration. On the other hand, words such as articles and demonstratives more rarely achieve this prominence, and where they do some special marking is often implied by the context. So in *Beowulf*, as Grendel approaches the high hall of the Danes, intent on slaughter and in greedy anticipation of a feast of corpses, the narrator intervenes to remark

> Ne wæs þæt wyrd þa gen,
> þæt he ma moste   manna cynnes
> ðicgean ofer þa niht.   Þryð-swyð beheold
> mæg Higelaces...   (734–7)
> (*It was by no means the outcome that he was to be*
> *allowed to partake of more of mankind after that night.*
> *The mighty kinsman of Higelac [Beowulf] watched...*)

47

In line 736 the usually insignificant *þa* (that) is stressed and alliterates (unlike the noun which it accompanies), because there is a point to be made, which is emphasised by the metrical pattern: Grendel will no longer feast on men 'after that night', because it is to be the very night in which he will lose his life at the hand of the waiting hero (see Fakundiny 1970, 139). Though this emphasis on the demonstrative is unusual, the fact that all the remaining nouns in the quotation except *niht* carry full stress, and that four of them also alliterate, is entirely characteristic.

The nominal phrase, then, is given a particular emphasis, and nouns and adjectives tend to carry most of the semantic weight. Indeed, poets seem at times to go to great lengths to avoid the use of finite verbs other than common ones such as 'to be' or 'to become'. When a Danish coastguard meets Beowulf and his men (257) he asks them to *gecyðanne hwanan eowre cyme syndon* (*literally* to make known whence your comings are), for which a modern English speaker would surely prefer something like 'make known where you have come from', using the verbal phrase 'you have come' rather than the odd-sounding nominal phrase 'your comings'. Similarly, in the same poem 'they request' is *hy benan synt* (364) (they are petitioners) and 'the monster grasped hold of him' is *him aglæca ætgræpe wearð* (1269) (the monster became grasping to him). In some cases the verb is avoided altogether, as in *æfter billes bite* (2060), literally 'after the cut of a sword', which would be more naturally expressed in Modern English by a clause such as 'after he had been cut down by a sword'.

An analysis of that part of the vocabulary of *Beowulf* which begins with the letter *b* has shown that virtually all nouns, adjectives, adverbs, and forms of *begen* (both) carry stress and alliteration, as compared with less than 60 per cent of non-finite verb forms and less than 30 per cent of finite forms (see Mitchell 1985, II.993).

No language, of course, poetic or otherwise, can function without effective predication, and certainly on those few occasions when a poet opts to give prominence to finite verbs the effect can be striking. For instance, the debauched drunkenness of Holofernes, Nebuchadnezzar's general, in *Judith* lines 23–4 is conveyed entirely by verbs: *hloh and hlydde, / hlynede and dynede* (he laughed and roared, bellowed and thundered), with even the further emphasis of rhyme on the last pair. Finite verbs are also used to good effect when the poet describes the great relish with which Grendel devours one of Beowulf's men:

he gefeng hraðe   forman siðe
slæpendne rinc,   slat unwearnum,
bat ban-locan,   blod edrum dranc,
syn-snædum swealh;   sona hæfde
unlyfigendes   eal gefeormod,
fet ond folma.   (740–5)

(*first he quickly seized a sleeping man, tore him without a second thought, bit into the bone enclosure [body], drank the blood from the veins, and swallowed him in huge pieces; in no time at all he had gulped down every bit of the lifeless man, feet and hands.*)

Another characteristic of Old English poetic diction is the extensive use of the lexical process known as conversion. Conversion involves the use of a word belonging primarily to a particular word-class as a member of a different word-class, as in the use of the noun 'brick' as an adjective in the phrase 'a brick wall'. In Old English poetry conversion most commonly involves adjectives which are used as nouns. This is commonly described as the 'absolute' use of the adjective. For example, in *The Dream of the Rood* (57), after the death of Christ on the Cross, *fuse feorran cwoman* (eager [i.e. eager people] came from afar); and later (63) *aledon hie ðaer limwerigne* (there they laid down limb-weary [i.e. the limb-weary man, Christ]). In view of the fact that there is grammatical agreement between noun and adjective in Old English, it is usually easy to determine the grammatical function of the adjective when it is used as a noun in this way, such as whether it operates as subject or indirect object. It is possible to interpret these as examples of the noun unexpressed or 'understood', but occurrences are so frequent as to make this an unsatisfactory explanation.

The ability of the poet to use adjectives without related nouns is assisted by the ease with which in Old English, poetry and prose, the pronoun subject can be understood from the verb. For example, *singeþ* means not only 'sings' but also 'he/she/it sings'. In *The Seafarer* (92) the poet describes a grieving old man with the expression *gomel-feax gnornað*. *Gomel-feax* is a compound adjective meaning literally 'old-hair', i.e. 'grey-hair[ed]', and the two words together mean 'grey-haired mourns'; this may equally well be interpreted as '[the] grey haired [one] mourns' or 'grey haired, [he] mourns' – the absence of a noun or pronoun leaves the exact situation unclear. Yet again, a suitably relevant noun may be in an adjacent line, as when before the Battle of Maldon a young soldier symbolises his resolve by allowing his hawk to fly free:

> he let him þa of handon   leofne fleogan,
> hafoc wið þaes holtes.   (7–8)

Some editors print the comma at the end of line 7, giving the sense 'he then allowed the dear [one] to fly from his hands, [the] hawk towards the wood'. Alternatively, without the comma the meaning could be 'he then allowed the dear hawk . . . ' A listener, or a reader of the manuscript, would, of course, have had no help from any punctuation (there is usually little or none in early texts) and would therefore have been free to understand either way or both.[1] The lack of obligation for the poet to be specific in such matters engenders a syntactic and semantic brevity which counterbalances other, more general tendencies towards elaboration.

This elaboration can also be seen in the considerable amount of special vocabulary. In creating it poets were greatly assisted by the capacity of Old English in general to expand its word stock. Much of the apparent complexity of the poetic language is semantic, rather than morphological, for the poets utilised the ordinary patterns of lexical enlargement which were used in all spheres of Old English. The processes were similar to those of Modern English, relying for the most part (in addition to the process of conversion already mentioned) on affixation and compounding.

Affixation is the adding of prefixes and suffixes to a base word in order to modify the meaning, thus *niman* (to take) alongside *beniman* (to take away) and *laec* (leech, doctor) alongside *laecdom* (medicine). Affixation is not specially significant in the vocabulary of Old English poetry. Prefixes are usually lightly stressed and do not carry alliteration unless they dominate the meaning. Suffixes are like those of prose, but words generated by the process of suffixation may be distinctive to poetry. For example, *eorlscipe* (courage), an abstract noun formed by the addition of the suffix *-scipe* (-ship) to the word *eorl* (noble warrior), is not found outside poetry. Patronymic *-ing* is another widely used suffix. It has the meaning 'child/follower/people of . . .' and is found in place names like Birmingham (the village of Beornmund's people) and Reading (the people of Reada). While not exclusive to poetry, patronymic -*ing* words may acquire a poetic colouring in a particular context. In *Beowulf*, for example, the Danish people are sometimes called *Scyldingas* (the people of Scyld), in preference to, or in addition to, the more ordinary *Dene*.

The other main process of word formation is compounding, in which one word base is added to another. The number and class of the words which could combine and the syntactic relationship of the elements is more restricted in Old than in Modern English, but compounding was none the less a productive means of lexical enlargement, and was especially important in creating new nouns and adjectives in poetry. Examples taken from the poetry are:

noun + noun = noun	heoro-sweng (swordstroke)
adj + noun = noun	an-floga (lone-flyer)
adv + noun = noun	ellor-sið (elsewhere-journey, death)
adj + adj = adj	hwæt-eadig (brave and prosperous)
adj + noun = adj	dreorig-hleor ([with] miserable face)
noun + adj = adj	heaþo-rof (battle-brave)
adv + adj = adj	wid-cuþ (widely known)
prep/adv + verb = verb	geond-þencan (to ponder every aspect)

The distinction between compounding and affixation is sometimes not great. In the noun *ofer-mod* (pride, haughtiness – *literally* over-spirit) and the verb *geond-þencan* (*literally* throughout think) the first element is formally a prepositional prefix, but in the first case it has the force of an adjective and in the second that of an adverb. Compounds may also be very similar to phrases. There is little to choose, for instance, between *woruld-cyning* (world-king) and *woruldes cyning* (king of the world), except inasmuch as the poet may prefer one or the other for metrical reasons, the second having five syllables, the first only four.

As an alternative to using the natural resources of their own language speakers and writers sometimes resort to borrowing from another. Old English loan words come predominantly from four sources: Celtic, French, Scandinavian and Latin. Celtic loans are found mainly in place names and do not affect the poetry. French words begin to appear in English writings only from about the end of the tenth century, none of them initially in poetic texts.

The small number of Scandinavian loan words in pre-Conquest poetry are confined to *The Battle of Brunanburh* and *The Battle of Maldon*, which tell of encounters fought between Anglo-Saxons and Vikings in 937 and 991 respectively. In *Maldon* (35) a Viking messenger demands tribute money, which, he says, will be used to establish *griđ* (a truce). In another place (149) an attacker of the English leader is referred to as *drenga* (a warrior). In *Brunanburh* the word *cnear* (small ship, trading vessel) appears twice (35, 53). Each of these loan words is restricted to descriptions of the Scandinavian side and may have been felt to be consciously 'foreign'. It may be that they were considered to give an appropriate Scandinavian 'flavour'. Latin exerted a greater influence, as might be expected of a language which was unchallenged in the spheres of commerce, administration, religion, and learning. Latin loans are found in English from the time of the earliest written records. Such words were so widely assimilated that examples belonging specifically to the poetic register are difficult to identify with confidence. Latin words certainly enrich the poetic vocabulary, loans such as *draca* (dragon) appearing alongside the native equivalent, *wyrm*, and *deofol* (devil) alongside *feond* (*literally* enemy, *whence* fiend). In compound words and phrases Latin elements combine freely with English, as in *win-reced* (wine-building, feasting-hall), cf. Latin *vinum*, and *rodores candel* (candle of heaven, the sun), cf. Latin *candela*. In *Beowulf* 1600 the Latin loan *non* (*modern* noon) has been used as evidence in establishing the context of the poem, since the word seems to have lost its original application to a religious service celebrated at the ninth canonical hour and to indicate merely a certain time of the day (Whitelock 1951, 6), from which it is deduced that the poem must date from a time late enough to have allowed this change of meaning to occur.

All these processes – but especially that of compounding – are employed to create the elaborate poetic diction which is one of the features contributing to the immediate impression of mannerism and artifice in Old English verse. While a boat or a ship may be simply *bat* or *scip*, a whole range of words may be substituted or added, as the context requires. Amongst the words which appear as variations upon *bat* or *scip* are the simplices (i.e. uncompounded words) *brenting, fær, naca, flota* (floater), *ac* (oak, i.e. oak-built ship), *wudu* (wood, i.e. wooden ship), *bord* (plank), *ceol* (keel), *stefn* (prow), and the compounds *sæ-bat* (sea-boat), *sæ-genga* (sea-goer), *wæg-flota* (wave-floater), *brim-wudu* (sea-wood), *wæg-þel* (wave-plank), *sæ-mearh* (sea-steed), *yð-mearh* (wave-steed), *sæ-hengest* (sea-stallion), *fearoð-hengest* (current-stallion), *wæg-hengest* (wave-stallion), *sund-hengest* (surge-stallion), and *wæter-þisa* (water-rusher). As for phrases, it happens that no genitive phrase of the type **yða mearh* (steed of the waves) is recorded for 'ship'.[2] But there are many distinctive nominal phrases of noun + adjective, such as *flota fami-hals* (foamy-necked floater) and *wudu wunden-heals* (twisted-necked wooden ship), which refer to the vessel as a whole.

The words in the above list range from the literal to the figurative: *bat* and *sæ-bat* express the plain meaning; *ac* and *wudu* express the concept more obliquely, by reference to the material from which a ship is made; *ceol* and *bord* indicate the whole by reference to only one part; and *wæg-hengest* and *wæter-þisa* evoke the image of a creature thundering over the billows. Words such as these may be interchanged to provide the poet with a large number of near-synonyms (depending, of course, on the appropriate alliterative and metrical circumstances). Alternatively, in the case of the compounds the constituent parts may be varied (e.g. *wæg-*, *sæ-*, *brim-*, *fearoð-*, *sund-*, and *yð-* for the general concept of 'sea' and *-mearh* and *-hengest* for 'horse'). The effect is to produce a general impression of elaboration and lexical richness and to mark the register as clearly belonging to the world of poetry.

For other objects and concepts there is a similar range of terms: the sun is (among other things) 'heaven-light', 'heaven-candle', 'God's candle', 'heaven's gem', 'the bright beacon of God'; heaven is 'the homeland', 'the joy-land', 'the eternal kingdom', 'the land of angels', 'the glory-place'; hell is 'the abyss', 'the hot region', 'the home of darkness', 'the death-hall', 'the deep pit', 'the house of torment', 'the serpent-hall', 'the fire-enclosure'; the devil is 'the harmer', 'the criminal', 'the guardian of hell', 'the distributor of death', 'the prince of enemies', 'the ancient enemy', 'the slayer of mankind'; a lord is a 'leader of princes', a 'protector of warriors', a 'friend of the people', an 'adviser of men', a 'gold-friend', a 'ring-giver'; and a princess is a 'noble queen of the people', a 'peace-weaver' and a 'peace-bond of peoples' (referring to the role of marriage in establishing peace treaties).

A surprisingly large number of words occur only once in the 30,000 or so lines of extant Old English poetry. These are sometimes referred to as *hapax legomena*, a Greek term meaning 'once-said words'. Many will not actually have been unique, and many may not even have been unusual. Some of the once-occurring compounds, for instance, are completely regular in terms of their morphological structure and consist of lexical elements which are common as simplices or as elements of other compounds. So natural was the tendency and so great the potential for new permutations that it is hardly surprising that some ordinary-looking words turn out to be unique. Thus, *guð-helm* (war-helmet) and *guð-sweord* (war-sword) happen to be unique in Old English poetry, but *guð-bord* (war-shield) and *guð-bill* (war-sword) do not. One can appreciate the uniqueness of *benc-sweg* (bench-noise, the sound of rejoicing along the benches in the meadhall), but the fact that the mundane *benc-þel* (bench-plank) occurs only in *Beowulf* is more likely to be a matter of chance. If more manuscripts had survived, further occurrences of what to us are unique words might possibly have been found – but then again, more texts would undoubtedly produce more hapax legomena, for hardly any poem is without them.

Some, though, are more likely to be the deliberate creations of individual poets – or, at least, they seem to be exactly right in context. Beowulf's lord is said to have died in battle *hiora-dryncum* (2358) (from sword-drinks), a poet is described, in the same poem, as *gilp-hlæden* (868) (laden with proud speeches), and in *Exodus* 485 as Pharaoh's soldiers pursue the Israelites across the Red Sea *multon mere-torras* (the sea-towers melted) and they were all drowned. Words like these seem to bear the mark of individual imagination, but one can never know for certain. The problem with any medieval poem is that there is always a suspicion that unique or unusual words may be simply the result of miscopying or misunderstanding by a scribe, or perhaps, if the text has been copied and recopied, by a whole series of scribes.

Let us look in turn at these simplices, compounds and phrases. If we begin with the simplices, we find that most of them are found also in the prose. It is hardly surprising that words which offer the 'plain' designation, such as *bat*, *scip*, *hlaford* (lord), *sweord* (sword), and *spere* (spear) are encountered across the whole range of Old English literature, that is, in both poetry and prose. More interesting for present purposes are those which belong more naturally in the poetic register and are rarely or never found in prose. For the concept 'warrior' these include *beorn*, *freca*, *hæleð*, *scealc* and *secg*. Although these are frequently interchanged, we would be wrong in regarding them as absolute synonyms. Each would have carried shades of meaning reflecting their origins − *beorn* , it is suggested, originally meaning 'bear', *freca* meaning 'greedy one', hence perhaps 'wolf', *hæleð* meaning 'hero', and so on (see Wrenn 1967, 49). Possibly certain words would have been marked as poetic in West Saxon (the dialect in which almost all Old English poetry survives) by the fact that they were non-West Saxon dialect forms: *mece* (sword), for which the regular West Saxon would have been **mæce*, is an example (see Sisam 1953, 126−8). Others might perhaps have become obsolete in ordinary, non-poetic usage, though this would be impossible to prove. Of our 'ship' simplices, surviving records seem to suggest that *ac, bord, brenting, ceol, naca, stefn* and *wudu* are all restricted (largely, if not entirely) to the poetic register. The etymologies of *naca* and *brenting* are uncertain, but *flota* is clearly connected with *flotan* (to float), while *bord, ceol* and *stefn* are examples of metonymy, or, more precisely, of that type of metonymy known as synecdoche, whereby the whole of something is signified by reference to only one part. In a similar way *ac* and *wudu* refer to the materials from which a ship is fashioned. Simple nouns like these are sometimes elaborated through modification by semantically rich adjectives, such as *sæ-geap* (sea-broad), *nægled-bord* (made with nailed boards), *famig-heals* (foamy-necked), *niw-tyrwyd* (newly-tarred) and *wid-fæðme* (wide-bosomed).

In nominal compounds the second element (the base) determines the gender of the word as a whole. It is also this which takes the inflexional ending and determines the function of the compound within the clause. The first element modifies the second in some way. The distinctive morphological structure of compounds and their potential for semantic richness mean that compounds feature prominently in all Old English poetry. Like the simplices, compounds are found in both poetry and prose, though a large number are again restricted to the poetic register. These include even the most straightforward combinations of simplices, such as *sæ-bat*. Others, such as *sæ-genga* and *yð-lida* are restricted to the poetry because their bases are not found (with comparable meaning) in the prose. *Sæ-wudu, wæg-bord* and all the other -*wudu* and -*bord* compounds show synecdoche in the base with the initial element supplying a simple functional/environmental context. *Brim-hengest* and *sæ-mearh*, however, are of a significantly different order: their first elements operate in the same way, but their bases involve a poetic image, suggesting that a ship can be imagined as a horse galloping over the sea. Figurative compounds and phrases of this sort are commonly called 'kennings'.

'Kenning' is a term borrowed from the thirteenth-century writings of the Icelander Snorri Sturluson. Writing about the language of the Norse court poets, the skalds, Snorri used the term 'kenning' to describe elaborate circumlocutions such as 'the burden of dwarfs' for 'sky', 'the daughter of Mundilfæri' for 'the sun' and 'Draupnir's precious sweat' for 'gold'. Some such terms are so elaborate and allusive that in order to understand them one has to know the background of legend and belief upon which they draw.

The kenning was never precisely defined by Snorri, and its application to Old English is in many ways problematic, since some have taken the term to refer to a wide range of nominal expressions – simplices, compounds and phrases – while others have preferred to restrict it to a particular variety of poetic compound or phrase. Rarely, if ever, does Old English poetic diction acquire the riddle-like quality of the Icelandic expressions mentioned above, and one assumes that terms such as *reord-berend* (speech-bearers) for 'people' and *seolh-það* (seal-path) for 'sea' would have been immediately understood by a contemporary audience without the need to puzzle out the meaning.

The Old English kenning (taking the word in its restricted sense) draws much of its meaning from the context, which discourages the listener or reader from taking the expression literally. It is a two-part periphrasis (i.e. an indirect expression) of which the base element expresses the thing with which the referent is being compared, while the modifier (the first element in the case of compounds) signals the true context and modifies the apparent disparity between the base and referent. For example, the kenning *sæ-hengest* has the referent 'ship'. The base -*hengest* (stallion) is a figurative expression for 'ship', while the modifier *sæ*- indicates that this is no ordinary stallion but one which moves upon the sea. On the other hand *sæ-genga* and *yð-flota* are literally, not figuratively, true: a ship actually *is* a 'sea-goer' and a 'wave-floater'. These expressions, therefore, are not kennings because they lack the essential figurative or imaginative quality. It is this quality which gives kennings their special appeal. Other examples are 'bone-chamber' and 'life-house' (body), 'head-gem' (eye), 'wind-enclosure' (sea), 'pleasure-snare' (sin), 'laughter-smith' (minstrel) and 'battle-snake' (arrow).

Sometimes the image implicit in the kenning is carried over into the wider context. For example, in *The Runic Poem* (66) we are told that *se brim-hengest bridles ne gymeð* (the sea-stallion does not heed the bridle). Here the image of the horse has determined the choice of the word *bridles* and we are encouraged to imagine the ship as thrusting forward like a runaway steed. The image is natural and unforced. On the other hand in the poem *Christ* (862–3) the poet compares human life to a voyage across a dangerous sea to the final safety of a heavenly haven

> hwær we sælan sceolon   sund-hengestas,
> ealde yð-mearas,   ancrum fæste.
> (*where we must tether our sea-stallions, old wave-steeds, firmly with anchors.*)

Here the pervading image of sea-horses is suddenly abandoned, and with the word 'anchors' we are abruptly brought back to the world of ships. The result is an uncomfortable mixture of metaphors which is far less satisfactory than the image of the *Runic Poem*.

However, even when dealing with the more literal compounds, we find that the semantic relationship of the two elements is not always as clear-cut as in the examples given above and that context sometimes has to be used as a guide to the most appropriate meaning. For example, in the word *wine-drihten* (lord) we find that the first element does not modify the base in quite the same way. The full meaning is the sum of both parts (friend + lord), the compound stressing the qualities of approachability, reliability and benevolence which a lord should possess. *Mon-dryhten*, however, probably means not 'man and lord' but 'lord of men', the elements having the same semantic relationship as in *þeod-cyning* (king of people). Kings, of course, cannot be other than 'kings of people', so there is a suggestion of tautology here, as in other words like *frea-dryhten* (lord + lord) and *ferhð-sefa* (mind + thought). However, we would be wrong to dismiss such terms too readily as tautologous. *Þeod-cyning* calls to mind *þeod-gestreon* (people-treasure), used in *Beowulf* 44 to describe the precious objects loaded aboard the funeral ship of the mighty king Scyld. This in turn calls to mind the breathtaking treasures of the seventh-century royal ship-burial at Sutton Hoo in Suffolk, in which jewelled regalia, rich weapons and symbols of royal office were heaped in profusion. If these were *þeod-gestreon*, they were priceless royal heirlooms, 'national treasures' in every sense of the word. By analogy *þeod-cyning* may indicate a king of particularly high status. For *beorn-cyning*, on the other hand, two meanings seem equally possible – 'warrior-king' or 'king of warriors'. The same is true of some adjectives: the man who is *winter-cearig* may be 'sorrowful *as* winter' (figuratively) or 'sorrowful *because of* winter' (literally), and the spear which is *feol-heard* may be 'hardened/sharpened *with* a file' or 'hard *as* a file', or perhaps both.

The literal meaning may, in any case, be irrelevant, misleading, or at best inadequate. In a perceptive analysis of poetic compounds evocative of desolation and wretchedness, E. G. Stanley (Stanley 1955, 434–41) shows how the first element of words like *morgen-ceald* (morning-cold) evokes a mood of gloom and misery. Morning, to Anglo-Saxon thinking, was a time of special misery, as were *uhtan* (dawn *or* the last part of the night) and the season of winter. The *morgen-longne dæg* of *Beowulf* 2894 makes no sense if taken literally, but is brilliantly effective in suggesting how the anxieties of the morning are increased and carried over later into the day as Beowulf's men await news of the outcome of his fight against the dragon. Likewise, warriors must grasp the 'morning-cold spear' (*Beowulf* 3021–2), while in *Resignation* 95–6 *him bið a sefa geomor, | mod morgen-seoc* (his thoughts are always sorrowful, his mood morning-sick). Conversely, when Beowulf promises that he will grapple with Grendel and destroy him during the night, so that people will be able to go without fear to the meadhall

> ﹀   siþþan morgen-leoht
> ofer ylda bearn oþres dogores,
> sunne swegl-wered   suþan scineð   (604–6)
> (*when the morning-light of another day, the bright-clothed
> sun, shines from the south upon the children of men*),

the greatness of the deed is accentuated by the fact that – if it comes off – Beowulf will have reversed the wretched associations of the morning, when the Danes in the past have so often had to creep to the meadhall to count their dead. *Uht-cearu* (dawn-sorrow) and *winter-cearig* (winter-sorrowful) convey similar feelings. Together with cold, frost, storms and the sea, they form an evocative network of associations by means of which sensitive undercurrents of anxiety could be suggested even in the midst of a scene of rejoicing.

Nominal phrases in which a qualifying genitive performs the same function as the first element of a compound are sometimes also included among the kennings, so long as the essential figurative quality is present. Admissible phrases would be *yða ful* (cup of the waves, sea), *worulde hrof* (roof of the world, sky), *roderes candel* (sky's candle, sun), *fugles wyn* (bird's joy, feather), *sumeres weard* (guardian of summer, cuckoo), *heafdes gimmas* (gems of the head, eyes), *wæl-gara wrixl* (exchange of slaughter spears, battle), and *eorla wynn* (delight of warriors, lord). Phrases such as *gold-wine gumena* (gold-friend of men, lord) and *beorht beacen godes* (bright beacon of God, sun) have the genitive after the noun, but otherwise the pattern is the same. Phrases of identical structure but lacking the metaphorical quality of the above examples would not be considered as kennings – for example *Dryhtnes word* (the word of God) and *wintres woma* (the tumult of winter). Phrases for Christian concepts, and especially for 'God', are more numerous and varied than any others. Some of these have parallels in Latin phrases, which in some cases may have influenced the English poets (Rankin 1909–10). These include *godes boda*, Lat. *nuntius dei* (messenger of God, angel), *feond mon-cynnes*, Lat. *hostis humani generis* (enemy of mankind, devil), and *sigores tacen*, Lat. *signum victoriae* (sign of victory, the Cross). Terms for 'God' include *fæder ælmihtig*, Lat. *pater omnipotens* (almighty father), *fæder swegles*, Lat. *pater celestis* (father of heaven), *heofenes weard*, Lat. *caeli defensor* (guardian of heaven), *lifes brytta*, Lat. *dator vitae* (giver of life), and *lifes fruma*, Lat. *fons vitae* (source of life). However, the similarities between Old English and Latin phrases are not so striking or so extensive as to imply wholesale dependence of the English poets upon Latin originals.

It has been mentioned that verbal phrases feature less prominently than nominal phrases in the Old English poetic diction. However, there is a small but significant exception in the case of expressions meaning 'live' and 'die'. The structure is usually verb + complement/object or complement/object + verb. Expressions for 'live' include *worulde brucan* (to enjoy the world), *blæd-daga brucan* (to enjoy days of prosperity), and *worolde wynne healdan* (to hold the joy of the world). Phrases for 'die' are more numerous and varied, and include *gewitan of worulde dreamum* (to go from the world's pleasures), *heonan gangan* (to go hence), *gum-dream of gyfan* (to give up the pleasures of men), *hleator alecgan, gamen and gleo-dream* (to put aside laughter, play and the joy of music), *flet ofgyfan* (to give up the hall), *gewitan on frean wære* (to go into the protection of the Lord), *feorh sellan* (to give up life), *aldor-gedal fremman* (to achieve separation from life), *grund-wong ofgyfan* (to give up the earth), *ellor scacan* (to hasten elsewhere), and *ceosan ecne ræd* (to choose everlasting gain). These are very much like present-day euphemisms for 'die', such as 'pass away' and 'depart this life'.

To illustrate the range and frequency of poetic terms, it may be helpful to list the words for 'sword' in the single 3182-line poem *Beowulf* (see Brady 1979). The uncompounded words are these: *sweord* (39 occurrences), *bill* (11), *mece* (9), *brond* (1), *heoru* (1), *seax* (1), and *secg* (1). It is impossible to be sure of the distinctions of meaning between these terms. *Sweord* is probably the general term. *Bill* and *mece* may refer to a particular type of long two-edged sword, while *seax* is a short one-edged weapon, the sort used to finish off a wounded opponent. But in general the distinctions between these uncompounded words are not well understood.

As for the compounds for 'sword', the more straightforward ones are *hilde-bill* (4 occurrences), *guð-bill* (2), *hilde-mece, beado-mece, guð-sweord* and *wig-bill*, in all of which the first element means 'war' or 'battle'. Equally straightforward is *wæll-seax* (slaughter-knife). *Maððum-sweord* (treasure-sword) stresses the rich ornamentation which made Anglo-Saxon swords highly prized possessions, and *wæg-sweord* means 'wave-sword', the first element probably referring to the wavy patterns on the sword blade produced by the forging process known as 'pattern-welding'. The *hæft-mece* (?haft-sword) with which Beowulf goes armed against Grendel's troll-mother seems to be a special type, perhaps a long-hilted, double-edged sword wielded with both hands. In *hilde-leoma* and *beado-leoma* the second element means 'ray or beam or gleam of light, flash of lightning'; the allusion is to the sword as a battle-light, perhaps literally, referring to the flashing blade, or figuratively, referring to the inspirational 'light' of a bravely wielded weapon. Clearly imaginative is *guð-wine* (war-friend), in which the weapon is personified as a faithful supporter in battle.

The above simplices and compounds relate to the sword more or less in its entirety. There are also many words which refer to parts of swords, e.g. *hilt* (5 occurrences), *fetel-hilt* (?ring-hilt), and *scenn* (?guard). Other words refer to the whole sword by means of one part (e.g. *ecg* 'edge [of the blade]') or by reference to the material from which it is made (e.g. *iren* 'iron'). Of a rather different status is the word *laf* (10 occurrences), meaning 'that which is left', which, when qualified by a noun in the genitive case, may refer to a sword as a bequest from an ancestor (e.g. *Eanmundes laf, suna Ohteres* 'the bequest of Eanmund, son of Ohthere') or as a manufactured item (e.g. *fela laf, homera laf* 'that which is left when the files/hammers have done their work', with a possible secondary meaning: 'the bequest of files/hammers', i.e. with the files/hammers personified and imagined as passing on the weapon as if by bequest). The latter are both circumlocutions for weapons forged by the smith and might refer to any such weapons – only the context supplies the correct meaning. In the case of *incge-laf*, however, the context is inadequate and the meaning of the word is lost.

Other genitive epithets for the sword are *giganta geweorc* (the work of giants), *wundor-smiþa geweorc* (the work of wondersmiths), and *enta ær-geweorc* (the ancient work of giants), all of which refer, either literally or figuratively, to the supposed miraculous origins of swords. Along the same lines is *eald-sweord eotenisc* (ancient sword of giants). This same sword is described by the unique compound adjective *sige-eadig* (victory-blessed). Also unique is the dative noun *hilde-gicelum*, which occurs when Beowulf hacks off Grendel's head, causing the corrosive blood to gush forth and melt the blade 'in battle-icicles'. Characteristic 'sword' adjectives found in *Beowulf* and elsewhere include *brun-ecg* (bright-edged), *heard-ecg* (hard-edged), and *scur-heard*, which literally means 'shower-hard', i.e. 'hard or unflinching in the storm of battle' or possibly 'hardened *by* the storm of battle'. In *Beowulf* a number of distinctive adjectives seem to refer to the process of pattern-welding mentioned above, for example, *hring-mæl* (ring-marked), *wunden-mæl* (plait-marked), *broden-mæl*, *brogden-mæl* (woven-marked), and *ater-tanum fah* (decorated with poison-twigs), all probably referring to the distinctive markings left on the blade by the process of twisting together a bundle of iron rods to ensure that the weapon is both flexible and strong. This is by no means an exhaustive list of words related to the concept 'sword' in *Beowulf*, but it is quite sufficient to demonstrate the lexical and semantic complexity.

Semantically this complex stock of poetic terms raises some interesting general and individual questions. A number of these are connected with the great cultural gulf between present-day society and that of the Anglo-Saxons, and our consequent difficulty in re-creating the values and ideals which the poets took for granted and which lie behind many of the effects they were aiming to achieve. T. A. Shippey has pointed out, in connection with *Beowulf*, how such things as boasting, drunkenness and physical violence were viewed differently. For instance, on the subject of drink,

> ale, beer, wine and mead are mentioned more than forty times in the poem, while there is no word for any item of food at all – the source, evidently, of many modern objections. Worse still, the characters view this with complacency. When Beowulf says to Unferth that he has said a great deal about Breca, *beore druncen* (531), he clearly means that Unferth is 'drunk on beer' and accordingly unreliable. The Danish queen Wealhtheow, however, once more causes semantic difficulty when she uses the same word in her idyllic description of Heorot (1228–31): 'Here every man is true to the other, kind-hearted and loyal to his lord, the thanes are united, the people are willing, the drunken retainers (*druncne dryhtguman*) do as I say.' Nervousness breaks out among many translators at this stage, with *druncne* rendered as 'carousing' or 'cheered with drink' or 'wine-glad' or even more circuitous paraphrase. But the problem is a cultural one; we cannot translate *druncne* as 'drunken' only because it seems to us not to collocate with words like 'true' and 'loyal' and 'united'. Our conventional wisdom says that drunkenness is associated with weakness of character.
>
> (Shippey 1978, 9)

A related problem is the difficulty of distinguishing between living and dead metaphors, between what was regarded as figurative and what was considered fact. Many words which today we regard as totally ordinary began life as metaphors – words like 'lord', Old English *hlaford*, from *hlaf* + *weard* (loaf + guardian) and 'lady', Old English *hlafdige*, possibly from *hlaf* + *dige* (loaf + kneader). Words like this had probably lost their picturesque associations by the time of the earliest written records, but it is impossible to be sure. When a poet used the word *gar-secg* (*literally* spear + man) for 'ocean', did he have in mind a Neptune-like personification? When he used *gewiofu* (weavings) for 'destiny', was he thinking of some mythological figures comparable to the Roman Parcae or Norse Norns who wove the thread of fate? When he used the expression *Welandes geweorc* (the work of Wayland, the legendary smith) with reference to a fine sword or suit of chainmail, or the phrase *enta geweorc* (the work of giants) to describe the ruins of a great Roman city, can we be sure that these were only figures of speech, or do they reflect an actual belief in Wayland and in giants? A similar problem arises when the poet of *Beowulf* describes the melting of a magical sword:

> Þæt wæs wundra sum,
> þæt hit eal gemealt   ise gelicost,
> ðonne forstes bend   Fæder onlæteð,
> onwindeð wæl-rapas.   (1607–10)
> (*It was a great marvel, in that it completely melted, very much like ice when the Father [God] releases the fetter of frost, unbinds the water-ropes.*)

Are *forstes bend* (fetter of frost) and *wæl-rapas* (water-ropes) picturesque images, or a 'scientific' explanation, in terms of contemporary thought, of the phenomenon of the formation of ice? Unfortunately we are not in a position to know.

Punning and wordplay in a written text are more difficult to recognise than in the same text read aloud. In the absence of intonational markers one looks for other clues, but it is rarely possible to be absolutely certain. However, Frank has given convincing examples from Old English biblical poetry of a type of etymological or pseudo-etymological wordplay called *paronomasia*. There are, for example, passages in which the author seems deliberately to be playing with the sounds of key words, such as at the beginning of the poem *Genesis A*:

> Us is riht micel   ðæt we rodera weard,
> wereda wuldor-cining,   wordum herigen.
> (*It is our great duty to praise with words the guardian of the heavens, the glory-king of hosts.*)

Frank notes that this triple paronomasia

> seems to be trying to persuade us that the poet's literary
> and Christian purposes are one, that nothing could be
> more natural or right in English than that the *weard*,
> king of *weroda*, should be praised in *wordum*.
>
> (Frank 1972, 212)

Poets were able to take advantage of the regular stressing of key
syllables in poetry by using the main alliterating lifts either side of
the caesura paronomastically to suggest a link not only of sound
but also of sense. Thus:

> Þa wæs Sarran   sar on mode   (*Genesis A* 2216)
> (*Then was Sarah sore in heart*)

and

> Hwæt, þu Eue, hæfst   yfele gemearcod...   (*Genesis B* 791)
> (*Lo, you, Eve, have marked with evil...*).

In the latter case the *f* between vowels was pronounced as *v*,
accentuating the association between 'Eve' and 'evil'. In Latin
texts the English poets had established models for wordplay like
this, a favourite example being that the original sin of Eve (Latin
Eva) was reversed in *Ave*, the first word of Gabriel's announcement
to Mary that she would bear a child, who through the Redemption
gave every Christian the means of overcoming Original Sin. So in
Old English religious poetry when we find 'God' coupled time and
again with 'good', and 'man' (O.E. *mann*) with 'sin' (O.E. *man*) it is
likely in many cases to be more than accidental.

The opportunities for such associations were very much
increased by the formulaic character of Old English verse, and, in
particular, by the recurrent collocations (i.e. habitual and
expected co-occurrences of words) that are found at every turn.
A glance at a concordance of Old English poetry (e.g. Bessinger
1978) shows that words tend to recur in twos and threes. For exam-
ple, forms of the word *leoht* (light) together with compounds in
which *leoht* is the first element are found in the verse in 232 places,
in 54 of which they collocate and alliterate with the word *lif* (life)
or one of its compounds or derivatives. In two-thirds of these cases

(36) the two words are in separate halves of the long line of verse, circumstances which suggest that they were not thought of as forming a concise alliterating phrase or formula. In the remaining eighteen cases the two words occur in the same half-line, including twelve in which the half-line is totally occupied by the formula *lifes leoht-fruma* (source of the light of life). *Liss* (joy) and *leof* (dear) are two words commonly found in proximity. While the currency of the formula *lifes leoht-fruma* may in this case have predisposed poets to link *leoht* with *lif*, many similar pairings cannot be explained in this way. Hundreds of such parallels occur, in both Christian and heroic poetry, and in many cases the words and phrases involved do not take part in the alliteration. Sometimes the similarities are not merely between individual words and phrases but between a number of them in succession.[3] No satisfactory explanation for this phenomenon has ever been proposed.[4]

Viewed uncharitably many such collocations could be thought of merely as clichés, and indeed in poorer poetry they sometimes seem to be just that. But they can also be used to striking effect. Alliterating words, for instance, may be semantically complementary, so emphasising qualities which the poet wishes us to associate with the subject. So the poet of *Beowulf* on twelve of the occasions when he mentions the evil Grendel by name links the name in the same line with the alliterating word *guð* (warfare, hostility), occasionally supplemented with a third alliterating word of related associations, such as *gryre* (terror) and *grim* (fierce). Fundamental associations are thus driven home, and whenever Grendel's name is mentioned it triggers connotations of hostility and fear (see Quirk 1963, 155–6). On the other hand, collocations may give rise to suggestive contrast between alliterating words. Beowulf and the dragon are sometimes contrasted in this way, for example by the alliteration of *dryhten* (lord) with *draca* (dragon, line 2402) and *leof* (dear one) with *lað* (hated one, line 2910). While the contrasted associations of Beowulf and the dragon are entirely to be expected, other collocations achieve their effect by bringing together words with jarringly dissimilar associations. So when Beowulf gets into an argument with the Danish councillor Unferð and accuses him of having been the slayer of his brothers,

> ... þeah ðu þinum broðrum   to banan wurde   (587)
> (... *though you became a slayer to your brothers*),

the associations of the first alliterating word, *broðrum*, are dramatically thwarted by the next, *banan* (slayer).

Lexical choice, then, was determined by many factors operating at one and the same time. The desire for complementary or contrastive collocation, often reinforced by traditional associations, was as important as the need to resolve metrical demands and effectively to convey the required sense. The balancing of these needs is a measure of the poet's skill, and the finest of the surviving verse shows how effectively this challenge was met.

5   Old English Verse:
Structure and Organisation

Syntax is that aspect of language study which is concerned with the ways in which small units of language combine to form larger ones. To take an analogy from house building, the systematic bringing together of materials such as bricks, mortar, timber and slates to make a house is akin to *syntax* in the same way as the calculation and ordering of the individual items from a breakdown of the architect's drawings is akin to *morphology*, the complementary branch of language study which looks at ways in which such things as clauses can be broken down into phrases, phrases into words and words into morphemes. Syntax, being an all-pervasive aspect of language, has inevitably been touched upon in Chapter 4 (e.g. in discussing the combination of simple words in compounds). The present chapter looks at the syntax of Old English poetry up to the level of sentence.

The chief syntactical embellishment, and one which invariably strikes those coming to Old English poetry for the first time, is the rhetorical figure known as 'variation'. This is a term invented in the nineteenth century and, as far as we know, there is no Anglo-Saxon equivalent.[1] Variation is a type of apposition, a common feature of English syntax, which is the placing together (cf. Lat. *appositus*) of nouns or nominal phrases, each with the same referent, in syntactically parallel constructions within a single sentence, but without any formal linking words. An example is 'Alfred, king of Wessex', where the proper noun 'Alfred' and the nominal phrase 'king of Wessex', both having the same referent (i.e. the historical Alfred), are placed side by side without any connecting word or words. If one allows that the appositive elements need not necessarily stand immediately together (e.g. 'Alfred appeared, king of Wessex') and that they need not be restricted to nouns and nominal phrases, one has arrived at the commonly accepted understanding of 'variation' in Old English poetry. These lines from *Beowulf* illustrate how this works in Old English:

> Him se yldesta   andswarode,
> werodes wisa,   word-hord onleac.   (258–9)
> (*To him the senior one answered, leader of the troop,*
> *unlocked his word-hoard.*)

The phrases 'the senior one' and 'leader of the troop' both refer to Beowulf and stand in a relationship of variation, even though they happen to be separated by the first verb. 'Answered' is similarly varied by 'unlocked his word-hoard', though the first is a simple verb and the second consists of object + verb.

The most straightforward form of variation is that which involves only nominal phrases, nouns and pronouns. Here the many simplices and compounds described in the last chapter are involved – in fact, their existence made variation possible, and variation in turn probably encouraged the use of the many synonyms and near-synonyms which are so characteristic of Old English poetic diction.

All the main elements of a clause – subject, object, verb, and adjunct – may be involved in variation. In particular, subject commonly varies with subject, and object with object. Examples could be given from almost any Anglo-Saxon poem. The following lines from Cædmon's *Hymn* show threefold variation of the subject and twofold variation of the object:

> Þa middan-geard   mon-cynnes weard,
> ece drihten,   æfter teode
> firum foldan,   frea ælmihtig.   (7–9)
> (*The guardian of mankind, the eternal lord, the*
> *almighty ruler afterwards adorned for mortals the*
> *middle-enclosure, the earth.*)

Variation involving verbs is also found, especially with verbs of speaking:

Satan maðelode, sorgiende spræc...   (*Genesis B* 347)
(*Satan made a speech, sorrowing he spoke...*).

Euphemistic expressions meaning 'to die' also tend to recur:

... gum-dream ofgeaf,   Godes leoht geceas   (*Beowulf* 2469)
(... *gave up worldly joy, chose God's light*).

Variation also occurs in the adjunct (i.e. that part of the clause which provides information which is supplementary to the main elements); for example, the Vikings at the Battle of Maldon advance *west ofer Pantan,/ ofer scir wæter* (west across the River Panta [Blackwater], across the bright water).

Variation may even involve whole clauses. In the opening lines of *Beowulf*,

Hwæt, we Gar-Dena   in gear-dagum,
þeod-cyninga   þrym gefrunon,
hu ða æþelingas   ellen fremedon
(*Listen! We have heard of the might of the Spear-Danes*
in days gone by, of the people-kings, how the princes
performed courageous deeds),

the final clause ('how the princes performed courageous deeds') is a variation of the nominal phrase ('the might of the Spear-Danes'), both being the object of the verb ('have heard') and referring to the same thing, i.e. what was heard.

Variation should be distinguished from similar constructions, such as enumeration:

Twelfe wæron
dædum dom-fæste,   dryhtne gecorene,
leofe on life.   (*Fates of the Apostles*, 4−6)
(*They were twelve, illustrious in their deeds, chosen*
by the lord, beloved in life.)

Here the three adjectival phrases descriptive of the apostles are an enumeration of distinct and separate qualities, rather than a re-statement of the same quality in varying terms. It should also be

remembered that the components of variation need to be closely
contiguous, normally operating within the same sentence, yet not
formally linked by any grammatical co-ordinator. For example, in
the following lines:

> [Ic] behold hreow-cearig   Hælendes treow,
> oððæt ic gehyrde   þæt hit hleoðrode.
> Ongan þa word sprecan   wudu selesta:
>
> (*Dream of the Rood* 25-7)
>
> (*Troubled and sorrowful I beheld the Saviour's tree,*
> *until I heard it talk. The most excellent wood then*
> *spoke words:*)

Hælendes treow and *wudu selesta* are two of some twenty-four expres-
sions in *The Dream of the Rood* for the cross on which Christ died.
Though they have the same referent, they are in separate sen-
tences, one as the object of *beheold* and the other as the subject of
ongan sprecan. These are variant terms, therefore, only in a loose
sense, not in terms of rhetorical variation. Similarly, the other
expressions for 'cross' in the poem as a whole cannot be said to
show variation in any strict sense of the word unless they occur in
the same sentence. On the other hand, words and phrases are not
necessarily excluded from participating in variation simply on the
grounds that they are in a different grammatical case. When
Grendel's mother takes vengeance for her son by carrying off the
noble Æschere, we are told some facts about the victim:

> Se wæs Hroþgare   hæleþa leofost
> on gesiðes had   be sæm tweonum,
> rice rand-wiga,   þone ðe heo on ræste abreat,
> blæd-fæstne beorn.   (*Beowulf* 1296-9)
>
> (*He was of men the most dear to Hrothgar of 'gesith'*
> *rank between the seas, a mighty shield-soldier, whom*
> *she destroyed in his bed, a renowned warrior.*)

Grammatically speaking, *hæleþa leofost* (the most dear of men) and
rice rand-wiga (a mighty shield-soldier) are both in the nominative
(subject complement) case, agreeing with *se* (he), whereas *blæd-
fæstne beorn* (a renowned warrior) is in the accusative (object)
case, agreeing with the immediately antecedent *þone ðe* (whom).

Despite these differences, the three phrases clearly refer, within the same sentence, to Æschere, and are examples of effective variation (see Brodeur 1959, 273).

As to the function of variation, a helpful and concise statement, relating to *Beowulf*, is given by Robinson. Though he actually speaks of 'apposition', Robinson regards this as equivalent to 'variation':

> Apposition, by its very nature, conditions readers to read the poem in a certain way. It is a retarding device and thus forces us to read reflectively, pausing to consider an object or action from more than one perspective as the poet supplies alternate phrasings for the same general referent. It is paratactic and so implies relationships without expressing them, thereby adding to the elliptical quality which is importantly present in the narrative as a whole. Apposition is predominantly nominal and adjectival and thus contributes to that sense of stasis in the narrative whereby a state or situation seems to be dwelled on in preference to 'a straightforward account of action' (Klaeber 1950, lxvi). Appositions also serve as transitional devices, enabling the poet to move swiftly and easily from one aspect of a subject to another – even within the limits of a single sentence. Beyond these effects, however, apposition functions in various ways to remind the poem's audience of the multiple levels of meaning present in words that make up the traditional Old English diction as it was adapted by the poet of *Beowulf*.
>
> (Robinson 1985, 60–1)

Brodeur, in a detailed study, also comes to the conclusion that variation

> restrains the pace of Old English poetic narrative, gives to dialogue or monologue its leisurely or stately character, raises into high relief those concepts which the poet wishes to emphasize, and permits him to exhibit the object of his thought in all its aspects.
>
> (Brodeur 1959, 39)

Klaeber gives examples from *Beowulf* of accumulations of variations 'for the sake of emphasis, as in characterizing a person, describing an object or a situation, and in address', but also points out passages which are effective because of the absence of variation in suggesting businesslike speech, incisive exhortations and rapid action (Klaeber 1950, lxviii). Greenfield explores these and other effects in a wider range of Old English poetry, drawing interesting analogies with recent English writings (Greenfield 1972, 60–83). Altogether, few critics would dissent from the view that variation is the single most distinctive feature of Old English poetic syntax.

A number of writers have drawn an analogy between variation in poetry and the geometrical and zoomorphic interlace that the Anglo-Saxons loved to use in their art. It was an art which tended towards abstraction. Curvilinear strands of knots and braids, or of animals with their limbs and bodies interwoven, were a favourite motif in metalwork, painting and sculpture. Leyerle (Leyerle 1967) sees structural interlace as a guiding principle of the *Beowulf* poet at every level, and illustrates its effects at text level by reference to lines 2354–9:

<blockquote>

No þæt læsest wæs
hond-gemota,   þær mon Hygelac sloh,
syððan Geata cyning   guðe ræsum,
frea-wine folca   Freslondum on,
Hreðles eafora   hioro-dryncum swealt,
bille gebeaten.

(That was not the least
of hand-to-hand encounters, where Hygelac was killed,
when the king of the Geats in the rush of battle,
the beloved friend of the people, in Frisia,
the son of Hrethel, died of battle-drinks [wounds],
struck down with the sword.)

</blockquote>

Although awkward in modern English [Leyerle writes], a translation following the original order of phrases shows the stylistic interlace... *Hygelac, Geata cyning, frea-wine folca, and Hreðles eafora* make one strand; *mon ... sloh, hioro-dryncum swealt,* and *bille gebeaten* make a second strand; *þær, guðe ræsum,* and *Freslondum on* make a third. The three stands are woven together in a stylistic braid.

73

This feature of style is familiar to readers of Anglo-Saxon poetry and is the literary counterpart for inter-lace designs in art that are decorative rather than structural.

(Leyerle 1967, 5)

Another analogy that points up the syntactical complexity of Old English verse in its use of variation and other rhetorical patterns is to an 'envelope' of words or ideas, or both, at the beginning of a group of verses and at the end. These sometimes give a sense of unity or logical completeness, as in this example from *The Battle of Maldon* 25–8:

Þa stod on stæðe,   stiðlice clypode
wicinga ar,   wordum mælde,
se on beot abead   brim-liþendra
ærænde to þam eorle,   þær he on ofre stod.
(*Literal translation: There on the bank stood, resolutely shouted,
the messenger of the vikings, spoke with words,
he who in boast announced the seafarers'
message to the ealdorman, where he stood on the bank.*)

Bartlett draws attention to the chiastic[2] structure of the opening and closing phrases, and, within the 'envelope' so formed, of the further chiastic patterning of the two genitives *wicinga* and *brim-liþendra*. She goes on:

A diagram of this short stanza-like verse group would be something like this:

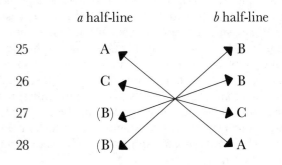

in which A is the place idea, standing on shore; B is the central idea of calling and delivering the message; C is the idea of the pirates' messenger. 27a and 28a are in parentheses to indicate that those half-lines are only partial or indirect expressions of the idea. The fact that *on ofre stod* should probably be read with a changed subject (Byrhtnoth instead of the *wicinga ar*) does not invalidate the scheme, which is dependent on verbal agreement of parts and logical unity of the whole. Reading the passage aloud will show the Envelope pattern even better than the diagram does. The diagram, however, shows better the possible origin of the Envelope pattern in simple chiasmus.

(Bartlett 1935, 10)

Bartlett gives many further examples of this and similar patterns in Anglo-Saxon verse, which show that such occurrences cannot be simply a matter of chance.

Whereas repeated words and phrases involved in the 'envelope pattern' are clearly there by design, others are so extensively and randomly scattered throughout Old English verse as to require a quite different explanation. Readers will be constantly stirred by a sense of *déjà vu*. Collocations (i.e. habitual and expected co-occurrences of words) are found in prose as well as in verse. They mostly involve nouns, adjectives and verbs. Some are naturally paired because of a semantic connection, e.g. *hungor and þurst* (hunger and thirst), *geong and eald* (young and old), *herian and lofian* (praise and glorify). Of these, a number are linked by alliteration, e.g. *eafoð and ellen* (strength and courage), *wlitig and wynsum* (beautiful and charming), *habban and healdan* (have and hold), others by rhyme, e.g. *bord and ord* (shield and spear), *frod and god* (wise and good), *healdan and wealdan* (hold and control). In some a combination of semantic and formal appropriateness explains their appeal: thus the natural pairing of *wer and wif* (man and woman) is accentuated by the fact that the nouns are alliterating monosyllables, while *duguð and geoguð* (experienced warriors and young, untried fighting men) are linked in meaning and in the fact that they rhyme. In the same way many traditional collocations in present-day English, such as *deaf and dumb* and *flotsam and jetsam,* seem naturally to belong together.

Recurrent collocations also take the form of phrases or short clauses. It is often the case that no obvious explanation for their recurrence can be found. Beowulf, for example, in preparing to fight the dragon (2524–5), vows that *nelle ic ... oferfleon fotes trem* (I will not flee ... the space of one foot), in strikingly similar terms to those in which Leofsunu at the Battle of Maldon (246–7) asserts his intention to resist the Danes (*ic ... nelle fleon fotes trym*). In both cases the avowed intention not to flee is followed by contrastive *ac ...* (but...) and the promise to fight bravely to the death.[3] Collocations on this level are so numerous and widespread that they cannot all be explained away either as borrowings from one text to another or as mere clichés. Rather they are features of a poetic idiom, partly dependent on subject matter and partly on form, with which literary users apparently did not feel uncomfortable, as they might today with such well-worn expressions. Familiar and traditional language seems to have been enjoyed and respected, and appropriateness valued more highly than novelty.

These recurrent words and phrases in Old English verse are known as 'formulae'. Their existence has long been recognised, but no fully convincing explanation of them has ever been given. An important, but controversial, attempt, however, was made by F. P. Magoun (Magoun 1953), who argued that they are carried over from a time when the poetry was extemporised and orally delivered. Magoun built his theory on pioneering work by Milman Parry and Albert Lord into Homeric and con-temporary oral versification in Yugoslavia, his personal contribu-tion being to develop their findings in the context of Old English. The theory holds that poetry in illiterate communities is com-posed by an 'oral-formulaic' process, whereby singers and poets make up their verse as they go along, not learning a fixed text but drawing upon a stock of memorised words and phrases that could be varied according to the demands of the subject matter and of any formal requirements, such as the need to alliterate or rhyme. The memorised word or phrase is the 'formula', and is defined by Parry as 'a group of words which is regularly employed under the same metrical conditions to express a given essential idea' (quoted in Lord 1960, 4). When a poem comes to be written down, of course, its text becomes fixed in a way that is quite uncharacteristic of the circumstances in which oral-formulaic verse flourishes.

Nevertheless, it is not difficult to see that extant written verse could well be described as 'formulaic':

Unferð maþelode,   Ecglafes bearn   (*Beowulf* 499)
(*Unferth spoke, the child of Ecglaf*)

Beowulf maþelode,   bearn Ecgþeowes   (*Beowulf* 529)
(*Beowulf spoke, the child of Ecgtheow*)

Wiglaf maðelode,   Weohstanes sunu   (*Beowulf* 2862)
(*Wiglaf spoke, the son of Weohstan*)

Magoun illustrates his theory by means of an analysis of passages from *Beowulf* and *Christ and Satan*. He defines a 'formula' (marked in the text below with solid underlining) as 'a word group of any size or importance which appears elsewhere in *Beowulf* or other Anglo-Saxon poems unchanged or virtually unchanged', and distinguishes it from a 'formulaic phrase or system' (marked with broken underlining), by which he means a group of words which is less closely paralleled but for which related groups can be found, conforming to the same verbal and grammatical pattern. For the parts left unmarked no supporting evidence can be found. The following is a short sample:

Hwæt, we Gar-Dena   on gear-dagum,
þeod-cyninga   þrym gefrugnon,
hu ða æðelingas   ellen fremedon!
Oft Scyld Scefing   sceaþena þreatum,
monigum mægþum   meodu-setla ofteah,
egsode eorlas,   syððan ærest wearð
fea-sceaft funden.   (*Beowulf* 1–7)
(*Listen! We have heard of the might of the Spear-Danes in days gone by, of the people-kings, how the princes performed courageous deeds. Often Scyld Scefing wrested the mead-benches from troops of enemies, from many tribes, after he had formerly been found destitute.*)

Several of the formulae at the beginning occur together: cf. *Exodus* 1 (*Hwæt, we feor and neah   gefrigen habbað*); *Andreas* 1 (*Hwæt, we gefrugnon on fyrn dagum*); *Fates of the Apostles* 63, *Elene* 364, 852 (*Hwæt, we þæt gehierdon ðurh halge bec*) ; etc. The formulaic phrase *fea-sceaft funden* in line 7a of *Beowulf*, however, has no closer analogue than *onfindað fea-sceaftne* in *Andreas* 181. Had more texts survived it would probably have been possible to classify a number of these formulaic phrases as formulae, along with other words and phrases which, on the basis of our limited records, are completely unparalleled. Even within *Beowulf*, Magoun claims, 'at least fifteen per cent of the verses of the poem are to all intents and purposes repeated' (Magoun 1953, 454).

The more controversial aspect of Magoun's theory is his assertion that

> the recurrence in a given poem of an appreciable
> number of formulas or formulaic phrases brands the
> latter as oral, just as a lack of such repetitions marks a
> poem as composed in a lettered tradition. Oral poetry,
> it may be safely said, is composed entirely of formulas,
> large and small, while lettered poetry is never formulaic.
>
> (Magoun 1953, 446)

In these terms, virtually all extant Old English poetry would have to be regarded as oral in origin. Yet some of the religious poems — the *Kentish Hymn*, the *Metres of Boethius*, the *Paris Psalter* and *The Phoenix* — are known to be translations from Latin, and are therefore thoroughly literary in origin. It therefore appears that, in these poems at least, the oral-formulaic style was used because it had become a matter of convention. And if this is true of the poems based upon translations, it cannot be asserted with any confidence that it was not also used for similar stylistic effect in other poems (see Benson 1966).

Other features of style are sometimes claimed to be dependent on an oral tradition:

> [The] absence of necessary enjambement is a character
> istic of oral composition and is one of the easiest touch
> stones to apply in testing the orality of a poem.
>
> (Lord 1960, 54)

Applying this to Old English verse one finds that in some cases the long line is indeed a self-contained syntactical unit consisting of a single clause, e.g.

Hringweald wæs haten   Herefarena cyning   (*Widsith* 34)
(*The king of the Herefaren was called Hringweald*)

and

Licgende beam   læsest groweð   (*Maxims I* 158)
(*A fallen tree grows least*).

The suggestion is that poems which make extensive use of these one-line syntactical units represent an early stage in the development of Old English verse. However, given the uncertainty about the dates of the poems, such an assumption would be unwise in the extreme.

The majority of surviving poems contain a mixture of end-stopped and run-on lines. This can be illustrated from *Beowulf*, in which there are end-stopped lines such as

Beowulf maþelode,   bearn Ecgþeowes   (529)

interspersed among – far more numerous – run-on lines such as

Swa mec gelome   lað-geteonan
þreatedon þearle.   Ic him þenode
deoran sweorde,   swa hit gedefe wæs.   (559–61)
(*In this way the loathsome ravagers often severely*
oppressed me. I attended to them with a precious sword,
as was fitting.)

The latter example consists of interlocking units, each of a line and a half. However, plurilinear units (as they are called) may be much longer than this. *The Wanderer* and *Judith* exemplify a very extensive use of the run-on style, with long sentences frequently beginning in the middle of a line, and with alliterative patterns rarely coinciding with the syntactical ones. Again, it would be unwise to regard such poems as a late development, since the more flowing, run-on style might simply have been a matter of individual preference. End-stopped lines seem also to have been used as rhetorical markers. In *Deor*, for example, a down-and-out poet summarises a series of sad tales, after each of which he consoles himself with the reflection

Þæs ofereode,   þisses swa mæg!   (7 etc.)
(*That passed, so may this!*)

Recurring six times, this line divides the poem into unequal sections, the last containing a direct observation on the poet's own plight and its hoped-for resolution. No other Old English poem is so divided, though *Beowulf* is set out in the manuscript in 43 numbered *fitts*, or sections. Each of these *fitts* finishes at the end of a line. However, some of the natural sections in *Beowulf* – the long paraphrases of the stories of Finn and Ingeld, for example – end midway through a long line. Counterbalancing this is the occasional use of a second half-line as an independent exclamatory clause, usually to mark the end of a passage of narrative or description before moving on to a new subject. The formula *Þæt wæs god cyning!* (That was a good king), is used three times in this way in *Beowulf*, indicating in each case that the poet has finished with the subject in hand and intends to pass on to another.[4]

A line which is end-stopped naturally tends to contain a single clause, and the feeling of simplicity, or even artlessness, which this engenders is accentuated in the wider context by a tendency towards the use of paratactic constructions. This affects the run-on passages as well. Parataxis is the juxtaposition of sentences or clauses which are not formally subordinated one to another. Two types are distinguished: The first is *asyndetic* parataxis, in which no connecting words at all appear between the sentences or clauses, e.g.

Ða aras mænig gold-hladen ðegn,   gurde hine his swurde;
ða to dura eodon   drihtlice cempan,
Sigeferð and Eaha,   hyra sword getugon.
                                        (*Finnsburg* 13–15)
(*Then arose many a gold-laden thane, girded himself
with his sword; then to the door went noble warriors,
Sigeferth and Eaha, they drew their swords.*)

The other is *syndetic* parataxis, in which co-ordinating conjunctions, especially *ond* (and) and *ac* (but), are used, e.g.

Wearp hine þa on wyrmes lic   and wand him þa ymbutan
þone deaðes beam.   (*Genesis B* 491–2)
(*He turned himself then into the form of a serpent and
then wound himself about the tree of death.*)

The converse of parataxis is *hypotaxis*, the use of complex sentences in which a main clause is accompanied by at least one subordinate clause, e.g.

> Ða wæs Guðlaces   gæst geblissad
> siþþan Bartholomeus   aboden hæfde
> Godes ærendu.   (*Guthlac A* 722–4)
> (*Then Guthlac's spirit was filled with joy, once*
> *Bartholomew had proclaimed God's message.*)

It has been claimed that parataxis is more primitive than hypotaxis, but this is not necessarily so, for delicate effects are as readily achieved by one as by the other. Also, the distinction between the two is often not clear-cut. Two factors are especially relevant here. One is the difficulty of distinguishing between parataxis and hypotaxis in the absence of guidance from a clear system of punctuation. The punctuation of all medieval texts, but especially of the Old English ones, is fraught with difficulty because the punctuation and capitalisation of manuscripts seems inconsistent and is not understood (see Mitchell 1980; Robinson 1985, 18–19). One editor of the riddles in the *Exeter Book* notes the difficulty of knowing sometimes even where one riddle ends and the next begins (Williamson 1977, 12–13). However, sporadic as the punctuation seems to be, there does appear to be some system in it. It often seems to be linked in some way to rhetorical markers, such as adverbs like *hwilum* (sometimes) and *nu* (now), and conjunctions like *ac* (but) and *swa* (as). Repeated words in correlative combinations, such as *þa...þa* (when...then) and *þær...þær* (where...there) were probably also used to signal the boundaries of clauses. Anglo-Saxon listeners would have responded very differently from how we today respond as readers. Certainly they would have had no use for the prescriptive, over-sophisticated, heavy punctuation of present-day editions, which usually forces the reader to accept only one interpretation of passages for which there may be a variety of possibilities. Old English verse was probably structurally, and therefore semantically, ambivalent, listeners being left to make sympathetic, imaginative choices from a range of alternatives. In connection with parataxis and hypotaxis, for example, how are we to distinguish the clausal relationship in the following description of the martyrdom of St Juliana?

> He bi feaxe het
> ahon ond ahebban   on heanne beam,
> þær seo sun-sciene   slege þrowade,
> sace sin-grimme,   siex tida dæges.   (*Juliana* 227–30)
> (*He commanded her to be hung by the hair and raised up*
> *on a high beam, where the one who was radiant as the*
> *sun suffered beating, very cruel torture, for six hours of*
> *the day.*)

The sense of the passage as punctuated is clear enough, but it would be equally satisfactory to begin a new sentence at line 229, *Þær seo*... (There the one...), as a result of which the construction would be transformed from hypotactic to paratactic.

The second factor which discourages too rigid a separation between parataxis and hypotaxis is that there is often a logical connection between juxtaposed clauses which creates an implied sense of connection even in the absence of formal grammatical markers. In *The Dream of the Rood*, for example, the Cross tells of its awesome duty in acting as the instrument of torture for the crucified Christ:

> Rod wæs ic aræred.   Ahof ic ricne Cyning,
> heofona Hlaford;   hyldan me ne dorste.
> þurhdrifan hi me mid deorcan næglum;
>   on me syndon þa dolg gesiene,
> opene inwid-hlemmas.   Ne dorste ic hira nænigum sceððan.
>   (44–7)
> (*I was erected as a cross; [and] I raised up the powerful*
> *King, the Lord of the heavens; [so] I dared not bend. They*
> *drove through me with dark nails; [from which] the wounds*
> *are clearly seen on me, open gashes of malice; [but] I dared*
> *not harm any of them.*)

The relationship of the clauses here would be perfectly clear even without the connecting words supplied in the translation within square brackets. To give a Modern English example: 'She went to hospital. She had been involved in an accident' clearly implies 'She went to hospital *because* she had been involved in an accident'.

The interrelationship of whole sentences is reflected in a feature of syntax which is widely, but unevenly, distributed in the poetry.

This is the enclosing of one short sentence within another in a parenthetic aside. This brief interruption is usually a single clause, and is often confined to a single half-line, more commonly the second, e.g.

> Iudas maðelade – gnorn-sorge wæg...   (*Elene* 655)
> (*Judas – he was suffering miserable anguish – declared...*).

The contexts in which such parentheses occur are varied, though they most often seem to come between a word meaning 'to speak' and the beginning of the speech itself, either describing the speaker's identity, appearance or mood (as in the example given), or the reaction of the audience, e.g.

> ongan ceallian þa   ofer cald wæter
> Byrhtelmes bearn   (beornas gehlyston):   (*Maldon* 91–2)
> (*Byrhtelm's son then called out across the cold water –*
> *warriors listened:*)

Other uses include the introduction of narrative detail, especially in the battle descriptions in *Exodus*, and of exclamatory reaction by the poet in condemnation of acts of wickedness or in praise of godliness. Opinions differ as to what constitutes a parenthesis, so it is impossible to give statistics, but the greatest number are found in *Beowulf, Juliana, Genesis, Andreas, Exodus* and *The Battle of Maldon* (see Krapp 1905; Mitchell 1985, 941–4). Altogether, the parenthetical construction seems to have been one of a whole range of rhetorical devices that the Anglo-Saxon poet had at his disposal.

The use of catalogues, an embellishment more commonly associated with Middle English poetry, is also a feature of the Old English poetic repertoire. The best known are those of *The Wanderer.* Here the first is a list of various forms of death:

>   duguþ eal gecrong
> wlonc bi wealle.   Sume wig fornom,
> ferede in forðwege: sumne fugel oðbær
> ofer heanne holm;   sumne se hara wulf
> deaðe gedælde;   sumne dreorig-hleor
> in eorð-scræfe   eorl gehydde.   (79–84)

(the band of retainers has fallen, proud by the wall.
War took some of them, carried them off; one a bird
carried over the high sea; one the grey wolf handed
over to death; one a sad-cheeked nobleman hid in an
earth-cave [grave].)

The recurrent syntactical pattern is accentuated by the repetition of the object *sumne* (one, a certain one) at the beginning of each short clause. Soon after there follows a plaintive series of five rhetorical questions, the first four introduced with formulaic *Hwær cwom . . . ?* and the last varied with *Hwær sindon . . . ?*

Hwær cwom mearg?   Hwær cwom mago?   Hwær cwom
    maþþum-gyfa?
Hwær cwom symbla gesetu?   Hwær sindon sele-dreamas?

(92–3)

(What has become of the horse? What has become of the
man? What has become of the treasurer-giver? What has
become of the places of feasting? Where are the joys of
hall?)

Following immediately upon this is a threefold lament:

Eala beorht bune!   Eala byrn-wiga!
Eala þeodnes þrym!   (94–5)
(Alas the bright cup! Alas the mail-clad warrior! Alas
the prince's might!)

This is quickly followed by a climactic series of reflections on worldly transience, emphasised again by the repeated syntax of the four clauses:

Her bið feoh læne,   her bið freond læne,
her bið mon læne,   her bið mæg læne.   (108–9)
(Here wealth does not last, here friend does not last,
here man does not last, here kin does not last.)

Though the concentration and variety of these lists is unusual within one short poem, each list is paralleled elsewhere, while in the case of *The Fortunes of Men* and *The Gifts of Men* each poem is, in effect, an extended catalogue.[5]

The essence of the catalogue is repetition. This is also employed in other ways for other effects. For example, in *Beowulf* 702–20, as Grendel approaches the high hall of the Danes intent on murder his relentless and menacing advance is conveyed by the repetition of the simple verb *com* (came) three times in nineteen lines. In each case the verb is emphasised by its place at the beginning of the clause, and expression of the subject is held back by intervening adverbs and prepositional phrases:

> Com on wanre niht
> scriðan sceadu-genga . . .   (702–3)
> (*In the dark night the shadow-goer came gliding . . .*)
>
> Ða com of more   under mist-hleoþum
> Grendel gongan . . .   (710–11)
> (*Then from the moor under the mist-slopes Grendel came striding . . .*)
>
> Com þa to recede   rinc siðian . . .   (720)
> (*Then to the hall the creature came journeying . . .*)

In each case the poet seems deliberately to have used the pleonastic (i.e. redundant) *com* + infinitive construction to accentuate the repetition while allowing himself scope for using a variety of infinitives, which in verbal phrases of this type are semantically the more important element.

Closely patterned repetition may involve *anaphora*, the repeating of words or phrases at the beginnings of successive syntactic units, as in the lines from *The Wanderer* cited above. The Seafarer, in the poem of that name, reflects that

> . . . nis þæs mod-wlonc   mon ofer eorþan,
> ne his gifena þæs god,   ne in geoguþe to þæs hwæt,
> ne in his dædum to þæs deor,   ne him his dryhten to þæs hold,
> þæt he a his sæ-fore   sorge næbbe,
> to hwon hine Dryhten   gedon wille.   (39–43)
> (*. . . there is no man on earth so proud of spirit, nor so
> fortunate in his gifts, nor so brave in his youth, nor so
> courageous in his deeds, nor his lord so gracious to him,
> that he is never anxious about his sea journey, as to
> what the lord may be pleased to send him.*)

Anaphoric *ne* continues over the next three lines, this time at the head of successive prepositional phrases:

Ne biþ him to hearpan hyge   ne to hring-þege –
ne to wife wyn   ne to worulde hyht –
ne ymbe owiht elles   nefne ymb yða gewealc.   (44–6)
(*He will have no thought for the harp nor receiving of
rings – nor for the pleasure of a woman nor delight in
the world – nor for anything except the rolling of the
waves.*)

Another rhetorical figure – that of *antithesis* – is sometimes achieved by interweaving negative sequences such as this with a complementary sequence of positives, either by using the simple adversative conjunction *ac* (but) in a 'not this but this' type of construction (e.g. *Phoenix* 14–20, 21–7, 60–4), or by simple juxtaposition without conjunctions:

Warað hine wræc-last,   nales wunden gold;
ferð-loca freorig,   nalæs foldan blæd.   (*Wanderer* 32–3)
(*The path of exile is his concern, not twisted gold;
a frozen heart-enclosure [breast], not the glory of the
world.*)

Antithetical formulae are sometimes separated by intervening clauses, as in (*Beowulf* 183–8):

Wa bið þæm ðe...   Wel bið þæm þe...
(*Woe is it for the one who...Well is it for the one who...*),

with the keywords *wa* and *wel* accentuated by alliteration at the head of successive sentences.

Although some of the examples given above involve a succession of negatives, the Old English poets were generally more moderate in their use of multiple negation than were the writers of prose. However, a strangely prevalent feature in the poetry is the expression of a positive concept by means of a negative grammatical construction, usually with a resultant sense of understatement. This figure is sometimes known as 'litotes', and is found throughout Germanic poetry and in other literature. Bracher (Bracher 1937, 920–1) gives a table showing the frequency of occurrence of this figure in individual poems, ranging from *The Riming Poem* (with an average which he computes as one in every 17 lines) to six poems in which it does not feature at all. *Beowulf* has an average of one occurrence every 34 lines. Two examples from *Beowulf* appear in the poet's comment on the fate of Hildeburh, daughter of Hoc, whose son and brother have both been killed while fighting on opposite sides in a quarrel between her husband's people and her own:

> Ne huru Hildeburh   herian þorfte
> eotena[6] treowe;   unsynnum wearð
> beloren leofum   æt þam lind-plegan
> bearnum ond broðrum;   hie on gebyrd hruron
> gare wunde;   þæt wæs geomuru ides!
> Nalles holinga   Hoces dohtor
> meotod-sceaft bemearn,   syþðan morgen com,
> ða heo under swegle   geseon meahte
> morðor-bealo maga.   (1071–9)
>
> (*Nor indeed did Hildeburh need to praise the good faith of enemies; guiltless, she was deprived at the shield-play of a son and a brother; they fell fated, wounded with a spear; that was a sad woman! Not without cause did the daughter of Hoc lament the decree of fate after morning came, when she was able to see in the daylight the death-destruction of kinsmen.*)

Here the wretched woman, having lost loved ones on both sides in this pointless dispute, is described as 'not needing to praise the good faith of enemies' and as lamenting 'not without cause'. A further example is the poet's comment on the death of Grendel,

> No his lif-gedal
> sarlic þuhte   secga ænegum   (*Beowulf* 841–2)
> (*Not at all did his parting from life seem sad to any of the men*),

where the true meaning is that the men were overjoyed. In *The Dream of the Rood* 123–4 the poet describes how he prayed '*þær ic ana wæs / mæte werede*' (where I was alone, with little company). Here the understatement (with little company) occurs in a relationship of variation with the positively stated adjective *ana* (alone), which points up the litotes. Various reasons have been suggested for the use of this figure. Irony, or even humour, is sometimes achieved, as in the Grendel example. The Hildeburh example perhaps gains a sort of perverse emphasis in the denial of the antithetical positive, much as a speaker today might describe as person as 'no fool'. Alternatively, these may be yet further examples of the Anglo-Saxons' pleasure in periphrastic or indirect language. As always, context is the main determining factor.

6 Middle English Poetic Diction

Middle English literature is substantially different from Old English in that a greater range has survived in a greater variety of dialects. The difference is accentuated because of the two centuries following the Norman Conquest, when written poetry in English virtually ceased to exist and the thread of continuity in vernacular writing was maintained only in prose. During these centuries it was not only the language that underwent substantial change, but also the practices of scribes, and in particular their orthographic (spelling) conventions. By the end of the Old English period the dominant West Saxon scribal tradition had produced a remarkably rigid spelling system throughout the country. When scribes had first begun to set English down in writing they probably attempted to reproduce phonetically the sounds they heard, but in the course of time their spellings ceased accurately to represent the spoken language and became increasingly out-of-date and conventional. The uniformity in the presentational conventions of late Old English texts makes it difficult to determine on the basis of spelling and handwriting alone exactly where a text was produced. This uniformity broke down after 1066 and it was not until the later fourteenth century that there was another movement towards a spelling standard of anything like the same stability.

The existence of diverse regional orthographies and the negligent attitude of the scribes of Middle English texts, few of whom before the fourteenth century had been systematically trained in the copying of English, add an extra layer of confusion to the situation. The cavalier scribal approach can be exemplified by reference to a thirteenth-century copy of Laȝamon's *Brut*, in which the scribe at one point mistook his place in his copy-text and accidentally reproduced the same short passage twice. On discovering his error he crossed out the reduplicated passage. However, despite this cancellation it is not difficult for us to compare and contrast the two. Although they were copied at probably the same time by the same scribe from the same copy-text, there are very striking differences, including the variations *after, æfter; aȝæin, aȝan; hælden, heolden; heh, hæh; iwræð, iwræð; strengðe, strene; uaste, uæste* (see Scragg 1974, 26 and plate 3). The copyist, like most of his contemporaries working with English texts, seems to have had no conception of a spelling standard and to have used variant forms at will.

The situation was also affected by an influx of professional scribes who had been trained in the French schools. These would have known nothing of the Old English spelling tradition, so when they came to write English they naturally based their spelling on the spoken language. As a consequence, many of the changes in pronunciation which had taken place during the Old English period are first recorded after the Conquest by Norman French scribes. They also to some extent used letters of the alphabet in a different manner from their Anglo-Saxon counterparts, preferring, for example, *o* to *u* in *loue* (love) (O.E. *lufu*) and *sone* (son, from Old English *sunu*) for reasons of orthographic convention rather than phonological change. Practices such as these accentuate, and even exaggerate, the apparent differences between Old and Middle English.

The post-Conquest centuries saw a huge expansion in the English lexicon, though the processes by which this was achieved had been operating in the years before. Most important in the creation of new words, as in Old English, were the processes of compounding, affixation and conversion. The use of compound words is less noticeable than in Old English poetry for two principal reasons. Firstly, the fashion for highly artificial, figurative compounds seems to have passed, and, secondly, compounding is especially useful in alliterative verse, which in Middle English constitutes only a part of the total corpus. It is in alliterative verse of the early Middle English period, however, and especially in Laȝamon's *Brut*, that we find the most extensive use of poetic compounds. Some of these originated in Old English, among them *blæð-fest* (famous), *feðer-home* (feather-covering), *særi-mod* (sorrowful), *sæ-werie* (sea-weary), and *wine-mæies* (friends and kinsmen). But the *Brut* and other early alliterative poems also contain compounds which are of the same type but which are not recorded in Old English, including *heorte-blod* (heart-blood), *leod-folk* (people) and *swerd-broþer* (sword-brother, companion in arms). The density of the occurrence of compounds, however, is a mere fraction of that of Old English. *Beowulf*, for instance, contains approximately 1070 compounds in 3182 lines, whereas the *Brut*, which of all the Middle English poems makes greatest use of compounds, has only about 525 in 16,095 (Sauer 1985; 1988, 186).

However, new compounds continued to be produced, some of them drawing upon borrowed words, and in later Middle English verse, both alliterative and non-alliterative, we often find imaginative and striking examples. They are of a rather different order than the traditional poetic diction, and some probably originated in everyday speech. A word like *blod-hounde*, for instance, although it is first recorded in a fourteenth-century poem, is sufficiently ordinary and descriptive to have had a non-literary origin. Similarly, a fifteenth-century lyric in which the poet complains about noisy blacksmiths who keep him awake at nights refers to them disparagingly as *bren-waterys* (water-burners, an allusion to their practice of plunging hot iron into water) and *cloþe-merys* (mare-clothiers). Although these terms have the appearance of imaginative literary coinages, a documentary reference to a 'Robertus Brennewater' dated 1252 suggests that Brennewater had been a colloquial nickname for a smith for many years previously and that the anonymous poet's inventiveness lay rather in utilising the term than in coining it. Compounds first found in the later Middle English poetry include colour adjectives such as *lilie-whit* and *note-broun*, which are condensations of similes and which would originally have had a freshness of which constant use has since deprived them. Two other compound terms which are still used are *love-longinge* and *bitter-swete*, although the latter in its first recorded occurrence (by John Gower) was a noun with the meaning 'a drink which is both bitter and sweet', and by extension 'an experience in which pain and pleasure are mingled'. *Wey-wending* is how an anonymous lyricist describes our 'passage through life', with a secondary meaning 'death, departure from life'. *Sloumbe-selepe* is not tautologous (as it might seem), but is suggestive of the 'deep, troubled sleep' which overcomes Jonah in the anonymous poem *Patience* (the first element being from Old English *sluma* with an intrusive *b*, as in present-day *slumber*). *Brustun-gutte* as a term for 'a greedy eater' in *The Castle of Perseverance* is sufficiently expressive to need no explanation. And *cok-crou wortes* are 'greens cooked the day before and kept overnight', though this expression (by John Lydgate) is another which looks like a colloquialism that has been borrowed into literature. All the above have their first recorded appearancé in the poetry.

Affixation is a more workaday method of lexical expansion, and one less likely to be used for conspicuous poetic effect. With regard to prefixes, only a relatively small number of those employed in Old English continued in use, including *a-*, *be-*, *bi-*, *for-*, *ge-*, *to-* and *ymb-*, which are found mainly in early Middle English (Burnley 1992, 446). In the case of these prefixes the etymological process continued to be the same, e.g. *be-* and *bi-* to form transitive from intransitive verbs (e.g. *biwailen* 'bewail') or from nouns (e.g. *besloberen* 'soil', from *slobber* 'slime') and *for-* to intensify the meaning of the base word, as in *fordolked of lufe-daungere* (mortally wounded by the power of love, *Pearl*, line 11). *Un-* is another prefix from Old English which continued in use, but its semantic range was reduced to the basic meaning 'not', as in Modern English. Additional morphological processes sometimes produced identical prefixes, as in *abed, aloft, aside, asleep* and *abroad*, which derive not from Old English *a-* but from prepositional phrases beginning with *on*. A number of English and Scandinavian affixes were closely related, and it is sometimes impossible to know which is the source of the Middle English form. The Scandinavian *umbe-* is preferred to English *ymbe-* (around) in the description of the Green Knight in *Gawain* 181:

> Fayre fannand fax vmbefoldes his schulderes
> (*Beautiful wavy hair enfolds his shoulders*),

and elsewhere in *Gawain* there are the infinitives *vmbeclyppe* (encompass), *vmbekesten* (cast about), *vmbelappe* (overlap), and the past tenses *vmbeteȝe* (surrounded) and *vmbeweued* (enveloped). Prefixes were also imitated from words borrowed from French and Latin. *Disapere* (to disappear) and *disencrese* (decrease [noun]), both first recorded in Lydgate, for instance, appear to be Middle English derivatives of borrowings like *disallowe* (to censure), disobeie and *dissimilacion* (dissimulation), all three first recorded in Gower.

Rather more of the Old English suffixes were retained than pre-fixes. An interesting one is *-mele*, from O.E. *-mælum*, meaning 'by quantities at a time', the nature of the quantity being defined by the base morpheme. The only example surviving today is *piecemeal* (by one piece at a time). In Middle English we find it in words inherited complete from Old English, such as *limmele* (limb by limb) in Laȝamon's *Brut* (referring to dismemberment), and in Middle English formations such as the aforementioned *pecemele* in the rhyming *Chronicle* of Robert of Gloucester. William Langland, author of *Piers Plowman*, seems to have been particularly fond of this suffix, and gives us *cuppemele* (cup by cup), *parcelmele* (piece by piece), *partimele* (little by little), *penimele* and *poundmele* (by a penny's worth / pound's worth at a time). The last is used ironically to describe the eagerness with which the ecclesiastical officials known as 'pardoners' gave out papal indulgences, or dispensations from sin, in exchange for money. The Old English derivational suffix *-lac* was used in abstract nouns (cf. present-day *wedlock*) and survived into Middle English alongside its Scandinavian counter-part *-leik*. The North-East Midland poet Orm shows a special fondness for the latter. Examples (in his characteristically idiosyn-cratic spelling) are *daffteleȝȝc* (modesty), *forrswundennleȝȝc* (apathy), *gredigleȝȝc* (gluttony), *herrsummleȝȝc* (obedience), *idelleȝȝc* (folly) and *modiȝleȝȝc* (pride). In *Gawain* we have *gryndel-layk*, a hapax legomenon from *grindel* (fierce, cf. Beowulf's adver-sary 'Grendel'). The Green Knight uses it sarcastically to disparage the bravery of Arthur's knights:

> Where is now your sourquydrye and your conquestes,
> Your gryndellayk and your greme, and your grete wordes?
>
> (311–12)
>
> (*What now has become of your proud bearing and your conquests, your fierceness, wrathful temperament, and boastful words?*)

The other main process which was productive of new words in Middle English is conversion. We especially come across verbs derived from other word classes, such as from nouns (e.g. *firen*, 'to set something on fire') and from adjectives (e.g. *lamen* 'to lame'). In verse, especially of the alliterative style, we encounter the same tendency as in Old English to use adjectives 'absolutely', as nouns.

Examples applied to the concept 'lady' are *þe clere* (the pure [one]), *þat cortays* (that courteous [one]), *þat gay* (that fair [one]), and so on. Some rather more extreme examples of the same process are found in *Piers Plowman*, where whole phrases, or even clauses, may be made to operate in positions where we normally find nouns and nominal phrases, as when Piers finds his workmen singing and drinking ale and the poet says sarcastically that they

> . . . holpen ere this half acre with 'How trolly lolly!' (VI.116)
> (. . . *were helping to plough this half-acre of land*
> *with 'How trolly lolly!' [i.e. not at all].*)

We have further examples in the same poem in names such as 'Robert Runabout' and 'Dame Worche-Whan-Tyme-Is'.

A small number of Middle English words were formed by what is known as *blending*, the process which in Modern English has produced such words as *smog* from *smoke + fog* and *brunch* from *breakfast + lunch*. Words believed to be formed by this process are found in poetry, e.g. *hathel* (man, warrior, hero) from the Middle English reflexes of Old English *hæleð* 'warrior' + *æðel* 'noble'. The word *burde* (lady, maiden of rank), which is very common in the register of courtly romance, may be a blend of *birde* (maiden) + *birthe* (child, descendant) + perhaps also *bride* (bride, with the common sound-change of *metathesis* , whereby the position of the *r* is shifted). In cases such as these it is impossible to be certain whether blending or some other lexical process is involved, but a number of words found in alliterative verse have been tentatively identified as blends, e.g. *schinder* (to shatter in pieces) and *sniter* (to fall [of snow]), and their occurrence may perhaps be attributed to the enforced lexical inventiveness of the poets working within the alliterative tradition (see Frankis 1983).

Word-formation by these methods was supplemented by extensive borrowing from other languages, in particular Scandinavian, French and Latin (see Serjeantson 1935). The only other languages to have a direct influence on the Middle English lexicon were Dutch and Flemish, which furnished a number of mainly maritime and commercial terms indicative of commercial contacts between England and the Low Countries. A few more general words from Middle Dutch are first found in the poetry, including *bous* (intoxicating drink, booze) in a humorous late-thirteenth-century lyric about the man in the moon, *dote* (a fool) in the

Proverbs spuriously ascribed to King Alfred (but probably dating from the twelfth century, 300 years after Alfred's death), and *polle* (head) in the fourteenth-century *Chronicle* of Robert Mannyng.

Scandinavian loan words in Middle English are associated particularly with everyday activities, with the sea, with the law and with the technicalities of local administration. They were slow to show themselves in any great numbers in written verse, the Scandinavian languages having had probably a lower status even than English in the early part of the period. They will undoubtedly have made a huge impact on the spoken language, especially in the areas of heavy Danish settlement in the North and East Midlands, though this is, of course, impossible to demonstrate. A verse text with a large number of Scandinavian borrowings is *The Ormulum*. Analysis shows (Serjeantson 1935, 81–4) that it contains about 120 Scandinavian loanwords, some of which are the earliest recorded examples of words which survive in present-day Standard English (e.g. *anngrenn* 'anger' (verb), *blome* 'bloom', *boþe* 'booth', *reʒʒsenn* 'raise' and *skerren* 'scare'). Important among them are the earliest recorded usages of the plural personal pronouns *they, their* and *them*, forms which did not become standard in London English until the fifteenth century. Orm also has the feminine third person singular pronoun *ʒho*, which, along with the form *scæ* in the annal for 1140 in the (prose) *Peterborough Chronicle*, is one of the earliest pieces of evidence for the development of the present-day pronoun *she*.

Also from the East Midlands between fifty and a hundred years later come the romances *King Horn* and *Havelok*, the former from near London and the latter probably from the region of Lincoln and Grimsby, where much of the action is set. Both have short lines of rhyming couplets. *King Horn* shows generalised Scandinavian influence in its vocabulary. An interesting first appearance is in line 212 of the Cambridge manuscript of this text:

Wel bruc þu þin euening!
(You do credit to your name!)

Þin euening is a case of *metanalysis*, or incorrect division between words, of *þi neuening*, from the verb *nevenen* (to name), which in turn is from Scandinavian *nefna* (to name). A connection here with the other romance is that *Havelok*, at lines 1398–9 and 2529–30, contains the imperfect rhymes *name:Rauen* (Hugh Raven, a personal name) and *grauen:name*. These seem to suggest that a scribe at some stage has removed original *naven* in both of these cases and substituted the more familiar *name*, so destroying the rhyme. *Naven* would be from Scandinavian noun *nafn* (name), which is not recorded elsewhere in Middle English but is the source of the verbs *nefna* and its Anglicised form *nevenen*, as in *Horn*. *Havelok* has over 120 Scandinavian borrowings, but far fewer first occurrences than in Orm's long poem. The first occurrences in *Havelok* include the noun *bulder-ston* (boulder-stone, cobblestone), the adjectives *mirke* (murky, dark) and *scabbed* (mangey), and the verbs *beiten* (to bait, torment with dogs), *callen* (to summon), *geten* (to obtain), *liften* (to lift), *lurken* (to hide), and *wesseylen* (to drink healths).

By the later fourteenth century, when writings in English started to be produced in great numbers, the Scandinavian element in the vocabulary was widely dispersed and well integrated. Because English and the Scandinavian languages are related descendants of Germanic, in many cases it is difficult to be sure which words have descended directly from Old English and which not. Otto Jespersen (Jespersen 1962, 61) has demonstrated how, even where a borrowing is not in doubt, processes of assimilation were at work to blur the distinction, as in the case of Old Norse *tîðende*, borrowed unchanged in Orm's *tiþennde* but later generally changed into *tiding(s)*, showing the influence of Old English *tid* and the common English ending *-ing*.

French loan words are different in character from Scandinavian loans. They are associated with a wider range of activities, often connected with administration and courtly life. Terms for clothes and for different classes of people are well represented amongst the oldest of them. Loans from French are found in the earliest Middle English poetry, which is of the late twelfth century, but not at first in any great numbers. The *Ormulum* has only eleven of French origin, in contrast to its numerous Scandinavian loans, which seems to suggest that Orm's North-East Midland dialect was in some way resistant to French influence. However, *Havelok* contains numerous words of French origin, despite the fact that both the setting of the tale and the provenance of the manuscript are located in strongly Scandinavianised Lincolnshire. This is largely because of the subject matter, and especially because of the numerous descriptions and catalogues in *Havelok* in which French-derived words tend to predominate.

We should perhaps be cautious about ascribing a preference for words derived from French (or any other language) to the author of a work, since the scribes themselves clearly had a hand in this, as can be shown when more than one manuscript survives. A good example is Laȝamon's *Brut* a poem of over 16,000 long lines, which survives in two roughly contemporary manuscripts of the third quarter of the thirteenth century (British Library Cotton Caligula A. ix and Cotton Otho C. xiii). Laȝamon was a conservative-minded writer, who looked to Old English traditions to provide models for his subject matter and style. He makes use of archaic English words, and shows a disinclination to use borrowed vocabulary. This conservatism is reflected to a greater extent in the Caligula manuscript than in Otho, of which the scribe is linguistically more progressive and makes many changes, to the extent that he might well be called a 'reviser'.[1] There are less than forty Scandinavian borrowings in the two versions, and most of them are words which are common generally in Middle English. It is interesting to note that the Otho scribe retains almost all of those used by the Caligula scribe and has a few more besides, namely *caste* (for which the Caligula version has *wurpen*), *legges* (cp. *sconken*), *may* (cp. *maide*) and *Þoris-dæi* (Thursday, cp. *Þunres-dæi*). There is greater disparity between the two versions with regard to the French loan words, of which there are almost eighty in Otho but far fewer in Caligula. Comparison shows that Otho in many places either substitutes different, less archaic English word or, as in the following examples, introduces French words and makes appropriate changes in the syntax in order to accommodate them:

MS Caligula	MS Otho
þe king wes al bærn-les (4484) (*the king was completely childless*)	þe king eyr nadde non (*the king had no heir*)
iherde þesne weop (5983) (*heard this weeping*)	ihorde þane cri (*heard that cry*)
æuerælche eorle and (8445) æuerælche beorne (*each earl and each* *noble warrior*)	ech earl and ech barun (*each earl and each baron*)
þe king ne rohte of æhte (14389) (*the king cared not for possessions*)	þe king of tresur ne rohte (*the king cared not for treasure*)

Some of the differences probably reflect the thematic preferences of the Otho scribe/reviser (who seems to be less interested in the old heroic imagery than is the scribe of the Caligula manuscript), while others are likely to result from his habitual use of more progressive language – it is impossible to distinguish between the two (cf. Wyld 1930, 2–21; Sergeantson 1935, 80–1, 117; Cannon 1993).

A statistical analysis of the evidence for a representative sample of all texts, i.e. prose and documents as well as verse, suggests that lexical borrowing from French began on a massive scale around 1200 and that a peak (or rather a high plateau) was reached in the first half of the fourteenth century (Dekeyser 1986). The subsequent decline in the number of French borrowings coincides with a rise in borrowings from Latin, particularly of the dignified, polysyllabic words which are known as 'aureate terms'. Aureate (i.e. 'gilded') terms are 'words designed to achieve sententiousness and sonorous ornamentation of style principally through their being new, rare, or uncommon, and approved by the critical opinion of their time' (Mendenhall 1919, 14). Even at this stage Latin continued to maintain its status in relation to the European vernaculars, and any flavour of Latinity was therefore likely to enhance the status of a literary work.

Aureate terms are found to a certain extent in the poetry of Chaucer, but principally in the works of the English and Scottish poets who admired and imitated him in the fifteenth and sixteenth centuries, and to a lesser extent in the Mystery and Morality Plays and in various prefaces and pageants which aspired to a lofty style. Some of these terms, such as *adjacent, eternal,* and *intercession* have settled into the language and are treated almost as naturally today as native words are, but others, such as *abusion, diverticle* and *equipolent,* have vanished without trace. It is often difficult to be sure whether such words were borrowed directly from Latin or via French, a language which, of course, is descended from Latin and at that time had many similar or identical items in its lexicon. But considerations of precise origin were immaterial to the users, so long as a grandiloquent style was achieved.

The English and Scottish Chaucerians wrote frequently in praise of Chaucer's 'elevation' of the English language to a level worthy of fine poetry. For example, Thomas Hoccleve praised his *ornat endytyng* (ornate composition), while William Dunbar applauded his *fresch anamalit termes celicall* (fresh, enamelled, celestial terms). This aureate, or enamelled, diction was, of course, only one aspect of Chaucer's style, but it is prominent among the features they attempted to imitate. John Lydgate was particularly prolific, and his voluminous works contain the first recorded examples of over 800 words of Latin or French origin which are either new borrowings or new formations, and many of which have been accommodated in the lexicon of present-day English (Mendenhall 1919, 46). Lacking their master's fine touch, however, the Chaucerians sometimes took matters to extremes, and this example from the opening of Dunbar's *Ane Ballat of Our Lady* shows how it could become an unbearable affectation:

Hale, sterne superne; hale, in eterne	*star of the heavens*
In Godis sicht to schyne;	
Lucerne in derne for to discerne	*light in darkness*
Be glory and grace devyne;	*by means of*
Hodiern, modern, sempitern,	*of today, of the present, eternal*
Angelicall regyne:	
Our tern inferne for to dispern	*gloom; dispel*
Helpe, rialest rosyne.	*rose*
Ave Maria, gracia plena:	*Hail, Mary, full of grace*
Haile, fresche floure femynyne;	
ȝerne us guberne, virgin matern,	*carefully guide us, Virgin*
Of reuth baith rute and ryne.	*Mother root and bark*
	[i.e. the totality]
	of compassion

Borrowing and the use of grandiloquent terms were not engaged in wholeheartedly by all poets, for some had aesthetic and social reasons for resisting, precipitating a debate which in the early Modern English period was to rage more furiously in the so-called 'inkhorn controversy'. So while the Chaucerians and others believed, like the classical rhetorician Sulpitius Victor, that 'big things should be put in big words', others wrote in favour of simplicity, such as Chaucer's contemporary Thomas Usk, who argued that

> rude [plain] wordes and boystous [uncomplicated] percen the herte of the herer to the innerest point, and planten there the sentence [meaning] of thinges.
> (*Testament of Love*, Prol. 7–9, in Skeat 1897)

Others demonstrated their reluctance in their writing practice. Orm, for example, shows a preference for English words over those derived from Latin, as in *dædbote* instead of *penitence* and *þeowwdom* instead of *seruise*. The anonymous contemporary author of a verse paraphrase of *Genesis and Exodus* also prefers *londes speche and wordes smale*, as he explains in his preface, and his lexical choice generally seems to bear this out, for he shows a clear preference for Germanic rather than Romance words. When he does make use of an unusual foreign word he glosses it immediately:

| Bigamie is unkinde ðing, | *unnatural* |
| On engleis tale, twie-wifing. (449–50) | *speech* |

This pairing of native and foreign words, originally for the sake of clarity, probably contributed to the development and popularity of the so-called 'doublet style', the mannerism whereby two expressions are used side by side without either adding to the meaning of the other, such as *honour and worship*, *prest and redi*, and *socour and help*. But this 'glossing' of Romance words can at best only be part of the explanation, since we also find pairs of simple native words (e.g. *lef and dere*) and French (e.g. *cuntek and strif*), and the idiom is even found in Old English, though mainly in prose (see Oakden 1935, 197, 235, 266, 314; Burrow 1971, 18–20).

Words and phrases from foreign sources sometimes remain unassimilated into the English lexicon. *Cordon bleu*, *enfant terrible* and *piste* are examples in Modern English. Even in Middle English, when new words were accepted at what must have been a bewildering rate, it was still possible to use foreign words and phrases for stylistic effect. The stanza from Dunbar's poem, quoted above, includes a complete line in Latin, giving the words of the angel Gabriel to the Virgin at the Annunciation. This line recurs in the same position in each of the seven stanzas, acting as a sort of refrain. In other poems the relative quantities of English and Latin are more equal, and alternate lines of each are not uncommon. Verse which mixes different languages in this way is called 'macaronic', and in Middle English is especially found in religious lyrics in which the poet is consciously wishing to achieve echoes of Latin hymns. But sometimes languages other than English are used in a less formal way. In the Chester Mystery Play of the Magi, for instance, the three kings who come seeking the infant Christ first encounter Herod and greet him in French, the language appropriate to a courtly context, while he replies in the same fashion before lapsing into English (VIII.153–60). In the Coventry Mystery Play on the same subject the herald who announces Herod delivers his whole proclamation in French (I.475–85). Herod in the Towneley Mystery Play uses only a few scraps of French, nothing more than *bewshere* (fine sir) and *ditizance doutance* (said without doubt, for certain), which are corruptions of *beau sire* and *dites sans doutance*. His parting words,

> Bot adew! – to the deuyll!
> I can no more Franch. (XVI.740–1) *know*

suggest that he is struggling to keep up appearances and that the playwright was aware of the comic potential of juxtaposing contrasting registers for satirical purposes.

It may be helpful to look at an example of Middle English verse to illustrate the relative proportions of native and borrowed words. *Pearl* is a late fourteenth-century poem found in the same manuscript as *Sir Gawain and the Green Knight* and is probably by the same poet, whose dialect places him in the North-West Midlands. The language exhibits both Scandinavian and French influence. The subject is the death of an infant child. The bereaved father dreams that he meets her in a beautiful land and converses with her across a river, and that his grief is lightened by her comforting words and her assurances that she is among the elect in Paradise:

> Thenne demed I to þat damyselle:
> 'Ne worþe no wrathþe vnto my Lorde,
> If rapely I raue, spornande in spelle.
> My herte watz al wyth mysse remorde,
> As wallande water gotz out of welle.
> I do me ay in hys myserecorde.
> Rebuke me neuer wyth wordez felle,
> Þaʒ I forloyne, my dere endorde,
> Bot kyþez me kyndely your coumforde,
> Pytosly þenkande vpon þysse:
> Of care and me ʒe made acorde,
> Þat er watz grounde of alle my blysse.'   (361–72)

(Then I spoke to that damsel: 'Let there not be any offence
to my Lord if I talk foolishly and rashly, stumbling in what I
say. My heart was all afflicted with a sense of loss, like
water gushing out of a spring. I put myself at his mercy
for ever. Do not rebuke me with cruel words, my dear beloved,
though I go astray. But kindly make known to me your
words of comfort, compassionately thinking of this: It was
you who brought sorrow and me together, you who until
then had been the foundation of all my happiness.')

Scandinavian borrowings are marked with double underlining. They consist of two complete words, plus the present participle suffix *-ande* (O.N. *-andi*) which is regular throughout the *Gawain* manuscript. French borrowings, marked with single underlining, are more numerous and are in prominent positions, including seven of the twelve rhymes. Words developed from Old English are by far the most numerous (65) and include several (*I, in, me, my, of, watz, wyth* and *at*) which occur more than once. These are the common pronouns, prepositions, articles and forms of the verb *to be* which convey grammatical meaning and do the unobtrusive 'spadework' of a language. Their numbers, and the syntactical relationships they represent, show that the basic structure of English is still very much as it was before the Conquest and that the borrowed words, for all their prominence, have perhaps a less fundamental importance than might at first appear to be the case.

Lexical choice was also governed by the genre within which a poet worked and by considerations specific to the subject. Language which is characteristic of a particular subject is known as *register*, and a distinctive vocabulary is usually the most noticeable feature of it. In the Middle English lyrics on Courtly Love, for instance, we can expect to find such words and phrases as *bour* (bower), *derne loue* (secret love), *hende* (gracious), and *nyhtegale* (nightingale), whereas in, say, the religious lyrics dealing with the Passion of Christ words like *blodi* (bloody), *bohte* (redeemed), *pine* (suffering), *þolen* (suffer), and *woundes wete* (bleeding wounds) tend to recur. Probably the registers would be more strongly differentiated were it not for the poets' frequent desire to explore the common features and ambivalences of physical and spiritual love. However, nowhere is the poetic register more distinctive than in poems which are alliterative in structure, especially those of the fourteenth and fifteenth centuries which are said to belong to the 'Alliterative Revival'. These poems make use of a vocabulary which, in part, is quite distinct from that of rhymed verse. Words of this distinctive type have been described as 'chiefly' or 'characteristically alliterative' (Oakden 1935, 175; Turville-Petre 1977, 71), meaning that they are infrequently, or in some cases never, found outside alliterative verse. By definition they belong to the poetic register, so a single occurrence in an alliterative context is not enough to prove that a word had this 'characteristically alliterative' status any more than the occasional appearance of a word in a rhyming poem is sufficient to deny it.

An important consideration, as in Old English poetry, was the need to create a large stock of alliterating words. For the concept 'man, warrior', therefore, the poet might use either a widely current noun, such as *kniȝt*, *lorde*, or *mon*, or one from a more restricted set, comprising *burne*, *freke*, *gome*, *hathel*, *lede*, *renk*, *schalk*, *segge*, *tulke*, or *wyȝe*. Similarly, for any generalised verb of movement ('to go' etc.), as alternatives to *go* and *ride* there were *bowe*, *caire*, *chose*, *drive*, *fare*, *ferke*, *founde*, *glide*, *hale*, *helde*, *kever*, *raike*, *schowve*, *seche*, *strike*, *tourne*, *wade*, *wende* and *win*. If a generalised complimentary adjective ('gracious, noble' etc.) were called for, the need could be met by a widely used word such as *comly*, *courteis*, *dere*, *fre*, *gentil*, *hende*, *lufly*, *worthy* or by a more restricted word such as *menskful* or *wale*. And an adverb expressive of prompt and speedy movement ('quickly' etc.) might be *bilive*, *deliverly*, *faste*, *ȝerne*, *hastily*, *kene*, *radly*, *swiftly* (all of which are found in the London English of Chaucer) or a word more characteristic of alliterative verse, such as *graithely*, *ȝarely*, *ȝederly*, *prestly*, *rapely*, *rekenly*, *skete*, *taitely* or *wyȝtly*.[2]

Characteristically alliterative vocabulary is more often found in alliterative poems of the North and North Midlands than in those from the South Midlands, and since it was in this sense regional it is not surprising that lexical items are sometimes drawn from the dialects of these regions. *Blesenand*, for example, means 'brilliant, splendid, glaring'. It seems to have been a northern variant of 'blazing', and is found several times in both *Wynnere and Wastoure* and *The Wars of Alexander*. *Happed*, an adjectival past participle of obscure etymology meaning 'wrapped up', is another northern word which is common in alliterative contexts. *Raxlen* 'to stretch, especially on awaking' is another example, and occurs in *Pearl* and *The Wars of Alexander*, while *donken* 'to moisten, to be moist', which occurs almost exclusively in Middle English alliterative contexts, is found also in Modern English dialects from Gloucester and Warwickshire northwards with the meaning 'to drizzle'.

Since the North and North Midlands were areas of heavy Scandinavian settlement, we naturally find in the dialects of these regions a relatively high concentration of Scandinavian loan words, and these, too, were readily absorbed into the alliterative verse. Scandinavian loans are less numerous than French. In *Sir Gawain and the Green Knight*, for instance, of the total number of approximately 2650 words over a thousand are loans, of which, so far as their etymologies can be determined, about 250 are Scandinavian and about 750 are French (Tolkien and Gordon 1967, 138). But the French words are more fully assimilated and therefore more familiar, whereas those of Scandinavian origin have a more prominent role in the alliterative register. Scandinavian words are specially effective in evoking hostile northern English topography. When Gawain anxiously surveys the landscape near the Green Chapel, where he is to meet the Green Knight (2163–7), it seems to him that the *skwez* (clouds, O.N. *ský*) are being *skayned* (scraped, O.N. *skeina*) by the *scowtes* (jutting rocks, O.N. *skúti*). Turville-Petre points out that *OED* does not record *scowte* elsewhere in English literature but that the word survives as a place name element in Kinder Scout, the highest point of the Peak District of Derbyshire, and in Scout Moor in Lancashire.

> The implication must be that this was a dialect word used regularly by the poet and his audience to describe the craggy peaks in the regions they lived in and through which Gawain (no soft southerner, he) is travelling. For an audience in the north-west midlands this word and a number of others like it would have conjured up the bleak and desolate landscape of the Peaks and the Pennines that they knew so well.
>
> (Turville-Petre 1977, 76–7)

Small wonder, then, that the topography of the Green Chapel has seemed so real and distinctive to readers of the poem that a number of them have attempted, on evidence from the poem, to locate this imaginary place in the real landscape of North Derbyshire and Staffordshire (e.g. Elliott 1984).

The receptiveness of the alliterative poets and their resourcefulness in extending their lexicon can be illustrated by reference to the many verbs, mentioned above, which are used to mean 'go, proceed'. Simplest of all are *fare* and *wade*, which inherited the plain meaning from Old English (*faran, wadan*) and *raike*, which inherited it from Old Norse (*reika*). Others had a reflexive form which gave the appropriate sense, including *helde* (to advance, turn oneself), *raike* (to betake oneself, set out), and *ricche* (to make one's way, proceed). Others had both transitive and intransitive application, including *drive, seche* and *chose*; thus in *Sir Gawain* we find both *chosen þe gate* (930) and *chosen to þe gate* (778, both meaning 'go/gone along the path'). Some special type of movement is in some cases implied by the word's etymology, though in the alliterative context the specialised sense is often disregarded in preference for the general sense 'go'; thus there is *ayre* (O.F. *errer* 'to wander'), *caire* (O.N. *keyra* 'to whip or spur a horse', *drive* (O.E. *drifan* 'to rush violently'), *glide* (O.E. *glidan* 'to glide') and *thring* (O.E. *þringan* 'to press, throng'). *Tourne* originally meant 'to turn' (O.E. *turnian*), and *bowe, helde* and *loute* originally meant 'to bend, bow' (O.E. *bugan, hyldan, lutan*). The half-line *bugon þa to bence* (they then proceeded to the bench) in *Beowulf* 327 shows that *bugan* was sometimes used intransitively with the generalised meaning 'went, proceeded' in Old English verse. And *mete* (from O.E. *metan* 'to measure by paces') shows a similar application in Middle English alliterative verse of earlier poetic usage.

A more remarkable survival, however, is the group of restricted poetic terms for 'man, warrior' alluded to above. This comprises eight words which have direct equivalents in Old English poetry (Middle English *burne, freke, gome, lede, renk, schalk, segge* and *wyʒe*, Old English *beorn, freca, guma, leod, rinc, scealc, secg* and *wiga*), plus a ninth, *hathel*, which is thought to be a blend of the Old English poetic noun *hæleð* (man, warrior, hero) and the adjective *æðel* (noble). A tenth word, *tulke*, is also of this group, but is unique in being a loan word, from Old Norse *tulkr* (spokesman, interpreter). These words are approximate synonyms. They are found only rarely outside alliterative verse and none has descended into Standard Modern English (though *freke* and *schalk* survive in dialect). Their affinity with words common in Old English verse (except in the case of *tulke*) has been taken as evidence of an unbroken tradition underlying the phenomenon of the Alliterative 'Revival' in the fourteenth century. In the absence of Early Middle English alliterative texts to illustrate the link, it is sometimes argued that the line of continuity took the form of an oral, and perhaps provincial, tradition. But the history of the individual words suggests a more complex situation, with poets perhaps 'rediscovering' the usefulness in alliterative verse of words which had continued to survive in differing senses and status (see Borroff 1962, 52–90 and Turville-Petre 1977, 14–17, 78–80). Whatever the case, the ten words in the group have been identified as of 'high alliterative rank', that is, as stylistically elevated words whose important status can be gauged from the fact that they are far more likely to bear the alliteration than not. The statistics speak for themselves. Comparison between *lede* and *kniȝt*, for example, reveals that in *Sir Gawain and the Green Knight* the former occurs 38 times in an alliterating position and not at all in a non-alliterating one. Similarly, in *Morte Arthure* there are 15 alliterating occurrences of it and no non-alliterating occurrences. Conversely, *kniȝt* is much less likely to alliterate, the ratio being 41 (alliterating) to 27 in *Gawain* and 22 to 99 in *Morte Arthure*. Taking our ten words listed above as a whole, the ratio of alliterating to non-alliterating occurrences in *Gawain* is a striking 263 to one. Whatever their history and precise range of senses, then, these words seem to be used, in addition to meeting metrical requirements, with a uniform stylistic purpose, namely to elevate and idealise the persons and subject matter and to imbue them with that characteristic quality which establishes the conventional parameters and stimulates expectations of traditional actions and values.

Considerations such as this remind us of the need constantly to strive to bridge the cultural divide between medieval times and our own and to try, however laboriously, to reconstruct associations which would instantly have come to the mind of a medieval listener or reader. This applies to the historical study of literature of any period, to verse, prose, alliterative and non-alliterative poetry alike. The fifteenth-century lyric *I sing of a Maiden* (Brown 1939, 119) illustrates this point :

I syng of a myden þat is makeles,   *maiden matchless/mateless*
Kyng of alle kynges to here sone che ches.   *she chose*

He cam also stylle þer his moder was   *as quietly*
As dew in Aprylle, þat fallyt on þe gras.   *falls*

> He cam also stylle to his moderes bowr
> As dew in Aprille, þat fallyt on þe flour.   *flower*
>
> He cam also stylle þer his moder lay
> As dew in Aprille, þat fallyt on the spray.
>
> Moder and mayden was neuer non but che —   *none but she*
> Wel may swych a lady Godes moder be.

In this unpretentiously skilful lyric there are many semantic layers of which a present-day reader might not be aware.[3] The epic formula 'I syng of...' sets up expectations of a lofty subject which, at one level, seem to be denied by the restrained simplicity of the language. The poet describes the miracle of the Immaculate Conception with a deliberate mixture of secular and religious imagery. Jesus is daringly pictured, with stanza-by-stanza progression, as a lover approaching the bed of his loved one. Words from the register of courtly love such as *bowr*, *flour* and *spray* balance phrases with devotional associations such as *kyng of alle kynges* and *Godes moder*. The word *makeles* in the first line is deliberately ambivalent, meaning both 'matchless, without equal' and 'mateless, unsullied by intercourse', a reference to the unique paradox which is more explicitly stated in the last stanza. Most semantically loaded of all is the unobtrusive word *dew*. While the present-day reader is likely to appreciate the aptness of the comparison between the implanting of the seed in Mary's womb and the mysterious stillness of the falling of pure and refreshing dew, he or she is unlikely to know without having been told that dew had established associations with the Holy Spirit because of the story of Gideon's Fleece (Judges 6.36−40). The dew represents the presence of the Holy Spirit and the Holy Spirit was the means of the Miraculous Conception, as any medieval person who had seen a picture of the event or listened to a sermon on the subject (i.e. every medieval Christian) would know. In medieval science and popular belief dew was also held to have fructifying properties. Word associations such as these are culturally engendered, and are inevitably lost as society changes. It is salutary to remember that we cannot hope to reconstruct more than a fraction of the semantic richness of the best medieval poems.

7 Middle English Verse: Structure and Organisation

Whereas Old English verse is almost exclusively alliterative, and, as we have seen, there was also a distinctive Middle English alliterative tradition, which flourished particularly in the fourteenth century and fifteenth centuries, the greater part of Middle English verse is patterned on end-rhyme. In addition, we find that the poets of rhymed poems often make use of alliterative features for ornament, just as the alliterative poets did of rhyme. Syntactic patterns are profoundly affected by the poet's adherence to one or the other of these traditions, and a brief consideration of the basic differences between rhymed and alliterative verse is therefore a good starting point for consideration of the structure and organisation of the verse.

End-rhyme is the familiar prosodic pattern whereby syllables are arranged to rhyme at the ends of lines of verse and sometimes at the end of syntactic units within the line ('internal rhyme'). Verse of this type usually has lines of fixed (or relatively fixed) numbers of syllables, unlike lines of Old English verse, in which the number of unstressed syllables is variable. End-rhyme is the exception in Old English, and in a fully developed structural form it is found only in *The Riming Poem*, where in each of the 87 lines the first half-line rhymes with the second, while the two are also bound together by the customary alliterative structure of Old English verse:

> Burg-sele beofode,   beorht hlifade,
> ellen eacnade,   ead beacnade.   (30–1)
> (*The castle-hall shook, towered bright,*
> *courage increased, wealth shone forth.*)

Apart from this and in some passages of poems by Cynewulf, rhyme in Old English is only used as an occasional ornament, either in fully rhyming syllables such as

> Byrhtnoð maþelode,   bord hafenode   (*Maldon* 42)
> (*Byrhtnoth spoke, brandished his shield*)

or with varying degrees of imperfect rhyme or assonance such as

> torn unlytel.   Þæt wæs tacen sweotol.   (*Beowulf* 833)
> (*great affliction. That was a clear token.*)

The line

> æfre embe stunde   he sealde sume wunde   (*Maldon* 271)
> (*time and again he gave some wound*)

is totally without alliteration (since *st-* does not alliterate with *s-*), but uses rhyme to link the two half-lines in a way which anticipates Laȝamon's *Brut*

> And mid swulche þinges   he ouer-com alle kinges.
> (*Brut* 9957).
> (*And with such things he overcame all kings.*)

The potential for end-rhyme was very great, given the ease with which Old English inflexional endings could be made to rhyme (as in the first *Maldon* example). But although some Anglo-Saxon poets were familiar with rhyme in Latin hymns and perhaps already made use of it in traditional formulae such as *frod and god* 'wise and good', there seems to have been resistance to it until French poets and patrons brought it into vogue after the Conquest. Rhyme in Middle English follows much stricter criteria than the occasional examples in Old English, and most rhymed verse conforms to the first category in the list of commoner types below. But even then there seems to have been considerable tolerance of partial and identical rhymes, as other types illustrate:

Rhyme: Initial consonants of words are different but the stressed vowel and succeeding consonants are the same. This can be *masculine rhyme*, where the rhymed element is a concluding stress (*lyf:wyf*), or *feminine rhyme*, where an unstressed syllable follows the final stressed one (*fable:able*).

Triple rhyme: Two unstressed syllables follow the final stressed one (*morowe:sorowe*, with pronunciation of final *-e*).

Identical rhyme: Identical words, syllables or homonyms rhyme (*men:men, lond:Engelond*).

Rhyme on syllables which are normally unstressed or weakly stressed. This is often found (*holinesse:simplesse; crying:king*), and may indicate that the usual stress pattern could be varied for the sake of rhyme.

Assonance: The vowels of the final stressed syllable are alike but not the consonants (*honde:stronge*).

Consonance: Consonants or consonant groups of the final stressed syllable are alike but not the vowels (*kuste:reste*).

The arrangement of rhymes in longer poems was usually in couplets, in lines of varying length. Much of the earliest rhyming verse takes this form, including *The Owl and the Nightingale, Cursor Mundi,* Robert of Gloucester's *Chronicle,* the beast fable of *The Fox and the Wolf,* and the romances *King Horn* and *Havelok.* Most of the later romances are also in couplets, though a significant group of 23, composed mainly in the fourteenth century in the East Midlands, is in 'tail-rhyme' stanzas. Tail-rhyme involves the linking of a series of couplets by individual lines based on one rhyme. For example, *Sir Launfal* has stanzas of twelve lines rhyming *aabccbddbeeb*, but stanzas of many different lengths are also found. Many other arrangements are possible, and greater variety is encountered as the period progresses. Shorter poems and lyrics exhibit a wide range of verse forms even in Early Middle English. For example, the thirteenth-century political satire *The Song of Lewes* rhymes *aaaabcb*, with internal rhyme in the *c* line. The last two lines form the refrain for each of the eight stanzas, and the eighth stanza is rounded off by an extra two lines, *aaaababcb*. Sophisticated effects like this were possible even at this early period. An example of the effective use of rhyme in later, fifteenth-century verse can be found in those plays of the Towneley (Wakefield) Mystery Cycle which were composed by an anonymous playwright known simply as 'The Wakefield Master'. He is author of five or six of the 32 surviving plays and made adaptations to others. His style is characterised by a unique, 13-line stanza, rhyming *ababababcdddc*.[1] The number of syllables varies from line to line. Despite the constraints of this complex form, the effect achieved is one of ordered naturalness, even where one line is divided between two speakers. In the following example (313−25) Noah and his wife come to blows:

Noe.	We! hold thi tong, ram-skyt,	*ram-shit*
	Or I shall the still.	*shut you up*
Vxor.	By my thryft, if thou smyte,	*upon my life*
	I shal turne the vntill.	*I'll turn on you*
Noe.	We shall assay as tyte.	*we'll soon see*
	Haue at the, Gill!	*take that*
	Apon the bone shal it byte.	*cut [he strikes her]*
Vxor.	A, so! Mary, thou smytys ill!	*by Mary! you're hurting!*
	Bot I suppose	*imagine*
	I shal not in thi det	*debt [i.e. having given less]*
	Flyt of this flett:	*go from this place*
	Take the ther a langett	*take this thong*
	To tye vp thi hose!	*[she strikes him]*

In verse in which end-rhyme is the norm the lack of it is usually taken as an indication of corruption in the transmission of the text, either from a failure of memory at the oral stage or from a deliberate or accidental change in copying. As we have seen, scribes sometimes modernised the language, changed the dialect, or simply failed to read properly from the exemplar. In some instances a knowledge of Middle English dialects can help to reconstruct a lost rhyme. In the romance *Sir Orfeo* we are told that when Orfeo was in the wilderness searching for his queen he suffered great deprivation and

In somer he lieuþ bi wild frut,
And berien bot gode lite.   (257−8)
(*In summer he lives on wild fruit and berries of no great quality.*)

This is the reading in the Auchinleck manuscript (*c.*1330), the best of the three in which the poem survives. The other two have different rhyme words which are not helpful to the issue. To understand why the rhyme is lacking it is necessary to look a little into the phonology. The Old English long vowel *y* (pronounced as in French *lune*) appears as a different vowel in differing dialect groups in Middle English. Broadly speaking, in the North and East Midlands it appears as *i*, in the South East, especially in Kent, as *e*, and in other areas of the South and in the West Midlands it remains substantially the same as in Old English but is usually spelt *u*. The Old English adverb *lyt* 'little', therefore, became respectively *lite, lete,* and *lute* in these areas. In the couplet from *Orfeo* the rhyme word *frut* is a French borrowing of which the vowel quality is not in doubt. To establish a good rhyme, therefore, the form *lute* is required. The language of the Auchinleck manuscript is thought to belong to the Middlesex area, but the inadequate rhyme suggests that the poem may originally have been composed in a rather more westerly dialect, or that the dialect of Middlesex had a more westerly colouring at the time when the poem came into being, or even that a mixed literary variety was in use which drew upon a range of regional features. It would be unwise to place too much weight on a fragment of evidence such as this, but where such imperfect rhymes are supported by other clues they can be very helpful in piecing together the linguistic background.

Rhymed verse often makes use of alliteration as a decorative feature, sometimes for special stylistic effect. In the Mystery Plays, for instance, alliteration may be used to dignify the formal speech of a patriarch or to convey the threat and bluster of a villain, like Herod in the N-Town Play *The Slaughter of the Innocents*:

> I ryde on my rowel, ryche in my regne!
> Rybbys ful reed with rape xal I rende!
> Popetys and pap-hawkys I xal puttyn in peyne,
> With my spere prevyn, pychyn, and to-pende!   (XX.9–12)
> (*I spur my horse on, magnificent in my royal power! I shall quickly tear apart ribs, red with blood! Babies and sucklings I shall put in pain, stab and torture them, test them on my spear!*)

A different use of alliteration emerged in the second half of the fourteenth century in the poems of the so-called Alliterative Revival. In these works the alliteration is structural, forming the primary pattern of the verse, just as end-rhyme does for rhyming poems. The fundamental principles are the same as in Old English, and this is why the fourteenth-century development is commonly seen as a 'revival', though continuity from Old English cannot be proved.

There are also some important general differences. One is the use in Middle English alliterative verse of a predominantly end-stopped line, with fewer sense units beginning and ending at the caesura than in Old English (Benson 1965, 112–17). Consequently, though Middle English alliterative verse still depends on parallel constructions, as did Old English, the parallels are more likely to consist of a whole clause rather than individual phrases:

> Þay boȝen bi bonkkez þer boȝez ar bare,
> Þay clomben bi clyffez þer clengez þe colde. (*Gawain* 2077–8)
> (*They travelled along hillsides where trees are bare,*
> *They climbed by cliffs where the cold clings.*)

Though it rarely marks the beginning of a major sense unit, the caesura still signifies a syntactic pause, and often, as in the two lines quoted, the main clause is completed in the first half-line. For this reason, the second half-line may be completed either by a subordinate clause which simply adds more information (as above) or by some formulaic filler or tag:

> A chaplet one his chefe-lere, chosen for the nones,
> Raylede alle with rede rose, richest of floures.
> (*Parlement of the Thre Ages* 118–19)
> (*A garland on his head, a beautiful one indeed,*
> *Set with red roses, most splendid of flowers.*)

Such differences resulted to some extent from general developments which occurred in the transition from Old to Middle English. The loss of inflexional endings and the disinclination of poets to compress meaning into poetic compounds, as had formerly been the practice, encouraged the development of a more analytic syntactic structure (i.e. one which makes more use of prepositions, articles and auxiliary verbs and which depends on word order to show relationships). The number of unstressed, 'small' but grammatically important words was consequently increased. For example, whereas in Old English poetry the concept 'God' was likely to be expressed by a traditional epithet such as *Drihten* or by a formulaic compound such as *heah-cyning* (high-king), in Middle English it might be expressed less compactly by a nominal phrase:

þe Soverayn þat syttez so hyȝe   (*Purity* 552)
þat syre þat syttes so hiȝe   (*Patience* 261)
he þat on hyȝe syttes   (*Gawain* 256)
þe wyȝe . . . þat vphaldez þe heuen and on hyȝ sittez
                                 (*Gawain* 2441–2)[2]

The rhythm is also affected by the increased number of small words. In Old English the stress commonly fell on the first syllable of a word, and the inflexional ending was always stressed weakly. This gave rise to a 'falling rhythm', as in *Rómana býrig* (city of the Romans, *Metres of Boethius* IX, 10); on the other hand, in Middle English the rhythm is characteristically rising, as in *the cétee of Róme* (*Morte Arthure* 440), where the unstressed syllables are encountered first.

It may also be a consequence of the lengthened line that a less restrained use of alliteration developed, with more syllables in each line alliterating together than was possible in Old English verse. Formerly care was taken to ensure that the first stressed syllable after the caesura (the 'headstave') alliterated with either or both of the main stresses in the first half-line (*ax/ax, xa/ax* or *aa/ax*), but never with the final stressed syllable of the long line. In Middle English, however, the final stressed syllable is sometimes included in the alliterative scheme (as in *Gawain* 2077–8, quoted above) and a third alliterating syllable sometimes appears in the first half-line:

In **W**est **W**alys, i**w**ysse,   syche **w**onndyrs þay **w**roghte.
                                  (*Morte Arthure* 322)

Other such 'non-standard' developments are found in Middle English, involving alliteration in excess of what was permissible in classical Old English verse. Conversely, lines are sometimes encountered which are deficient in alliteration, though there is sometimes a suspicion that they have been corrupted in the course of transmission. *Piers Plowman* is a striking example: in places it lacks any alliteration at all in the second half of a line (between

2.1 per cent and 4.5 per cent of lines in the three versions of the poem are like this), and occasionally there is none in the whole of the long line (0.7 per cent to 0.9 per cent). This looser type of alliterative verse sometimes comes close to being a sort of rhythmic prose.[3]

Many devices, both traditional and new, were used by poets to serve their prosodic needs. Authors of rhyming poems, for example, for whom the number of syllables in each line was more rigidly prescribed by their chosen verse-form than for poets of the rhythmic alliterative line, seem to have taken advantage of contemporary uncertainty and difference of practice concerning the loss of inflexional endings, particularly in the case of the pronunciation of final -e. Final -e usually represents a separate unstressed syllable in Middle English verse (until about the middle of the fourteenth century, at least), so a word such as *bridde* has two syllables and *nyhtegale* four. Other inflexional endings, such as the final -es in *lordes*, were also pronounced. Adjectival -e, in particular, has a complicated history. Some adjectives (e.g. *milde, swete*) have -e in their uninflected (subject) form because it is an etymological inheritance from Old English. Others have -e because it indicates the plural, or because it is a marker of the old Germanic 'weak' form, which was used with the definite article, the demonstrative, or a possessive pronoun (the, this, that, my, your etc.). The following sequence is therefore found:

good boke, yong wif	('strong' singular)
þis goode boke, his yonge wif	('weak' singular)
goode bokes, yonge wives	(plural)

The situation was changing throughout the period, with final -e ceasing to be pronounced earlier in northern districts than in the South. It remained a feature in written English long after it had died out in the spoken language, but as time went by final -e in verse came to be used as a separate syllable only where metrical conditions required it. All this caused considerable confusion, especially when manuscripts came to be reproduced, for scribes often either disregarded final -e in places where it was required by the metre, producing deficient lines such as

And, at þe þre[ë] day[ë]s endë   (*Handlyng Synne* 9185)

or inserted it in places where there was no historical justification, such as in *Sir Orfeo* 79–80, where unhistorical *-e* in *wete* has spoilt the rhyme:

> Sche froted hir honden and hir fet,
> And crached hir visage – it blede wete.
> (*She rubbed her hands and her feet and*
> *scratched her face till it was wet with blood.*)

In general, the lack of consistency in the use of *-e* probably reflects the fluidity in this respect of colloquial practice – a latitude some poets seem to have turned to their advantage.[4]

A similar exploitation of the changing linguistic context can be seen in the use of the prefix *y-* on verbs. In the South and in the West Midlands a *y-* prefix appeared in Early Middle English as a marker of the past participle (a development of Old English *ge-*), and this was gradually lost during the course of the Middle English period. In the fourteenth century its retention or otherwise was sometimes a matter of personal choice on the part of the poet, and the metrical context was sometimes a determining factor: Compare and contrast, for instance, the following couplets:

> Amorwe þe vndertide is come,
> And Orfeo haþ his armes ynome   (*Orfeo* 181–2)
> (*The next morning has arrived, and Orfeo has taken up his arms*)

> So long he haþ þe way ynome
> To Winchester he is ycome.   (*Orfeo* 477–8)
> (*He has travelled so far that he has arrived at Winchester.*)

The former shows the use of the *y-* prefix on only one of the past participles, whereas the latter (in which the *y-* is needed in order to supply the required number of syllables) has it on both, though the same verbs are involved in the same rhymes in each case.

Flexibility was also possible in matters of phrasal syntax. In the nominal phrase, for instance, a device that could be used to gain or lose a syllable was the omission of the definite or indefinite article in circumstances in which Modern English would include it (and vice versa). Thus Gower omits the definite article when referring to Albinus

> Which bar corone of Lombardie   (*Confessio Amantis* I.462)
> (*Who bore the crown of Lombardy*),

but includes it, somewhat inconsistently, in

> Tho was the vertu sett above
> And vice was put under fote.   (*Confessio Amantis* Prol. 116–17)
> (*Then virtue was exalted and vice repressed.*)

A similar freedom of choice was available in other contexts, such as after the adjectives 'each' and 'every', where the indefinite article was not historically the norm:

> In ech a court wher she is maistresse
>   (Lydgate, *Fall of Princes* II.2251)

The now familiar combinations *many a, such a,* and *what a* began in this period to appear.

Another freedom within the nominal phrase was the range of possible ways in which the genitive could be formed, and one suspects that prosodic considerations may at times have determined choice. Old English has a variety of different genitive inflexions for different classes of noun, and for different numbers and genders, but these were mostly reduced to -*s* in Middle English. A major new development, though, was the genitive construction with *of*, which appeared in late Old English and grew by the fourteenth century to become a frequently preferred form in written use. It seems, however, from statistical analysis of a selection of prose and verse texts, that poets resisted the use of the *of* genitive (Mustanoja 1960, 75). Apart from the inherent conservatism of the language of poetry, this is probably owing to the greater flexibility afforded by the more compact, inflected form. Where the *of* genitive *is* used in verse the syntax is sometimes adapted:

> I finde hou whilom Adrian,
> Of Rome which a gret lord was,
> Upon a day as he per cas
> To wode in his huntinge wente...
>   (Gower, *Confessio Amantis* V.4938–41)

(I find how once upon a time Adrian, who was as great lord of Rome, as he by chance was going to the woods to hunt . . .)

Another Middle English development is the 'group genitive', that is, the application of a genitive inflection to a phrase containing more than one noun. The type of group genitive in which the nouns are in apposition is found in Early Middle English:

Þe Laferrd Cristess karrte   (*Ormulum* 56)
(*The Lord Christ's chariot*).

Another type, in which the main noun is qualified by another in a prepositional phrase, is first found in Chaucer:

God of Loves servantz   (*Troilus* I.15)
(*God of Love's servants*).

This is, of course, now standard in Modern English (e.g.'the Queen of Sheba's throne'). But Middle English much more commonly splits the genitive group around the noun that governs it, and this sometimes falls in easily with the prevailing rhythm of the line of verse:

For mi lordes loue, Sir Orfeo   (*Orfeo* 518)
(*For my lord Sir Orfeo's love*)

Þe prestes doghtyr of þe tounne   (*Handlyng Synne* 9030)
(*The priest of the town's daughter*).

The syntax of the prepositional phrase allowed similar scope for freedom of stylistic choice. Some of the non-standard patterns found in verse are as follows:

Preposition placed in final position in prepositional phrase (for rhyme):

He ete and dranc þat was his will,
And siþen his sone he called him till.
                    (*Cursor Mundi* 3711–12)
(*He ate and drank whatever he wanted, and then called his sone to him.*)

Preposition placed in final position in prepositional phrase (alliterative verse):

> The haþel heldet hym fro, and on his ax rested.
>
> (Gawain 2331)
>
> (*The man turned back, and rested on his axe.*)

Preposition separated from associated noun or pronoun (deferred for rhyme):

> And whan my lord him drynkiþ to
> Þe coppe he schal to wille vp do.
>
> (*Kyng Alisaunder* (MS L) 4184−5)
>
> (*And when my lord drinks his health he will gladly steal the cup.*)

Preposition brought forward (for rhyme):

> Þe werst piler on to biholde
> Was al of burnist gold.   (*Orfeo* 367−8)
>
> (*The meanest pillar that could be seen was all burnished gold.*)

Preposition brought forward (alliterative verse):

> And profrede Piers this present to plese with Hunger.
>
> (Langland, *Piers Plowman* VI 295)
>
> (*And offered this gift to Piers for him to appease Hunger with it.*)

These variations in the syntax of the prepositional phrase, however, are as nothing when compared with those encountered in the verbal phrase, where the scope was so much greater. The infinitive, for example, offered scope for flexibility and individual choice. Three different forms were available − the word by itself (with or without inflexional ending) and with *to* and *for to*. There were some established patterns of usage (such as the single-word infinitive after common auxiliary verbs), but choice on the grounds of style was frequently possible. If extra syllables were required, the infinitive might be preceded by *for to*, which originally expressed purpose (as in *com to him forto here*, 'came in order to hear him', *Orfeo* 440), but which was reduced in the course of time simply to an infinitive marker. If fewer were needed, either of the other forms could be used. It is not uncommon to find a mixture of forms, even in close proximity one to another.

It was also possible, where an auxiliary was present and the sense clear, for the infinitive of a verb of motion to remain unexpressed. This had also been possible in Old English verse, and Middle English poets took advantage of the flexibility this offered:

> Whider þou gost ichil wiþ þe,
> And whider y go þou schalt wiþ me. (Orfeo 129–30)
> (*Whither you go, I will [go] with you,*
> *and whither I go, you shall [go] with me.*)

Conversely, pleonastic verbal expressions are also found, such as *come* accompanied by the infinitive of a verb of motion (a practice also carried over from Old English), in a way which is comparable to Modern English *came* plus present participle:

> Ase he com ride be a cost... (*Beues of Hamtoun* 1023)
> (*As he came riding along a coastal path...*)

The infinitive in such constructions seems to have become the main carrier of the verbal idea, usually expressing manner or purpose, and consequently these periphrases were felt to have more descriptive colour than the finite verb alone.

Negation was another area in which freedom could be exercised. In Early Middle English the standard method was to place the negative adverb *ne* immediately before the finite verb. In the case of certain common verbs – *have*, *will*, and some forms of *be* – the negative adverb and the verb were sometimes run together to give forms such as *nam* for *ne am*, *nas* for *ne was* and *nil* for *ne wil*. An additional negative adverb, such as *nought*, *nat*, *nawt* or *not*, was sometimes placed after the verb. The original purpose of this was to make the negation more emphatic, but in time this aspect was weakened and the *ne* began to disappear, so that by the middle of the fourteenth century *nat* or *not* alone, placed immediately after the finite verb, had become the standard way of expressing the negative. In verse other positions are found, with the negative sometimes placed first for emphasis:

Nat purpose I make othir testament.

(Hoccleve, *Regement of Princes* 4320)

(*I do not intend to make another will.*)

Multiple negation is common, again for emphasis, and there is no sense of one negating word cancelling another, as in present-day English. We therefore find such lines as *Þu nart noȝt to non oþer þinge* 'you are useless for anything else' (*The Owl and the Nightingale* 559) and *neuer him nas wers for noþing* 'he had never been more upset about anything' (*Orfeo* 98). Figurative periphrases of the negative are also encountered, especially where the verse is quoting or imitating colloquial speech, e.g. *I nolde fange a ferthyng* (I wouldn't accept a farthing, *Piers Plowman*, V.558).

Yet another feature carried over from earlier times is the so-called 'ethic dative', a pleonastic personal pronoun associated mainly with the first and second persons:

So wiste I me non other red.　　　　(*Confessio Amantis* I.108)

(*So I did not know what to do [for myself].*)

Closely related is a variety of reflexive pronoun found with verbs (usually intransitive) expressing motion or fear:

Þe king him rod an huntinge　　　　　　　(*King Horn* 645)

(*The king rode out hunting*)

Men feeren hem in al the toun.

(Gower, *Confessio Amantis* III.454)

(*People are afraid throughout the town.*)

The use of the reflexive pronoun in this way seems to be more prevalent in verse, and in many instances, including the above, the preference can be explained on metrical grounds (see Fischer 1992, 239).

The use of *do* as an 'empty' auxiliary verb (e.g. 'He on the ground did fall') is first recorded in literature from about 1300, and its frequent, early occurrence in poetry suggests that metrical considerations may have had an influence in its development. Auxiliary *do* may have developed from causative *do*, which is found extensively in Old and Middle English contexts, e.g.

Þe king dede þe mayden arise.   (*Havelok* 205)
(*The king caused/ordered the maiden to arise.*)

At times it is impossible to be sure whether cause is implied or not:

Grim dede maken a ful fayr bed   (*Havelok* 659)
(*Grim had a very beautiful bed made/prepared*
or *Grim did make [i.e. made] a very beautiful bed*),

and it is possibly from such ambiguous instances that the habit developed of using *do* as a mere periphrasis (see Visser 1969, 1488–1502). Whatever its origins, it proved useful to poets, especially in providing an extra, unstressed syllable and in allowing the accompanying verb to be placed at the end of the line in a rhyming position. Extra unstressed syllables and rhyme words were, of course, of no interest to the poets of Old English alliterative verse, and it was not until rhyme and iambic metre came into vogue that literary examples are found. In a similar way *gan* (commenced) and its variant *can* in combination with an infinitive came to be used in a weakened sense, equivalent to the past tense. We therefore find such examples as

Ac, as sone as sche gan awake,
Sche crid, and loþli bere gan make   (*Sir Orfeo* 77–8)
(*But as soon as she awoke she cried out and made a dreadful din*),

where the context shows that all sense of 'commencing' has been lost. This feature is exclusive to verse, and, as with other features, its development may well have been a matter of prosodic convenience. As with *do*, *gan* and *can* each provide an extra syllable useful to iambic metre and allow the main verb to make the rhyme. For the same reasons alliterative poets had little use for auxiliary *gan*. In *Sir Gawain*, for example, there are only two instances in the long, non-rhyming alliterative lines, but as many as twenty in the five short rhyming lines (the 'bob and wheel') with which each stanza ends (see Visser 1969, 1572).

Certain tenses of the verb are also marked in verse, among them the present tense as a variant of the preterite (the so-called 'historic present'). This had not been a prominent feature of Old English, and the small number of instances that have been noted in pre-Conquest literature are all confined to the poetry (see Visser 1966, 705–26). Recorded examples of the use of the historic present remain rare until the fourteenth and fifteenth centuries, when they begin to appear in increasing numbers, especially as variations within long series of regular preterites, mostly in verse narratives such as those of the romances, the works of Chaucer and Gower, and in poems of the alliterative tradition. The following is an example of the mixed style, with the narrative shifting between past and present forms:

> His wif unto the see him broghte,
> With al hire herte and him besoghte
> That he the time hire wolde sein
> Whan that he thoghte come ayein:
> 'Withinne,' he seith, 'tuo monthe day.'
> And thus in al the haste he may
> He tok his leve, and forth he seileth,
> Wepende, and sche hirself beweileth,
> And torneth hom, ther sche cam fro.
>
> (*Confessio Amantis* IV, 2951–9)
> (*His wife brought him to the sea and besought him with all her
> heart that he would tell her the time when he expected to return.
> 'Within two months', he says. And thus, with all the haste he
> may, he took his leave and sails forth. And she herself,
> weeping, laments, and turns home to where she came from.*)

Even during the period of the extensive use of the historic present in verse, it remains extremely rare in prose. A consequent hypothesis is that its usefulness in rhyme and metre may have been responsible for its popularity as a stylistic device. For example, the historic present form sometimes participates in rhyme:

> The blode braste owt at hys eerys,
> And hys stede to grownde he berys   (*Syr Tryamowre* 790–1)
> (*The blood burst out at his ears, and he bears his steed to the ground*),

where historic present *berys* is used as opposed to non-rhyming past tense *bore*. It also sometimes provides an extra syllable essential to the scansion:

There he lygges in the felde,
Many men one hym byhelde   (*Sir Perceval of Gales* 65–6)
(*Where he lies in the field, many men on him beheld*),

where disyllabic *lygges* is used, as opposed to monosyllabic *lay*. It is not easy, however, adequately to explain why the historic present is also used extensively in alliterative verse, unless it is through some process of analogy.

Also common in similar contexts is the use of the perfective aspect, involving the present tense of the verb *have* or *be* followed by a past participle (the 'present perfect'). Generally speaking, the verb *have* is used with transitive verbs and *be* with intransitive:

He herde a vois, which cride dimme,
And he his ere to the brimme
Hath leid, and herde it was a man,
Which seide, 'Ha, help hier Adrian,
And I wol yiven half mi good.'
                    (Gower *Confessio Amantis* 4967–71)
(*He heard a voice, that cried out faintly, and he has put his ear
to the edge [of the pit] and heard that it was a man, who said
'Hey, help me here, Adrian, and I'll give you half my goods!'*)

The choice of the perfective aspect is associated with time-orientation. *Hath leide* implies something of the speed of the action – immediately the strange voice has been heard the rescuer is listening at the edge of the pit. The perfective, like the historic present tense, is also often said to convey immediacy, bringing to a past event the intensity of a present experience. Its popularity in narrative verse, also, may be explained by its usefulness in rhyme and metre. Simple couplets of narrative sometimes depend upon it entirely, e.g.

The messengere ys come and gone,
But tydyngys of Tryamowre herde he none,
                    (*Syr Tryamowre* 1030–1)

where the expression *ys come and gone*, as opposed to *came and went*, is essential to both rhythm and rhyme.

124

A similar freedom to that with which phrases are treated in verse is also found at the level of clause and above. Since Middle English makes less use than Old English of inflexional endings as a means of expressing the relationships between words, word order became more firmly fixed and there were therefore fewer opportunities for variation, except where poets wished to achieve a special stylistic effect. Thus, while subject/verb/object order is the norm within the clause, the object/verb/subject pattern is found approximately four times more often in verse than in prose (Fischer 1992, 371–3). Complete relative clauses could also be separated from their antecedents, as in

> My Lorde þe Lamb louez ay such chere,
> Þat is þe grounde of alle my blysse   (*Pearl* 407–8)
> (*My Lord the Lamb, who is the foundation of*
> *all my happiness, always loves such demeanour*),

where the subordinate clause refers to *My Lorde þe Lamb*, not to the contiguous *such chere*. Also in verse, presumably in the interests of compactness, relative pronouns could be omitted:

> On auenture his wiit him brohute
> To one putte wes water inne   (*Fox and Wolf* 70–1)
> (*By chance his cleverness brought him to a well [which] water was in*),

and in such cases one wonders to what extent the poets were utilising the syntactical patterns of colloquial speech.

In general, the language of Middle English poetry was probably closer to the spoken English of the time than either the language of Old English poetry, which was strikingly mannered, or the poetry of the fifteenth century and later, which the use of a literary standard increasingly distanced from the language of ordinary speech. A consequence of this probable closeness is that features which are associated with colloquial speech are often found in Middle English verse. In the popular romances, for example, paratactic constructions are not uncommon, both with simple co-ordinators (syndetic parataxis) and without (asyndetic parataxis):

Sum stode wiþouten hade,
And sum non armes nade,
And sum þurth þe bodi hadde wounde,
And sum lay wode, ybounde,
And sum armed on hors sete,
And sum astrangled as þai ete;
And sum were in water adreynt,
And sum wiþ fire al forschreynt.   (*Orfeo* 391–18)
(*Some stood without heads, and some had no arms, and some
had wounds through their bodies, and some lay mad, tied up,
and some sat armed on horseback, and some [had been] choked
as they were eating, and some had been drowned, and some
[had been] shrivelled up by fire.*)

The fates of the victims in Orfeo's ghoulish vision are described in a
series of syndetic paratactic clauses, each linked, for rhetorical
effect, by the simple co-ordinator *and* at the beginning of each
line. Commonly, though, and in contrast, clauses may be simply
juxtaposed in asyndetic parataxis. This is particularly useful in
narrative, to move the story along at a good pace. A separate
action is often stated in each line and conjunctions dispensed with
altogether:

Þe foules of þe water ariseþ,
Þe faucouns hem wel deuiseþ;
Ich faucoun his pray slouȝ.   (*Orfeo*, 311–13)
(*The birds rise from the water, the falcons see
them clearly; each falcon killed its prey.*)

Lines like this are often difficult for the present-day editor to punc-
tuate. Conventional punctuation is often inadequate when the
'punctuation' is, as here, provided by the syntax.

   The use in these contexts of subordinate clauses (hypotaxis) was
more restrained. In the following example hypotaxis is used in
conjunction with asyndetic parataxis for special effect, as Sir
Orfeo, after ten years in voluntary exile, reveals his identity on his
return to his faithful steward in a series of conditional subordinate
clauses:

126

Steward, herkne now þis þing!
ȝif ich were Orfeo þe king,
And hadde ysuffred ful ȝore
In wildernisse miche sore,
And hadde ywon mi quen owy
Out of þe lond of fairy,
And hadde ybrouȝt þe leuedi hende
Rȝt here to þe tounes ende,
And wiþ a begger her in ynome,
And were miself hider ycome
Pouerlich to þe, þus stille,
Forto assay þi gode wille,
And ich founde þe þus trewe,
Þou no schust it neuer rewe.   (*Orfeo* 557–70)
(*Steward, now listen to this: If I were King Orfeo, and had
suffered great misery in the wilderness for ten long years, and
had rescued my queen from the otherworld, and had brought the
gracious lady right here to the edge of town, and had taken
lodging here with a beggar, and had myself secretly come here
to you like a poor man, in order to test your faithfulness, and
had found you as true as I have, on no account would you ever
regret it.*)

The main clause of Orfeo's self-revealing statement comes only in
the last line. The rest consists of a string of co-ordinate clauses, all
of which are dependent on the conditional ȝif. In rhetoric this is
known as a 'periodic sentence', i.e. one in which the most signifi-
cant element is deliberately held back for the sake of climax.

Stylistic effects could be achieved by contrasting relatively
simple syntactic structures such as these with more complex ones.
For instance, it has been shown that in *Sir Gawain and the Green
Knight* the major characters are differentiated by means of their
patterns of speech:

Gawain's *cortaysye* is expressed most fully in the *way* in
which he says what he says . . . One of the first things one
notices [in his first speech] . . . is the presence of a number
of particularly circumlocutory phrases . . . The sense one
has in moving through the passage is of the skirting of a
series of obstacles, the overcoming or evading of one

difficulty after another: the syntax seems to wind itself along, to move two steps sideways for every step forwards. This effect is heightened by the profusion of parenthetic phrases inserted before the main point of each clause is reached...There are parentheses and subordinate clauses even within the subordinate clauses.

The Green Knight's bluffness [in contrast] is expressed through a series of short sentences, usually linked by 'and' – by co-ordination as opposed to the elaborate subordination of Gawain's idiom. Where Gawain's speeches are full of conditional and subjunctive verbs, the verbs here are most often in the simple present or past indicative, or else, significantly, in the imperative...Where Gawain is subtle, the Green Knight is brusque.

(Spearing 1972, 44–9)

The Green Knight's style of speech is even carried over to his *alter ego*, Sir Bertilak, whom Gawain does not realise is the same person, but whose concealed identity is revealed to the linguistically perceptive listener or reader by his distinctive style of expression (see Clark 1966, 362–6).

Subtle effects like this could be achieved despite the fact that Middle English verse, like Old English, is often formulaic, with poets dealing not so much in arresting new terms – 'oft thought but ne'er so well expressed' – as in established terminology, which to the present-day reader can often seem no more than cliché.'Formula' has already been defined, in the context of Old English, as 'a group of words which is regularly employed under the same metrical conditions to express a given essential idea'.[5] Recurrent formulae are also a feature of Middle English verse, and are particularly common in the rhymed romances and in poems of the Alliterative Revival.

The following examples, from the romances *Havelok, Beues of Hamtoun,* and *Guy of Warwick,* illustrate common patterns. Firstly, there are those formulae which provide the rhyme and may occupy as much as half of the complete line:

Þe king þar of	was glad and bliþe	(*Beues* 529, 905)
And Beues	was glad and bliþe	(2497)
Of whom þat he	was glad and bliþe	(*Guy* 1924)
And made hem	glad and bliþe	(*Havelok* 1246)

In each of the examples above the formula occupies virtually the whole of the predicate (the part of the clause other than the subject), but formulae are rather more likely to be adjuncts, since adjuncts are the most mobile of the elements in a clause and the most freely added:

Þai gonne schete	be ech a side	(*Beues* 882)
Wiþ gret ioie	be ech a side	(2162)
Þe cri aros	be ech a side	(4438)

The adjunct commonly, as here, consists of a prepositional phrase, of which the formulaic structure may be recognised, despite variation, so long as the final noun – the important rhyme word – is left intact:

And mi lond destrud	in ich a side	(*Guy* 2878)
Gret slauȝter worþ	in eiþer side	(*Beues* 4130)
Þar was ioie	be eueri side	(3962)
He was beset	in boþe side	(4399)

While the formula, particularly in the shape of the prepositional phrase, is most useful to the composer or reciter at the end of the line, it also conveniently supplies a suitable beginning:

In þe world ne worþ man of so gret miȝt	(*Guy* 4263)
In is world	is better non at nede	(6120)
In al þis werd	ne haues he per [*equal*]	(*Havelok* 2242)
In al þis world	nis þer man	(*Beues* 1101, 1113)

Glad and bliþe in the first set of examples above is one of those repetitive word pairs, or 'doublets', noted in the previous chapter. Most commonly consisting of co-ordinate constructions with *and* or *ond*, they contain more or less synonymous, antonymous or otherwise associated words and occur as stock phrases, often associated with typical themes. Their range and variety can be briefly exemplified from *Havelok*. Some, such as *glad and bliþe, answerede and seyde,* and *quen and leuedi,* are of the tautologous type which we still have in present-day English in such phrases as *honest and true, really and truly* and *lo and behold.* Some are common collocations because of a natural association of meaning, including *siluer and gold, hond and fet,* and *eten and drinken*. Others consist of paired opposites, such as *riche and poure, yunge and holde, heye and lowe* or *brune and blake* (dark and fair), which the *Havelok* poet uses figuratively to mean 'all and sundry'. A number of this sort refer to specific social classes, including *clerc ne prest* (contrastively co-ordinated, as is common), *knith ne sweyn*, and *king ne kaysere*. The last is an example of an alliterating pair, of which others in *Havelok* are *fed and fostred, wind and water* and *strong and stark* (another instance of tautology).

Recurrent alliterative phrases are among the most interesting of all the formulae and have been extensively studied.[6] A large number are completely unexceptional and were probably drawn from everyday speech, such as paired nouns like *lordis and ladis* (a pair which occurs about 30 times in non-rhyming poems of the Alliterative Revival as part of the formal alliteration), paired verbs such as *wepe and weile* (about 13 times), and semantically associated verb + noun pairs like *lese ... lif* (lose ... life, about 16 times).[7] Some of the most common alliterating collocations can be traced back to Old English, including *londe and lede* (land and people) and *man upon molde* (man upon earth), of which the former is found in two and the latter in twelve Old English poetic contexts. Many formulae in Middle English, however, involve one or more post-Conquest borrowed words, and are not therefore traceable so far back. Thus in Middle English *more and mountain* is based upon the Old English phrase *more ond munte*, but the second element has been changed in favour of a similar French-derived word.

Common syntactic patterns in the alliterative phrases are noun + noun, adjective + adjective and verb + verb, often co-ordinately linked (*faith and fellowshipp, comly and clene, deluen and diggen*), noun or adjective qualified by a genitive phrase (*blode of thi bodi, fayre of face*), and verb + direct object (*drynke a drawȝte*). Words qualified by prepositional phrases other than the genitive are numerous (*floures in feldes, fairest on folde* [on earth], *dares for drede* [cowers for fear]). In the long lines of alliterative poetry phrases produced by such means fitted most naturally into the first half-line, for the second required only a single alliterating syllable to link it with the first.

Formulae are sometimes difficult to differentiate from tags, which are conventional phrases, virtually meaningless in themselves, which are used to fill out the verse. They are found even in the best poetry, rhymed and alliterative, particularly where the verse form makes demands on the poet, such as in the short, rhyming 'bob and wheel' of *Sir Gawain*. Tags consist mainly of set phrases, such as *in londe, on felde* and *vnder sonne*, but others are based on syntactic patterns that allowed slight variation, such as *to seye þe soþe, to speke þe soþe* and *to telle þe soþe*. The fact that such diffuseness was tolerated has much to do with the conventions of oral delivery and the fact that in the long poems which are so characteristic of Middle English a relaxed and predictable style of expression could be as comfortable for the listener or reader as it was helpful to the poet. In such a context tags have their part to play:

> These can properly be regarded as a form of verse-articulation, especially suitable for spoken verse, and of minimal artistic importance. Genuine formulae, on the other hand, can exist as a sort of stylised verbal equivalence, where a certain series of phrases, rigorously formalised in content, are the recognised stimulus, through their traditional associations, for a certain poetic response, a form of descriptive shorthand. Tags are not meant to be noticed, but formulae are, and it is the mark of an inferior romancer that he reduces conventional formulae to the level of tags.
>
> (Pearsall 1977, 149)

Finally, it is worth noting that a number of the characteristic syntactic structures of Middle English verse were encouraged through contemporary rhetorical practice, and some were codified and promoted in treatises on rhetoric.[8] Rhetoric is the art of persuasion in speaking and writing by means of the effective use of language. Standard patterns, or 'figures', of rhetoric, such as repetition and contrast, are extensively found in even the simplest Middle English verse – not because all Middle English poets had made a formal study of rhetoric, but because such things could be learned from the writings of others, from public orations, and to some extent from ordinary speech. It is clear that medieval poets, whether trained in rhetoric or not, appreciated the linguistic complexity of English and understood very well how linguistic structures could be manipulated to serve their needs.

8. Linguistic Varieties

In dealing with this subject I wish, for the sake of convenience, to make use of the variety classes distinguished by Randolph Quirk and Sidney Greenbaum in *A Grammar of Contemporary English* (Quirk and Greenbaum 1973, 1–9). The model is a simple one:

> *Variety Classes*
> Region
> Education and social standing
> Subject matter
> Medium
> Attitude
> Interference

Probably the most easily recognisable of these variety classes is that which is based on region and has the well established label 'dialect'. Within dialectal areas there is further variation according to education and social standing, there being a polarity between educated and uneducated language. Uneducated language (by definition spoken, rather than written) is usually closely identified with a regional variety, but educated language more commonly transcends dialectal boundaries. By virtue of the fact that educated English has acquired implicit status in social, educational, religious and administrative spheres, it has come to be referred to as 'Standard English', but this is not a concept that was relevant for the medieval period. Linguistic variety which is dependent on subject matter is often referred to as 'register', and involves adjustments which all speakers and writers make as they change from one subject to another. If the subject in hand is cookery it will call for a

131

different register than if the subject is, say, bee-keeping. Most typically this involves switching from one set of lexical items to another, such as from 'marinating' and 'suet' to 'queen' and 'hive', but phonology, morphology and syntax may also be involved. The next variety class is associated with medium. The main conditioning factors here are speaking and writing, for between the two there are many situational and semiotic differences. Writing usually has to be more careful and explicit than speech, since the person or persons who are being addressed are not actually present. Furthermore, a writer has to struggle with conventional orthography (spelling, punctuation, etc.) in an attempt to get across what a speaker can much more easily convey by various subtle nuances of stress, rhythm, intonation and tempo. Variety according to attitude is the fifth type, and proceeds from a speaker's or writer's attitude to the listener or reader. The distinction is made, for instance, in the level of formality — formal to a stranger, informal to a friend — with resultant differences of style. Finally, varieties according to interference result from traces left by one language upon another, as when a person has acquired the use of a new language but continues to use constructions from the native language that are not idiomatic in the newly acquired one. Such influence can sometimes be seen in medieval works that have been translated into English from another language.

As far as Old English is concerned, the variety of which we have overwhelmingly the most information is regional, though this results more from ignorance of other variety classes than from an abundance of dialectal evidence. Most of what survives, as has been said, is in the dialect of Wessex. Of the three other major dialects, Mercian is not represented in surviving verse. The nearest thing to it is the interlinear gloss to the Latin psalms and hymns of the *Vespasian Psalter*, though there is no attempt to give this any of the form characteristic of Anglo-Saxon verse. In contrast, the two items that remain of verse in the Kentish dialect — a free paraphrase of Psalm 50 and a short hymn, both apparently of the tenth century — are in the typical vernacular prosodic form, but are not particularly interesting in respect of their content. Northumbrian verse is rather better represented. There is the fourteen-line *Leiden Riddle*; there are five lines of verse said to have been composed by the Venerable Bede on his death-bed; there is the Northumbrian version of Cædmon's *Hymn*, the circumstances of which have already been mentioned; and there are the lines from the poem

The Dream of the Rood, carved in runic letters on the stone cross from Ruthwell in Scotland. Also in runes are the inscriptions on the front and on one side of the small, eighth-century, whalebone Franks Casket, now in the British Museum, which can be transcribed into lines of verse. The inscription on the side, like the carved scene it accompanies, is not properly understood, but the one on the front, which borders scenes of the Magi and Wayland the Smith, makes reference to the source of the bone:

> Fisc flodu ahof   on fergen-berig;
> warþ gasric grorn,   þær he on greut giswom.
> Hronæs ban.
> (*The flood lifted up the fish on to the cliff-bank;*
> *the whale became sad, where he swam on the shingle.*
> *Whale's bone.*)

It is specially interesting that all of these Northumbrian texts except those on the Franks Casket survive also in West Saxon versions, though the relationship in each case is different. The *Leiden Riddle*, so called because it is preserved in a manuscript in Leiden University in the Netherlands, has a counterpart in a riddle of the Exeter Book. Both derive from the same Latin original. They exhibit too many similarities for it to be possible that they are entirely independent translations. Apart from phonological and grammatical differences which are dependent on dialect and date, there are small variations (such as the use in a couple of places of singular forms in the West Saxon against the plural in the Northumbrian), and one major difference, in that the West Saxon version has introduced two completely new lines at the end, in place of those of the Northumbrian version.

Bede's Death Song is included in a number of manuscripts of a Latin account of Bede's death, ranging in date from the ninth century to the twelfth. Two versions survive. The earlier is in the Northumbrian dialect, the later in West Saxon. What probably happened was that as time passed copies of the *Song* were made increasingly to conform to the Late West Saxon literary 'standard', which had become established as the natural medium for important texts. Other differences between the versions (such as *deoth-daege* 'death-day' in the Northumbrian version as opposed to *deaþe* 'death' in the West Saxon) are relatively minor.

The story of Cædmon's miraculous acquisition of the gift of poetry was first told in Latin by Bede in his *Historia Ecclesiastica Gentis Anglorum,* I.24. In describing the song that Cædmon sang after being instructed in his dream Bede says simply 'this is the sense of it' and proceeds to summarise, carefully adding afterwards 'this is the sense but not the exact order of the words'. In its Old English form, therefore, the *Hymn* is not an integral part of Bede's account. In those manuscripts in which it appears it was added as a sort of appendix. Bede's *Historia* was one of those works which King Alfred in the ninth century considered an essential educational text, and which he therefore ordered to be translated into English, by which he meant, of course, into West Saxon. In the West Saxon version of Bede's history the *Hymn* itself replaces the paraphrase. Of the twelve copies of Cædmon's *Hymn* found in manuscripts of Bede's Latin *Historia,* four are in the Northumbrian dialect and eight in the West Saxon. There are also five copies of the Old English translation of Bede, which have the West Saxon version fully integrated into the text. There are minor variants in the extant texts, and one which is more significant: while in Bede's Latin heaven is said to have been created as a roof *filiis hominum,* 'for the sons of men' and in the two earliest Northumbrian copies *aelda barnum,* 'for the children of men', the other two Northumbrian texts have *eordu bearnum,* 'for the children of earth'. These differences suggest the existence of two distinct traditions, which is borne out by similar variation in the surviving West Saxon texts. The phrase *eordu bearnum* is unique, whereas *aelda barnum* (or more commonly the West Saxon *ylda bearnum*) is a formula which recurs eight times in other poems and is closely paralleled by *hæleða bearnum* (9 times), *monna bearnum* (8) and *fira bearnum* (3), each of which has very similar meaning. 'Children of earth', the unique wording, may have been the earlier of the two, with 'children of men' being substituted because of its greater familiarity. In most other respects the texts are so similar that it has been suggested that particular care may have been taken to preserve this most venerated of poems without change or corruption (Wrenn 1967, 96).

The remaining poem to have survived in both Northumbrian and West Saxon is *The Dream of the Rood.* The Northumbrian version is inscribed on the edges of the Ruthwell Cross, which probably dates from the early eighth century, and the fuller West Saxon version is written in the early eleventh-century Vercelli Book. The poem is a dream vision, in which the dreamer experiences a vision of Christ's cross, which describes to him the ordeal of the Crucifixion, after which the dreamer contemplates Christ's victory and the hope of eternal life. The Vercelli text contains 156 lines, fifteen of which are found, in whole or in part, in the Ruthwell text, which is confined to that part of the poem in which the cross itself speaks. The following is an example:

Ruthwell (partially reconstructed):
+ Ondgeredæ hinæ God almehttig,
þa he walde on galgu gestiga,
modig fore allæ men.
Buga ic ni dorstæ...

Vercelli 39–42:
Ongyrede hine þa geong hæleð (þæt wæs God ælmihtig),
strang ond stið-mod;   gestah he on gealgan heanne,
modig on manigra gesyhðe,   þa he wolde mancyn lysan.
Bifode ic þa me se beorn ymbclypte;   ne dorste ic hwæðre
    bugan to eorðan.
(*The young man (who was almighty God) stripped himself,
strong and firm-minded; he climbed the high gallows, a brave
man within sight of many people, when he wished to redeem
mankind. I trembled when the man embraced me; however, I
dared not bow down to the earth.*)

As can be seen, the Ruthwell text does not consist of complete lines of verse, and there are some differences of construction (such as the auxiliary *walde* appearing with *gestiga* [wished to climb], rather than with an equivalent of *lysan* [wished to redeem]). Two main possibilities suggest themselves: either that the inscription inspired the composition of the longer poem, or that the sculptor chose and modified extracts from an existing poem, which may or may not have been like the Vercelli version. Which of these is the more likely is difficult to say, especially since the Ruthwell text is brief and incomplete.

Very little is known about varieties of Old English other than regional, especially in as much as they affect the poetry. In terms of education and social standing West Saxon clearly acquired, from the time of King Alfred, a status beyond that of other regional varieties. As time passed it became natural for it to be used for writing down works as diverse as Bede's *Death Song* and early Kentish laws, even though the originals of these had been in other dialects. But had more texts survived from other areas the picture would probably look very different. The problem is that we are dealing only with written material — circumstances under which distinctions of education and social standing are difficult or impossible to detect.

The third variety is that which is related to subject matter. Different registers for different subjects of Old English verse can indeed be distinguished in broad terms, especially where poetic compounds are involved, words like *goldwine* (gold-friend, lord) and *eorlscipe* (prowess) naturally being characteristic in heroic verse, just as words such as *ælmihtig* (almighty) and *rodor* (sky, heaven) are in religious. Another example is the so-called 'gnomic' use of the modal auxiliary *sceal,* a verb which implies a blend of necessity, obligation and duty, and, occurring commonly in a series, gives a characteristic syntactic shape:

> Geongne æþeling sceolan   gode gesiðas
> byldan to beaduwe   and to beah-gife.
> Ellen sceal on eorle,   ecg sceal wið hellme
> hilde gebidan.   Hafuc sceal on glofe
> wilde gewunian,   wulf sceal on bearowe,
> earm anhaga,   eofor sceal on holte,
> toþ-mægenes trum.   (*Maxims II* 14–20)
> (*Good comrades shall encourage a young nobleman to battle*
> *and to the giving of rings. Courage shall be in a warrior. The*
> *sword shall endure battle against the helmet. The wild hawk*
> *shall grow accustomed to being on the glove. The wolf shall*
> *live in the forest, a wretched, solitary creature. The boar shall*
> *be in the wood, strong in the might of its tusks.*)

It has also been suggested that, apart from genre-related distinctions such as these, there existed a special literary variety of Old English which transcended geographical boundaries:

> More attention should be given to the probability that
> there was a body of verse, anonymous and independent
> of local interest, which was the common stock for the

entertainment or instruction of the English peoples. A poem, wherever composed, might win its way into the common stock. The native metre, based primarily on the alliteration of stressed syllables, carried well because in this essential the usage of seventh-century Northumbria and tenth-century Wessex was the same; but any local dialect forms that affected the verse-structure were a handicap to circulation. A poet might prefer to take his models from the common stock rather than from the less-known work of his own district. In this way poems could be produced that do not belong to any local dialect, but to a general Old English poetic dialect, artificial, archaic, and perhaps mixed in its vocabulary, conservative in inflexions that affect the verse structure, and indifferent to non-structural irregularities, which were perhaps tolerated as part of the colouring of the language of verse.

(Sisam 1953, 138)

Some scholars, however, explain the situation differently, claiming that the mixture of dialectal features sometimes found in Old English verse results from the use of non-West Saxon sources or from the transmission of manuscripts by non-West Saxon scholars and scribes. Poets and transcribers certainly seem to have been conscious of a characteristic verse register, using such things as unsyncopated (i.e. uncontracted) forms in the present tense of verbs (e.g. *bindeð* 'binds') rather than the syncopated forms characteristic of prose *(bint)*, and retaining distinctively Anglian forms (e.g. *aldor* 'lord') in preference to those typical of West Saxon prose *(ealdor)*. But whether this constitutes a fully developed poetical variety is uncertain.[1]

Varieties according to medium, mainly a matter of speech as opposed to writing, cannot be clearly identified in Old English because, of course, of the one-sidedness of the evidence, which is not only in written form but, as far as the poetry is concerned, in an elevated and artificial variety that is far removed from the language of ordinary speech. The claim has been made (Von Lindheim 1951) that a cluster of words found in the Old English *Riddles* which are rare in other verse may possibly be colloquialisms, since the *Riddles* are the only Anglo-Saxon poems to treat homely, and sometimes frankly obscene, subjects. These words include *nebb* (nose), *steort* (tail), *þyrel* (hole) and *wamb* (belly). The *Riddles* provide, admittedly, the sort of context in which colloquialisms might be expected, but the suggestion is not one that can be put to the test in any way. Allegedly oral characteristics have, of course, been paramount in the hypotheses of the oral-formulaicists, whose original proponent (with regard to Old English), Magoun, claimed that oral poetry is composed entirely of formulae and that lettered poetry is never formulaic (Magoun 1953, 446). This extreme view has now been extensively modified, for, while some formulae may indeed have originated in orally transmitted traditions, they also became characteristic in written verse.[2]

Varieties according to attitude – formal and informal – are distinguishable in Old English poetry only in broad terms, between such extremes as, on the one hand, Satan's address to the devils of hell in *Genesis B*, 356–441, with its elaborate, hypotactic structure, and, on the other, the simple earnestness of passion in *Wulf and Eadwacer*, the lament of a woman who is separated from her lover. Formal language, however, is best exemplified in *Beowulf*. The poet has a special interest in etiquette, and several times mentions with approval that one character or another was *cynna gemyndig* (mindful of good manners), *cuþe . . . duguðe þeaw* (understood the etiquette of the court), or *meþel-wordum frægn* (enquired with formal words). Introductory formulae of the type

> Hroðgar maþelode,   helm Scyldinga   (456)
> (*Hrothgar spoke, protector of the Scyldings*)

signal formal discourse, and we notice extensive variation in Beowulf's address to King Hrothgar, especially when Beowulf craves an indulgence:

> Ic þe nu ða,
> brego Beorht-Dena,   biddan wille,
> eodor Scyldinga,   anre bene:
> þæt ðu me ne forwyrne,   wigendra hleo,
> freo-wine folca . . .   (426–30)
> (*I now wish to ask you, protector of the Bright-Danes,*
> *prince of the Scyldings, one favour, which I trust you*
> *will not deny me, defender of warriors, noble friend*
> *of the people . . .*)

In addition to the personal pronoun *þe*, four different terms of address are used, which surely must reflect the formality of the language. In contrast, his speech to, say, the coastguard is much more direct and practical.

Interference, the last of the variety classes, can sometimes be detected in those Old English poems which are translations from Latin. Some of the translations are quite close to the original, particularly the *Paris Psalter*, the *Metres of Boethius*, the *Kentish Psalm*, and parts of *The Phoenix*, and in these poems constructions are sometimes encountered which are more characteristic of Latin than of Old English. The *Kentish Psalm*, for example, appears to contain in line 51 an example of the 'accusative absolute', a construction sometimes found in Latin but extremely unusual in Old English. Similarly, the *Paris Psalter* 118.10 contains an uncharacteristic use of the negative, which probably reflects the Latin original (Mitchell 1985, I, 690). Latin, however, was not the only language to cause interference. In 1875 Sievers speculated that the Old English poem *Genesis B* was a translation or paraphrase from Old Saxon, an hypothesis which was dramatically vindicated when fragments of a version of the original poem were discovered in 1894. Comparison shows that some of the hapax legomena or very rare words in *Genesis B* are modelled on the Old Saxon, including *hearm-scearu* (affliction, O.S. *harm-skara*), *giongorscipe* (service, O.S. *jungarskepi*) and *romigean* (to try to obtain, O.S. *rômon*). Some other words in *Genesis B* are less rare in Old English but seem, under the influence of the original, to be used in a special sense, including *cræft* (host, army, O.S. *kraft*), *geongra* (servant, O.S. *jungaro*) and *leoht* (world, O.S. *lioht*).[3]

It is also worth noting what is possibly the first deliberate literary use of an interference (or related) variety in an English text – in the speech of the Viking messenger who, in *The Battle of Maldon* 29–41, demands tribute money from the East Saxons in exchange for peace. Robinson notes that

> Locutions of Scandinavian origin as well as locutions that are simply unique in Old English are prominent in the speech, and it seems likely that these features were intended to suggest to an Anglo-Saxon ear the menacing voice of a foreigner.

> (Robinson 1976, 26)

The word *grið* ('peace') in this speech has already been noted as the earliest recorded occurrence in English of that Scandinavian loanword. Furthermore, the *gar-ræs* (storm of spears) which is threatened unless the English comply is found nowhere else in Old English, but has an exact counterpart in *geir-rás* in Old Norse. The construction *syllan sæ-mannum on hyra sylfra dom* (give to the seamen according to their own assessment) is an exact parallel of the Scandinavian legal term *selja sjálfdæmi*. This and other evidence is convincingly presented by Robinson, who concludes:

> While it must be conceded that the emergence of hitherto undiscovered Old English texts might show one or another of these features to be less peculiar than it now appears to be, it seems unlikely that the entire cluster of Scandinavicisms and unidiomatic phrases in so short a space should be either illusory or accidental.
>
> (Robinson 1976, 27)

Turning now to Middle English, we have rather more information on variety types than we have for Old English, though, once again, it mostly concerns regional varieties. Many more examples of a range of regional dialects survive than in Old English, principally because for much of the period no one of them enjoyed particular prestige. Only through painstaking analysis, such as that used to produce *A Linguistic Atlas of Late Mediaeval English* (McIntosh et al. 1986), is a clearer picture beginning to emerge. It is also possible, in the case of Middle English, to prove a contemporary awareness of regional dialect. John Trevisa, a translator who several times commented on contemporary language, distinguished three broad dialects in the fourteenth century, which he called Southern, Midland, and Northern, and offered explanations as to why Northern English was so harsh and unattractive (he thought it was because the people of the north were not much more than *strange men*, i.e. 'foreigners', and because the king's court seldom went north). There are also explicit comments on the practice of translation from one Middle English dialect to another. The author of the Northern Middle English poem *Cursor Mundi*, for instance, says that some of his material was originally in 'Southern English' and that he therefore had to translate it 'into our own language':

In sotherin englis was it draun,   *composed*
And turnd it haue i till our aun   *translated*
Langage o northrin lede,   *people*
Þat can nan oiþer englis rede.   (20061–4)

Middle English authors were certainly able to imitate dialects. The earliest literary example occurs in Chaucer's *Reeve's Tale*, lines 4022ff., where two Cambridge undergraduates from 'Strother, fer in the north' are given an exaggeratedly Northern style of speech. Another well-known example of the use of dialect in Middle English is found in the fifteenth-century Wakefield *Second Shepherds' Play*, with the entry of Mak the sheepstealer. In speaking to the shepherds Mak adopts a Southern English dialect for comic effect:

Mak:
    What! Ich be a yoman,
    I tell you, of the kyng,
    The self and the some,   *same*
    sond from a greatt lordyng,   *messenger*
    And sich.   *suchlike*
    Fy on you! Goyth hence
    Out of my presence!
    I must haue reuerence.
    Why, who be ich?   (XIII.291–9)

Mak's imitation involves a sprinkling of clearly southern forms, such as *ich be*, instead of *I am*. And the imperative *goyth* is a Southern dialect form, of which the Northern form is *goys*. This linguistic foolery would presumably have been a cause of mirth for the original Yorkshire audience. But the shepherds are in no mood to play along with him, and one of them tells him to 'take outt that Sothren tothe, and sett in a torde!'

The second of our variety classes, education and social standing, related as it is to the concept of a 'standard', begins to assume importance in the later Middle English period, particularly in the development of a literary standard based upon dialects of the Central Midlands and in the wide adoption after about 1430 of 'Chancery Standard', the variety used by the London administrators. Although there were many experiments to produce an acceptable

'Educated Standard', this was never achieved. The attempt in the fifteenth century to elevate English by importing 'hard words' from the classical languages was not lastingly successful (Shakespeare is still ridiculing the excesses of this movement in the language of Holofernes, the schoolmaster in *Love's Labours Lost*). An interesting exploration of this aspect of educated Middle English is found in the fifteenth-century moral play *Mankind,* the author of which seems very interested in the whole subject of language, so much so that he makes it a theme of his play. The only righteous, and pre-sumably educated, character, Mercy, who is a male cleric, uses a heavily Latinate vocabulary:

> Mercy ys my name by denomynacyon.
> I conseyue ȝe haue but a lytyll fauour in my communycacyon.
> (122–3)

The reaction of the worthless Newguise, to whom he is speaking, is

> Ey, ey! yowr body ys full of Englysch Laten! (124)

After listening to many lines of Mercy's high-flown Latinate speech we might feel tempted to share this distaste. But, in terms of con-temporary thinking, we would be wrong. The character Man-kind, who represents the average Christian person, refers to Mercy's style of speech as 'louely wordys... swetere þen hony' (225). Mankind's own speech, which is base and scatological when he is under the influence of the vices, changes to a variety similar to Mercy's own when he reforms and comes to a state of grace:

> O Mercy, my suavius solas and synguler recreatory,
> *sweet; comfort*
> My predilecte spesyall, ȝe are worthy to hawe my lowe!
> *have; love*
> For wythowte deserte and menys supplicatorie, *means*
> ȝe be compacient to my inexcusabyll reprowe.
> *compassionate; shame*
> (871–4)

Conversely, the base and uneducated variety of English, which is plentiful in the play in the speech of the vices, is described as *large* (i.e. 'vulgar', or, as we might say today 'broad'). And it has its own stylistic differentiation, 4- and 8-line stanzas being used by Mercy, as opposed to tail-rhyme stanzas by the vices:

> Nowadays:
> I prey yow hertyly, worschyppull clerke,   *worshipful scholar*
> To haue þis Englysch mad in Laten: *made into*
>
> 'I haue etun a dyschfull of curdys,
> Ande I haue schetun yowr mowth full of turdys'.
>   *shitten*
> Now opyn yowr sachell wyth Laten wordys
> Ande sey me þis in clerycall manere!   *scholarly*
> Also I haue a wyf, her name ys Rachell;
> Betuyx her and me was a gret batell;
> Ande fayn of yow I wolde here tell   *gladly*
> Who was þe most master.   (129–38)

Notice again the awareness of educated and uneducated varieties in the reference to 'clerical manner' (i.e. the educated variety of English, which is, thankfully, incapable of expressing this scatological couplet).

Varieties dependent on subject matter, the next of our classes, are also distinguishable in Middle English. It is easy to observe, for example, that the language used in medieval romance is distinct in many ways from that used in works of religious instruction. In the case of the two extant versions of Laȝamon's *Brut*, it has been suggested that the Otho scribe deliberately expunged words associated with alliterative contexts, such as *athel* (noble), *barn* (man), *blanke* (horse), *Drihten* (God), *folde* (earth) and *grith* (peace), all of which are more fully represented in the Caligula manuscript, and included wherever possible words that assume thematic prominence in romance texts, such as *tresour*, *knave* (man), *pes* (peace), *kinedom* (kingdom) and *knight* (Cannon 1993, 198). Use of an appropriate register is only to be expected, whatever the period, whatever the subject and whatever the language. But it is possible also to detect that users of Middle English sometimes show an awareness of this variety to the extent that they consciously make use of it for particular effect. In a sense Nowadays' challenge to Mercy to express his rude words in an educated, Latinate style shows an understanding of this. Mercy cannot do it partly because he would not wish to sully his lips and partly because his Latinate English simply lacks the appropriate lexical items. But a rather better example of this type of linguistic variation is found in the York Mystery Play of *The Harrowing of Hell* (XXXVII.107–10). When Christ descends into Hell to release the souls from Limbo the devils are thrown into panic:

> I Diabolus:
>> Þei crie on Criste full faste
>> And sais he schal þame saue.
>
> Belsabub:
>> ȝa, if he saue þame noght, we schall,
>> For they are sperde in speciall space.   *imprisoned*

The exchange relies upon a play on the word *save*. *MED* gives a variety of meanings, including 2, 'to bring to salvation' and 7a, 'to lock up'. The reason why the word-play is possible is because *save* in relation to Christ is meant to be taken spiritually (i.e. Jesus will bring them to salvation), while Beelzabub's use of the word belongs to the physical, material world (i.e. he will keep them locked up). In other words, the first is from the theological register and the second is from the administrative register of prisons and security.

The problem with our next variety class, that which is associated with medium, is that, as with Old English, all surviving Middle English exists only in written form, so comparison of spoken and written varieties is not possible. But we can go some way towards it by reference, once again, to medieval plays, for in some of these the language seems to be conditioned by the context of the play in performance, and, in fact, often cannot be understood without consideration of it. In the play *Mankind*, for example, the character Newguise returns from an escapade of theft and violence:

> Make space, for cokkys body sakyrde,
>> make space!   *God's sacred*
> A ha! well ouerron! God gyff hym
>> ewyll grace!   *out-run; evil*
> We were nere Sent Patrykes wey,
>> by hym þat me bought.   *redeemed*

I was twychyde by þe neke; þe game
    was begunne.
A grace was, þe halter
    brast asonder: *ecce signum!*   *behold the sign*
The halff ys abowte my neke;
    we hade a nere rune!   *close shave*

                                    (612–17)

There is no stage direction, and the speech can only be under-
stood by reference to the supposed context. For instance, the first
line is addressed to the audience, who for this play would have
been closely gathered round the acting area. This is not the only
point in the play where the actors call for the audience to make
room. The next line seems to relate to a person who has been
chasing him. Newguise has out-run him, and shouts a parting
curse in his direction. He next tells the audience, in graphic and
colloquial terms, that he was about to be hanged on the gallows,
presumably having been apprehended for his misdeeds, when the
rope happened to break. '*Ecce signum*' ('behold the sign, proof'), he
says, indicating the noose which is still around his neck.

As so often with the gifted playwright of *Mankind*, and also with
the so-called Wakefield Master, author of the best plays in the
Towneley (Wakefield) Mystery Cycle, the contextual explicitness
which is normal in writing is simply not present. A director's ima-
gination is often called for to make theatrical sense of a speech by
means of a gesture or prop or some other performance device. In
other words, the language of the plays sometimes comes closer to
the variety associated with spoken, rather than written, English.
This is not to say that the playwrights had an objective under-
standing of the difference, but they were certainly able to make
use of spoken and written varieties in an extremely sensitive way
as the dramatic context required.

Variety according to attitude, the fifth category, characteristi-
cally involves differences in the level of formality. Middle English
had built-in linguistic structures for expressing such distinctions,
particularly in the use of the personal pronouns *thou* and *thee* as
opposed to *you* and *ye*. Originally it was a matter of distinction
between singular and plural, but by the late fourteenth century
you and *ye* came to be considered the polite forms of address, *thou*
and *thee* the familiar or affectionate. But a misplaced *thou* was seen

as patronising or derogatory, so a complex hierarchy of attitudes could be implied, as illustrated here:

> Bot euer ich haue yloued þe   *I have always loved*
> As mi liif, and so þou me.
> > (*Sir Orfeo*, 123–4, familiar singular)

> And if þow rechez me any mo,   *give*
> > I redyly schal quyte.   *repay*
> > (*Sir Gawain*, 2324, impolite singular)

> Madame, if ye wolde haue rowthe...   *pity*
> > (Gower, *Confessio Amantis*, I.47, polite singular)

> And though ye deye for doel,   *die of pain*
> > the devel have that recche!   *cares*
> > (*Piers Plowman*, VI.120, impolite plural)

> Childre, hu habbe ȝe ifare?   *prospered*
> > (*King Horn*, 1388, polite plural)

By use of the appropriate (or inappropriate) personal pronoun, speakers and writers were able to convey shades of formality and informality, of approval and disapproval, of artlessness and irony, even without recourse to the many other lexical and syntactic means by which this rigidly hierarchical society made its feelings apparent and enforced the *status quo*.

Finally, there are features of Middle English, as of Old English, that come close to what we might regard as interference variety. Properly speaking, this arises when a non-native speaker or writer unwittingly imports features from another native tongue. In Middle English poetry, however, the closest we get to it is when anomalies are carried over in the course of translation from other languages. Thus it happens that in *Sir Orfeo*, which is believed to be translated or adapted from an Old French or Anglo-Norman work, there are several features that are more typical of French than of English (see Bliss 1966, xl–xli). One is the expression *fowe and griis* (variegated and grey fur, 241) in rhyme with *biis*, where there is a distinct possibility that Old French *vair et griis* has been only partially translated, so as not to destroy the rhyme. Another is the couplet

> He cleped togider his barouns,   *called*
> Erls, lordes of renouns...   (201–2)

where the plural form of *renouns* in rhyme seems similarly to have been carried over from a French original. A third is the name *Traciens* (Thrace, 47, 50), which has the form of an Old French masculine singular adjective, which suggests that it may be a distortion or misunderstanding of a phrase such as *reis Traciens* (Thracian king). If this last example is indeed a mistake it is comparable to words and phrases in the moral play *Everyman* which probably arose from misunderstanding of the Dutch original *Elkerlijc*. Thus *O godlic wesen* (O divine being) has become *O goodly vysyon* (O goodly vision, *Everyman* 582), *waer* (true) has become *ware* (aware, 435), and *regneren* (rule) has become *renne* (run, 72). It has been suggested that some of these errors may represent not what the translator saw but what he heard in the course of dictation (see Conley 1975).

It is worth noting, by way of conclusion, that the word 'variety' with the meaning 'a different form of something' is not recorded until 1617, and the use of the word in a linguistic sense is, of course, much later still. In Middle English the word *diversite* seems to have served.[4] But if people of the middle ages were as linguistically aware as some of the above examples suggest, we should not automatically assume (as is often the case) that *diversite* meant only regional diversity (i.e. dialect). Writers of medieval English poetry had at their disposal the same range of varieties as we have in present-day English and frequently used them to make subtle linguistic distinctions, of which we need to be aware in our reading if we are to enjoy the literary richness to which they contribute.

9 Examples of Analysis: *Beowulf* and *Sir Gawain and the Green Knight*

Beowulf, 2241–77

The last survivor of a noble tribe buries the heirlooms of his people in a barrow. The treasure hoard is discovered and guarded by a dragon.

Beorh eall-gearo

	wunode on wonge wæter-yðum neah,	
	niwe be næsse, nearo-cræftum fæst;	
	þær on innan bær eorl-gestreona	
5	hringa hyrde hord-wyrðne dæl,	[2245]
	fættan goldes, fea worda cwæð:	
	'Heald þu nu, hruse, nu hæleð ne mostan,	
	eorla æhte! Hwæt, hyt ær on ðe	
	gode begeaton. Guð-deað fornam,	
10	feorh-bealo frecne fyra gehwylcne	[2250]
	leoda minra þara ðe þis [lif] ofgeaf,	
	gesawon sele-dream. Nah, hwa sweord wege	
	oððe fe(o)r(mie) fæted wæge,	
	drync-fæt deore; dug(uð) ellor s[c]eoc.	
15	Sceal se hearda helm (hyr)sted-golde	[2255]
	fætum befeallen; feormynd swefað,	
	þa ðe beado-griman bywan sceoldon;	
	ge swylce seo here-pad, sio æt hilde gebad	
	ofer borda gebræc bita irena,	

20   brosnað æfter beorne.   Ne mæg byrnan hring   [2260]
      æfter wig-fruma   wide feran,
      hæleðum be healfe.   Næs hearpan wyn,
      gomen gleo-beames,   ne god hafoc
      geond sæl swingeð,   ne se swifta mearh
25   burh-stede beateð.   Bealo-cwealm hafað   [2265]
      fela feorh-cynna   forð onsended!'
      Swa giomor-mod   giohðo mænde
      an æfter eallum,   unbliðe hwe(arf)
      dæges ond nihtes,   oð ðæt deaðes wylm
30   hran æt heortan.   Hord-wynne fond   [2270]
      eald uht-sceaða   opene standan,
      se ðe byrnende   biorgas seceð,
      nacod nið-draca,   nihtes fleogeð
      fyre befangen;   hyne fold-buend
35   (swiðe ondræ)da(ð).   He gesecean sceall   [2275]
      (ho)r(d on) hrusan,   þær he hæðen gold
      warað wintrum frod;   ne byð him wihte ðy sel.

(*A mound stood all ready on land near the waves of the sea, newly built near a headland, secure because the way of getting into it had been cleverly disguised; the keeper of the ornaments carried into it that part of the noble warriors' treasure, of plated gold, that was worthy of being placed in the hoard, and spoke these few words: 'You, earth, now keep these possessions of noblemen, since heroes do not have the opportunity to do so! Indeed, good men once took it from you. Death in battle, a terrible deadly evil, has carried off each of the men of my people, of those who gave up this life, who had experienced joys in the hall. I do not have anyone who can bear the sword or polish the gold-plated cup, the precious drinking-vessel. The band of experienced retainers has hurried on somewhere else. The strong helmet must be deprived of its plates, of its finely-worked gold; the polishers lie dead, who were accustomed to make the war-masks shine; and likewise the suit of chainmail, which has felt the bite of swords over the crashing shields, crumbles like the man himself. Nor can the ring-mail follow the war-chief very far, remain near to the warriors. There is no pleasure at all from the harp, no joy of the song-wood, nor does the good hawk fly through the hall, nor the swift horse beat its hooves in the castle court. Baleful death has carried away many of the race of men!' In this manner one man, sad of heart, put into words his grief for them all, went about wretched by day and by night, until the surge of death touched his heart. The ancient dawn-ravager, who, in flames, seeks out barrows and flies at night engulfed in fire, found the delightful treasure hoard standing open; creatures on earth are very afraid of it. Its nature is to find the hoard in the ground, where, old of years, it stands guard over the heathen gold; for all that, it is by no means better off.)*

These lines come from a part of the manuscript that is badly damaged. As a consequence they illustrate some of the fundamental problems that confront editors of medieval texts, particularly texts which, like *Beowulf*, survive only in one manuscript. All the leaves of the book were damaged by fire in 1731. This particularly affected the outer margins, which became brittle as a result of charring. The edges continued to flake away over a number of years until the decay was arrested in the nineteenth century by mounting each leaf in a paper frame. Editors therefore have to rely on a variety of evidence, including two late eighteenth-century transcripts made in preparation for the first edition, which show that more could be read at that time than can be seen today.[1] In keeping with normal scribal practice the text was written to fill the manuscript page from the right margin to the left, so the lost letters do not always fall at the beginning or end of the lines of verse as set out here. The *d* of *dæl* (5) and *es* of *nihtes* (33), for example, appear in the early transcripts but are no longer visible. The part of the manuscript from which these lines come is particularly badly damaged, and even in 1787 some words were not recoverable. Examples are the words *fe(o)r(mie)*, *dug(uð)* and *(hyr)sted-golde* (13–15), which have had to be hypothetically reconstructed. In the case of the *(hyr)stedgolde* the reconstruction takes account of the need for alliteration. There are also places where the scribe appears to have omitted something. In line 11, for example, although there is no gap in the manuscript an alliterating word is missing from the second half-line. The generally preferred restoration is *lif*, but *leoht* is also a possibility, since the expressions 'gave up this life' and 'gave up this light', meaning 'died', are both attested elsewhere. Editors also make changes where they believe a scribe may have miscopied a word, such as *s[c]eoc* (14), in which the *c* has been omitted, and also *þara* (11), which in the manuscript is written *þana*. At times the difficulties are such that the resultant text leaves much to be desired, as in the lines in question, for even with restorations and emendations the sense is often not free of grammatical problems, such as the awkward shift from the singular verb *ofgeaf* to the plural *gesawon* (11–12).

Aside from all this, the passage is rightly appreciated. It contains that part of the poem in which an explanation is given of the background of the hoard of treasure guarded by the dragon which Beowulf later slays, and by which he himself is slain. The poet imagines the precious objects being placed in the barrow long ago by a nobleman, the last survivor of a once-great society. Before committing them to the earth he thinks back to former times when the treasures were put to good use. The tone is emphatically elegiac, and the language and theme are strongly reminiscent of poems such as *The Wanderer, The Seafarer* and *The Ruin*. The poet then imagines how, on the death of the last survivor, the dragon comes across the open hoard. It was believed to be in the nature of such creatures to seek out treasure hoards and to guard them jealously. In this case the subsequent theft of a single precious cup by one of Beowulf's people is enough to enrage the dragon, who rains fire on the surrounding countryside. The hero is called upon to put a stop to it, a feat he eventually achieves, but only at a terrible price.

Words may have a more precise meaning than at first appears. *Niwe* (3) is a case in point, for the pre-Christian Anglo-Saxons practised both secondary and primary interment in barrows; in the former they buried their dead in existing prehistoric mounds, such as those of the Bronze Age in Wiltshire, the Peak District and the Yorkshire Wolds, while in the latter they threw up burial mounds of their own, like that of the rich chieftain at Benty Grange in Derbyshire and – most famous of all – the large mound covering the ship-burial at Sutton Hoo. *Niwe*, therefore, is technically specific, and may also have carried connotations of prestige. The mound in question is also *wæter-ýðum neah* (2), literally 'near water-waves', which seems somewhat tautological unless *wæter* is taken to have its common meaning (in Old English verse) 'sea', in which case the barrow on a headland near the sea is again reminiscent of Sutton Hoo. Also technically exact is *beado-griman* (17), which literally means 'war-masks', referring to helmets of the Sutton Hoo type, of which a full face-mask is a prominent feature. The impressive replica of the Sutton Hoo helmet now on display in the British Museum underlines the importance attached to the polishers who made such things shine. Appreciation of the semantic richness of the verse is thus enhanced by such reference to the material context upon which the poet drew.

As always in Old English verse there are many words with more or less the same meaning. Simplices of this type include *beorn* (20), *eorl* (8), and *hæleð* (7, 22), each of which means 'man, warrior' and carries, in the poetic context, strong connotations of nobility. All are confined to Old English verse, though *eorl* with other meanings is quite common in prose. *Fyras* (10) also means 'men, warriors', but differs in that it only occurs in the plural, while *duguð* (14) is a collective noun referring to the best, tried warriors, as opposed to the aspiring but inexperienced *geoguð* (youth). *Leod* (11) is a more neutral word for 'man', and commonly occurs in the plural, as here, with the meaning 'people, tribe'. *Gode* (9) is an adjective used 'absolutely', i.e. as a noun, meaning 'good men'. Other uncompounded near-synonyms are *sweord* (sword, 12) and the metonymous *iren* (19), and also the verbs *hwearf* (28) and *sceoc* (14), both of which here have the general meaning 'went', though the normal meanings in prose are more precisely 'turn' *(hweorfan)* and 'hasten' *(scacan)*.

The 37 lines of this passage contain 22 compounds, consisting of 20 nouns and 2 adjectives. Some of these are literal, the intended meaning being the sum of the meanings of the parts, as in *guð-dead* (war death, death in battle, 9), *drync-fæt* (drink-vessel, drinking-cup, 14) and *fold-buend* (earth dwellers, occupants of the countryside, 34), each of which comprises two simple nouns. Those in which the first element is an adjective (*giomor-mod*, sad of mind, 27) or an adverb (*eall-gearo*, all ready, completely prepared, 11) are, in effect, compressed descriptions – extremely compressed in the case of *nearo-cræftum* (3), of which the adjective element means 'narrow, difficult of access' and the noun 'skill, cunning', the plural dative case-ending *(-um)* giving adverbial force, 'by means of the skills of making access difficult'. Other compounds draw meaning from the heroic context. *Sele-dream* (hall-joy, 12) and *gleo-beam* (glee-wood, 23) can only be understood by reference to the idealised conviviality and merrymaking of warrior society, as described in Germanic literature, of which singing or recitation to the accompaniment of a harp at festivities in the hall is an important element. The broader values of such a society need to be known to appreciate what the speaker feels he has lost. Similarly *uht-sceaða* (dawn-ravager, 31) draws force from the special misery the Anglo-Saxons associated with *uhta*, the time just before daybreak. Compounds that rely on these rich associations are similar to those figurative circumlocutions called 'kennings'. But they are not kennings in the strictest sense, for in each case the second element is literally true: a harp is literally 'wood' and a dragon is literally 'a ravager'. The only compound in this passage which is not entirely literal is *hord-wynn* (hoard-joy, i.e. joy-giving treasure, 30). But even this is not a kenning, because the abstract and somewhat figurative second element is modified by the literal first.

Compounds are well represented among the hapax legomena, those words that occur only once in the extant literature.[2] *Beado-grima, bealo-cwealm, guð-deað, here-pad, hord-wynn, hord-wyrð, nearo-cræft, nið-draca, uht-sceaða, wæter-yð* and *wig-fruma* are hapax legomena, and the remaining compounds are restricted to the register of Old English verse. Uncompounded hapax legomena are much less frequently found, the only example in this passage being the verb *bywan* (to polish, 17). However, even if a word is unique its constituent elements may have illuminating associations. Within *Beowulf*, for example, the compound *uht-sceaða* is paralleled by *uht-floga* (flyer at early dawn, dragon, 2760) and *uht-hlem* (crash at early dawn, 2007), both of which are also unique. *Wig-fruma* (war-leader, 21) calls to mind other *-fruma* compounds with *dæd-, hild-, land-, leod-* and *ord-*, and suggests a second element of which the poet of *Beowulf* was particularly fond.[3] In the case of *eorl-gestreon* (treasure of noble warriors, 4) the first element has connotations of quality or degree, similar to *þeod-gestreon* (people's treasure, 44).

Phrases sometimes are used in preference to compounds. The commonest type, which is not particularly distinctive of verse, is the nominal phrase comprising noun and adjective. The word order is variable, but there is a tendency for the noun to precede in a first half-line (*drync-fæt deore*, 14a) and for the adjective to precede in a second (*fæted wæge*, 13b), the difference probably being the result of metrical pressures. More typical of the poetry are phrases consisting of a noun with a preceding genitive modifier, such as *hringa hyrde* (guardian of rings, 5) and *eorla æhte* (possessions of warriors, 8). These have a similar semantic ranges to those of the compounds. *Eorla æhte*, for example, is close to *eorl-gestreon* (4).

154

In terms of the syllabic and alliterative structure *Beowulf* is often regarded as representing 'classical' Old English verse. It is noticeable that the lines are generally short, a good proportion of the half-lines containing no more than the minimum permissible number of four syllables (e.g. 1b, 5ab, 6ab, 8a). In 4b the half-line is filled by only one word. Metrical patterns are unexceptional, with Sievers' Type A predominating.[4] In the successive second half-lines 2b and 3b metrical and grammatical patterns are almost identical, each being a Type A verse consisting of a four-syllable compound noun in the dative case followed by a one-syllable preposition/adjective. Other patterns similarly recur, helping to create a sense of diversity constrained by order.

The formulaic character of the verse is well demonstrated by reference to Bessinger's *Concordance to the Anglo-Saxon Poetic Records* and to repeated words and phrases within *Beowulf* itself. Some words and phrases recur in identical form (allowing for minor orthographic differences), and thus could be termed 'formulae' in the strictest sense advocated by F. P. Magoun. These include *borda gebræc* (19), *drinc-fæt deore* (14, cf. 2306), *feorh-bealo frecne* (10, cf. the identical phrase in *Beowulf* 2537a) and *hran æt heortan* (30). In each case the ready-made alliteration makes them immediately suitable for the first half-line. *Fea worda cwæð* (6) is also the cue formula for a speech at *Beowulf* 2662b. *Dæges ond nihtes* (29) is different in that the phrase is common in poetry and prose and was probably part of everyday speech, as 'by day and by night' is today. The phrase *an æfter eallum* (28), despite its sense of ready-made completeness, does not appear elsewhere. It is what Magoun would term a 'formulaic phrase', rather than a 'formula', i.e. a phrase of which the same pattern is found elsewhere but not the identical words. Thus *an æfter eallum* is closely related, both lexically and syntactically, to *an æfter anum* and *an æfter oðrum*, both meaning 'one after the other'. Similarly, *hringa hyrde* (5) is semantically and syntactically close to *hordes hyrde* (keeper of the hoard, 875), *frætwa hyrde* (keeper of ornaments, 3133) and *sinces hyrde* (keeper of treasure, *Genesis* 2101). One stage further removed from formulae proper are words that habitually alliterate together but do not occur in syntactically comparable phrases. *Nacod* and *nið*, for instance, collocate in this way in line 33 and also in *Daniel* 632, *Juliana* 187 and *Beowulf* 2585.

The compression of the verse into compact lines has already been remarked upon. This is partly achieved by the rigorous omission of words which carry little lexical meaning, such as articles, relative pronouns, conjunctions and even some verbs. Thus *fea worda cwæð* (6) could mean 'he spoke few words' or 'he spoke a few words' or 'he spoke these few words'. After the auxiliary verb *sceal* (15) the infinitive *wesan* or *weorðan* is required to accompany the past participle *befeallen* (must be/become deprived), but it is omitted. Such omissions often create a paratactic syntax, as in line 33 ('hairless malice-dragon [which] flies by night') and in the middle of 28, where a conjunction such as *and* is implied. An alternative would be to repunctuate to create smaller sense-units. Such omissions are found in all Old English verse. Less explicable are sporadic occurrences of such words where their omission might rather have been expected, notably the definite articles (or demonstratives) *se* (15, 24) and *seo* (18) which seem to add nothing of any consequence. The relative pronouns *þa ðe* (17), *sio* (18) and *se ðe* (32) and the conjunctions *oð ðæt* (until, 29) and *þær* (where, 36) create a contrastive hypotactic structure, as does the correlative *nu . . . nu* (7), which gives a sense close to that of the conjunction 'since'.

Personification is a device which was frequently used by the Anglo-Saxon poets, who went so far, in *The Dream of the Rood* and the *Riddles*, as to invest inanimate objects with the power of speech. The whole of the speech of the Last Survivor is addressed directly to *hruse* (earth/ground), with use of the second person pronouns *þu* and *ðe* (7, 8). A lesser degree of personification is maintained throughout. Thus *wunode* (2) regularly means 'dwelt', but here is used figuratively and with a hint of personification with the sense 'existed, was situated'. Similarly, *guð-deað* (death in battle, 9) and *bealo-cwealm* (baleful death, 25) are imagined as carrying the soldiers off, the *here-pad* (corselet, 18) is imagined as decaying like the dead man, and the suit of mail (*byrnan hring*, 20) is imagined as accompanying (or, rather, being unable to accompany) the warrior on his last journey. The dragon is also personalised, here and elsewhere, but we should remember that masculine pronouns are used in the description of him in 30–7 for the reason that both *uht-sceaða* and *nið-draca* are nouns of the masculine gender, not because the poet imagines him as such.

The poet, on the whole, is careful of such matters. Only occasionally is grammatical concord not observed. In line 8 the earth is commanded to accept the *æhte* (possessions) of noble warriors. *Æhte* is a feminine noun in the plural accusative case, but in the next sentence the more generalised neuter accusative singular pronoun *hyt* has been substituted. What follows in 9–12 is particularly difficult to unravel, but the poet seems to be referring to the death of 'each of the men of my tribe who gave up *(ofgeaf,* singular) this life, [who] had seen *(gesawon,* plural) the joys of hall'.[5] Such irregularities as this uncomfortable change from singular to plural are not unparalleled in *Beowulf,* and can usually be explained as a sudden shift of logic – in this case from thinking of the individual man to thinking of the many who experienced warrior society and passed away.

Variation, the chief rhetorical figure of the Anglo-Saxon poets, is used to embellish both the speech and the narrative. The main examples are *eorl-gestreon / fættan goldes* (4–6), referring to the part of the treasure carried into the mound, *guð-dead / feorh-bealo frecne* (9–10), referring to death, *fæted wæge / drync-fæt deore* (13–14), referring to the drinking-cup, *hearpan wyn / gomen gleo-beames* (22–3), referring to the joy of the harp, and *eald uht-sceaða / nacod nið-draca* (31–3), referring to the dragon. The adjectival phrases in lines 1–3 are a list of the different attributes of the barrow, not examples of variation.

Other features of rhetoric are specific to the committal speech itself. It is a consciously crafted set-piece. The direct address to the earth is a form of apostrophe, and is accentuated by the interjection *Hwæt* (8), a declamatory call for attention found at the beginning of a number of Old English poems, including *Beowulf* itself. Longer sense units are interspersed with shorter (e.g. 14b), but in general the sentence structure is complex, with more subordination than is typical of the poem as a whole. In essence the speech is based upon a catalogue of what has passed, but, instead of a simple list, the speaker's line of thought is followed from one thing to the next. He moves from observations on worldly possessions as a whole and from generalised comments on death (7–12) to more specific examples of his loss. Emphasis is often on symbolic objects and what they represent (12–25). He refers to the sword (no one will carry it), to the cup (no one will polish it), to the helmet (no one will repair and refurbish it) and to chain-mail (which will decay like human flesh). Battle is thought of in terms of the crashing together of shields and the cut of swords. Then follows a sequence of lines (20–5) expressed in the grammatical negative. The emphasis is still on representative symbols of the good life – the corselet, the harp, the hawk, the horse – but the catalogue structure is more apparent than previously. Finally (25–6) there is the generalised observation, in the form of a deliberately understated *litotes*, by which the speech is brought to an end.

This last remark is an example of a type of generalised gnomic utterance which can be found throughout the passage. Gnomic statements embody accepted wisdom and incontestable truths. They often make use of the verb *sculan*, which refers to the performance of an act in accordance with one's nature or custom or duty. Thus the helmet *sceal* (15) be deprived of its decoration because it is the nature of such things to decay in the ground. The habits and behaviour of dragons were particularly seen as being prescribed by their nature and instincts:

> Draca sceal on hlæwe,
> frod, frætwum wlanc.   *(Maxims* II 26–7)
> *(The dragon shall dwell in the barrow, ancient,*
> *exulting in its treasures.)*

In the passage from *Beowulf* (32–5) it is noticeable that the poet moves from description, in the past tense, of the activities of this dragon in particular, to more generalised comment, in the present tense, on behaviour which is typical of dragons in general – seeking out barrows and flying at night enveloped in flame. Gnomic *sceall* is again used (35) to emphasise that it cannot resist searching for the hoard and guarding it for many years. Finally, the half-line gnomic statement with which the passage ends is used both to round-off this section, as is typical, and to give a generalised truth in keeping with the moral position of the Christian poet.

Sir Gawain and the Green Knight, 713–62

At midwinter Sir Gawain rides on his horse Gringolet in search of the Green Chapel

> Mony klyf he ouerclambe in contrayez straunge,
> Fer floten fro his frendez fremedly he rydez.
> At vche warþe oþer water þer þe wyȝe passed   [715]
> He fonde a foo hym byfore, bot ferly hit were,
> 5   And þat so foule and so felle þat feȝt hym byhode.

So mony meruayl bi mount þer þe mon fyndez,
Hit were to tore for to telle of þe tenþe dole.
Sumwhyle wyth wormez he werrez, and with wolues als, [720]
Sumwhyle wyth wodwos, þat woned in þe knarrez,

10 Boþe wyth bullez and berez, and borez oþerquyle,
And etaynez, þat hym anelede of þe heȝe felle;
Nade he ben duȝty and dryȝe, and Dryȝtyn had serued,
Douteles he hade ben ded and dreped ful ofte. [725]
For werre wrathed hym not so much þat wynter nas wors,

15 When þe colde cler water fro þe cloudez schadde,
And fres er hit falle myȝt to þe fale erþe;
Ner slayn wyth þe slete he sleped in his yrnes
Mo nyȝtez þen innoghe in naked rokkez, [730]
Þer as claterande fro þe crest þe colde borne rennez,

20 And henged heȝe ouer his hede in hard iisse-ikkles.
Þus in peryl and payne and plytes ful harde
Bi contray caryez þis knyȝt, tyl Krystmasse euen,
    al one; [735]
        Þe knyȝt wel þat tyde
25   To Mary made his mone,
        Þat ho hym red to ryde
        And wysse hym to sum wone.

Bi a mounte on þe morne meryly he rydes [740]
Into a forest ful dep, þat ferly watz wylde,

30 Hiȝe hillez on vche a halue, and holtwodez vnder
Of hore okez ful hoge a hundreth togeder;
Þe hasel and þe haȝþorne were harled al samen,
With roȝe raged mosse rayled aywhere, [745]
With mony bryddez vnblyþe vpon bare twyges,

35 Þat pitosly þer piped for pyne of þe colde.
Þe gome vpon Gryngolet glydez hem vnder,
Þurȝ mony misy and myre, mon al hym one,
Carande for his costes, lest he ne keuer schulde [750]
To se þe seruyse of þat syre, þat on þat self nyȝt

40 Of a burde watz borne oure baret to quelle;
And þerfore sykyng he sayde, 'I beseche þe, lorde,
And Mary, þat is myldest moder so dere,
Of sum herber þer heȝly I myȝt here masse, [755]
Ande þy matynez to-morne, mekely I ask,

45 And þerto prestly I pray my pater and aue
        and crede.'
  He rode in his prayere,
  And cryed for his mysdede,   [760]
  He sayned hym in syþes sere,
50 And sayde 'Cros Kryst me spede!'

(He climbed over many a high rock in alien regions, and having wandered far from his friends he rides as a stranger. At each ford or river the knight crossed he found an enemy before him – unless it were quite exceptional – and so evil and fierce that he was obliged to fight. The man comes across so many strange things in the hills that it would be too difficult to describe a tenth of them. At times he fights against dragons, and also against wolves, at time against trolls of the forest who lived in the crags, against both bulls and bears, and at other times against boars, and ogres, who pursued him from the high moor. Had he not been brave and resilient, and had he not served God, without doubt many a time he might have been killed or have met his death. For battle did not afflict him to the extent that it was worse than the winter weather, when the cold, clear water was shed from the clouds and froze before it could fall on the faded earth. Nearly slain by the sleet he slept in his armour more than enough nights among bare rocks, where the cold stream runs splashing from the mountain-top and hung over his head in hard icicles. In this way, in danger and in pain and in wretched hardships, this knight rides alone through the region till Christmas Eve. Without doubt, the knight made his complaint at that time to the Virgin Mary, asking that she should guide him where to ride and bring him to some dwelling.

In the morning he rides briskly into a very deep wilderness, amazingly wild, with high hills on each side and thick woods below of huge hoar-oaks, a hundred together; the hazel and the hawthorn were entwined with each other, with rough, ragged moss spread everywhere, and with many miserable birds there in the bare branches, which pitifully chirped out of distress from the cold. The man hastens beneath them on Gringolet, through many a marsh and quagmire, totally alone, concerned about the circumstances he was in, lest he should not manage to see the service of that dear Lord who on that very night had been born of a maiden in order to end our sorrows. And therefore, sighing, he said, 'I beseech you, Lord, and Mary, mildest mother so dear, for some sheltering place where I may be able devoutly to hear mass and your matins tomorrow – humbly I ask, and to that end I eagerly say my Pater Noster, Ave and Creed.' He rode in prayer, lamenting his sins, and crossed himself many times, saying 'May Christ's Cross help me!')

Like the manuscript of *Beowulf*, that of *Sir Gawain* is unique, but it presents fewer problems. By the time it was written, about 1400, it had become the custom to write lines of verse separately, rather than in continuous lines of equal length. Capitalisation is sporadic in the manuscript and punctuation non-existent, so these have been inserted by the editor, as is the normal practice with all medieval texts. The word-division of the manuscript has also been standardised according to present-day practice, so combinations such as *forto* and *ahalue* (7, 30) have been separated. Only three words in these two stanzas have required editorial emendation: in line 14 the manuscript has the positive *was* instead of *nas* (was not), but the latter seems to give better sense; for *schadde* (was shed, 15) the manuscript has the plural *schadden* where the singular is required; and in 39 manuscript *seruy* appears to be a scribal error for *seruyse*. Other inconsistencies, such as *and/ande* (45/44) are a reflection of the variable orthographic system in use at the time the manuscript was made. Þ was still used at this time, but was beginning to give way to the digraph *th*. In this passage þ is regularly used as an initial consonant, but in a final position *th* is more common (e.g. *hundreth* 31), and medially either may be found (e.g. *oþer/wrathed* 3/14).

The verse form, with its stanzas of a variable number of unrhymed alliterative lines followed by five shorter lines rhyming *ababa* (the first known as the 'bob' and the last four as the 'wheel'), is unique. The general characteristics of the long lines are similar to those of Old English verse. The commonest pattern has two alliterating elements in the first half-line with one in the second, the latter falling on the headstave, i.e. on the first lift after the caesura (e.g. 1, 3, 5). However, the number of syllables is greater than in the lines from *Beowulf*, and some lines have three alliterating sounds in the first half (e.g. 20, 30, 39). Line 11 shows that words beginning with different vowels could alliterate with each other and with words beginning with *h* (*etaynez, anelede, heȝe*). In three instances the same alliterating sound is used in two adjacent lines (4–5, 8–9, 12–13) and in one case the same alliterating sound extends to three lines (30–2). In line 17 the group of consonants *sl* is treated as one alliterating sound, but this is not always the case in *Gawain* (cf. *And þou schal se in þat slade þe self chapel*, 2147).

The poet's skill has ensured that, despite the artificial verse form, neither syntax nor lexical choice appears forced. On the contrary, the style is generally fluent and idiomatic. Meaningless phrases and other redundant words are avoided: perhaps only the latter part of 4 and the rhyming tag *þat tyde* (24) could be so described. In 13 there is a distinction between *dreped* (slain) and *ded* (dead, from a variety of possible causes), so the line is not tautological, as it might first seem. The words *misy* and *myre* (37) perhaps refer to distinct varieties of quagmire, and are not necessarily repetitious. Even the short 'bob' in each of these stanzas (23, 46) is meaningful, which is not always the case elsewhere in the poem.[6] None the less, despite the sense of naturalness, the language is artificial and remote from that of ordinary speech.

In terms of grammar, perhaps the most striking feature is the mixture of tenses of the main verbs, most being in the preterite but approximately a quarter being in the historic present. The use of the two within close proximity and even within the same sentence (e.g. 1–2, 19–20) seems odd to the modern ear. Given the apparent randomness of the poet's use of the historic present, it is not possible to argue that he has chosen to use it on stylistic grounds, such as to give immediacy to Gawain's plight. Its extensive and patchy use in *Gawain* and other alliterative verse remains unexplained. Other verbal forms distinguished in this passage include the subjunctive (e.g. *nade, hade*, 12–13, but without final *-e* in *had*, 12) and the impersonal *hym byhode* (5). The present participle ends in *-ande* (*claterande*, 19, *carande*, 38), as is normal in *Gawain*, except that in *sykyng* (41) we have one of only two exceptions in the whole poem. Definite and indefinite articles are used extensively – unlike the practice in Old English verse – a feature in this passage being the tendency to use the former with a general, rather than a particular, sense (e.g. *þe hasel and þe haȝorne*, 32, and *þe colde*, 35).

Syntax is manipulated in the disposition of accented syllables coincident with the alliterating syllables. This is achieved by various unobtrusive methods, such as placing the *of* genitive in some instances before the noun or adjective it modifies (e.g. 31, 40) and in other instances after it (e.g. 35, 39). Similarly, adjectives may precede nouns (e.g. 6, 15) or follow them (e.g. 1, 34), prepositions can occur before the noun or pronoun they govern (e.g. 1 and generally) or after (e.g. 4), and infinitives may be preceded by *to* alone (e.g. 39, 40) or by *for to* (e.g. 7). Major components of clauses – subjects, objects, adjuncts – are placed in a variety of positions relative to the verb (e.g. object/subject/verb/adjunct 1, subject/verb/object/

adjunct 4, object/adjunct/subject/verb 6). It is through the, almost imperceptible, management of choices such as these that the characteristic syntax is achieved.

Rhetorical variation, so common in Old English verse, is absent here, with the single exception that in lines 36–7 *mone hym al one* could be described as a variation of *þe gome vpon Gryngolet*. Variation is not generally found because it relies upon asyndetic parataxis, something which is not extensively used in *Gawain*. Apart from lines 1–2 and 44, the relationship between clauses is overwhelmingly hypotactic. Sentence structure is predominantly complex (in the technical sense), the many subordinate clauses giving a sense of sophistication and control. The change of subject in line 14 from the dangers of men and beasts to the hardships caused by the winter weather is elegantly managed. Also, despite the fact that the subject matter would lend itself very easily to the use of long catalogues, these are not employed. Anaphora, a characteristic of catalogue rhetoric, is similarly avoided, except in lines 8–9 and 33–4. The language is much less formulaic than that of Old English verse. There are a few habitual alliterating collocations, such as *slay/slepe* and *mery/morn* (17, 28), but no recurrence of more sustained idiom other than the 'brevity formula' of line 7, which echoes the poet's assertion in the middle of his description of the Green Knight in an earlier part of the poem that

> Þat were to tor for to telle of tryfles þe halue   (165)
> (*It would be too difficult to describe half the details*).

Gawain's prayer (41–6, 50) makes use of conventional reverential formulae, such as 'myldest moder', 'prestly I pray' and 'Cros Kryst me spede', the syntax of the last probably being modelled on Old French *crois Crist* (see Tolkien and Gordon 1967, 98). Juxtaposition of the general and the particular is used in a variety of ways. On the one hand we are given graphic images of details such as the icicles and the pitiful birds (20, 34), and on the other told more generally of *mony klyf* (1), *mony misy and myre* (37), *vche warþe* (3), and so on. *Hundreth* (31) is, of course, only a general term for an indeterminately large number, as is the expression *mo þen innoghe* (18). *Innoghe* here could mean 'many', in which case this is an hyperbole, or 'enough', in which case it is a *litotes* (understatement) similar to those found in Old English.

The vocabulary is both conservative and forward-looking. Old English poetic diction is reflected in words such as *wormez* and *etaynez* (8, 11), which, in the senses which they have here, were probably beginning to look archaic by the time *Gawain* was composed, and by metonymic *yrnes* (17), though Old English heroic poetry *iren* invariably means 'sword' rather than 'armour'. *Wyʒe* (3) and *gome* (36) are words inherited from Old English verse. Along with *mon* (6, 37) and *knyʒt* (22, 24) they are used to refer to Gawain when the third personal pronoun is not used. There is also a range of synonyms, or near-synonyms, for various forms of 'go' (*caryez* 22, *floten* 2, *glydez* 36, *passed* 3, *ryde* 26). All such features are reminiscent of Old English verse. On the other hand, despite this conservatism, there are many signs that the poet has been receptive to a variety of means of lexical expansion.[7] The principal methods in *Gawain* are those found in the ordinary, non-literary language of the fourteenth century, notably affixation, compounding, conversion and borrowing. Thus we have in this passage *douteles* (13, which is French-derived *doute* + the Old English suffix *-leas*, an example of both borrowing and affixation), *haʒþorne* (32, 'hedge' + 'thorn', an example of compounding), and *colde* (35, an adjective used 'absolutely' as a noun, an example of linguistic conversion). Apart from the fact that *douteles* is not recorded earlier than in *Gawain*, there is nothing particularly distinctive about these words and their use, and all can be found in a variety of poetic and non-poetic contexts.

In the sphere of borrowing, however, the poet shows exceptional imagination and inventiveness, as well as a great willingness to draw upon a range of source languages and dialects. There is a total of 403 word occurrences in these two stanzas, but if we allow only one example of repeated words of the same word class, such as *and* (25 occurrences) and *to* (8 occurrences), the total is reduced to 345. Almost all of these repeated words (some 96 per cent) are derived from Old English, indicating that most of the unremarkable but important grammatical function-words are native in origin. Conversely, this means that a greater proportion of the more prominent, lexically rich words are borrowed from other languages – in the case of these two stanzas from French, Scandinavian and Latin. The etymological situation, however, is complex, and for various reasons it is impossible to give precise numbers. For example, some words borrowed from these languages had already been taken into Old English, including *werre*

(14, from the Norman dialect of French), *costes* (38, from Scandinavian) and *masse* (43, from Latin), so this blurs the distinction between Old English and the other languages. Furthermore, since Old English and Scandinavian are related Germanic languages, it is not always possible to say from which of these two a particular word has derived. Thus, *ferly* (4) may be from ON *ferligr* or from O.E. *færlic*, perhaps by way of the unrecorded Anglian form *feorlic*, which might have been expected in the North-West Midlands region in which the poem originated. Taking such factors into account it seems that approximately 83 per cent of words are from Old English, 9 per cent from French, 6 per cent from the Scandinavian languages, and 2 per cent direct from Latin.[8]

Most of the borrowed words were neither unusual nor distinctive of poetry, so the raw figures are not particularly significant in themselves. But others do indeed stand out. Scandinavian words, despite their smaller numbers, include several that were probably unusual and of limited currency. *Warþe* (3), for example, seems to be from Old English *waroð* (shore), but influenced by Old Norse *vað* (ford). The form *warthe* is recorded in Lincolnshire and northwards from the sixteenth century onwards, with the sense 'crossing place, ford'. The usual word for 'ford' in the poems of the *Gawain* manuscript is simply *ford*, but the poet has possibly used the more unusual word here for alliterative convenience, drawing perhaps upon his own dialect (see Haworth 1967). Similarly, *wone* (dwelling, 27) seems to combine senses associated with Old English *wunian* (to dwell) and its derived noun *wone* (the action of staying or remaining) with senses associated with Old Norse *van* (hope, expectation). *OED* draws a comparison with Norwegian *von* (place where one expects to find something, fishing place, hunting ground). Turning to the French-derived words in the passage, one of the most interesting is *anelede* (11). It appears to be from Old French *aneler* and ultimately from Latin *anhelare*, meaning 'to breathe'. In Old French it acquired the sense 'to breathe heavily, puff, get wind of, scent'. Here in *Gawain* the context suggests the meaning 'pursued', perhaps with associations of puffing and panting as the *etaynez* furiously chased the knight from the high fells. This may be an example of the poet's inventiveness, for the word is nowhere else recorded with this meaning. Also interesting are other effects engineered by the poet, such as the retention of the French pattern of stress on the borrowed word *prayere* (47) for the sake of rhyme, which is contrary to his practice in non-rhyming positions.

Even some of the more familiar-looking words do not here have the same meanings as in present-day English, including *bryddez* (small birds, 34), *contrayez* (regions, 1, 22), *forest* (wild uncultivated land, 29), *herber* (lodging, 43), and *straunge* (alien, 1). Since Gawain was so anxious, *meryly* (28) clearly does not have its common meaning 'merrily'. It is one of a group of adjectives and adverbs of which the meaning in *Gawain* and other verse sometimes seems to be contextually determined. The semantic range of *meryly* covers 'cheerfully, joyfully, heartily, jovially, sweetly, attractively, correctly, properly, brightly and briskly', and probably something of the last is intended here.[9]

Notes

I INTRODUCTION

1. However, it appears that drastic alteration such as this could also be made by scribes (see pp. 88–9. Compare also the two extant versions of Laȝamon's *Brut* (see below, pp. 96–7).

4 OLD ENGLISH POETIC DICTION

1. The punctuation of this passage is discussed at length in Mitchell (1980), 409–12.

2. The symbol * is the conventional indication of a theoretical form, one which does not actually occur. Though there is no such genitive phrase for 'ship', there are many referring to other things, such as *morðres brytta* (distributor of crime, villain) or *wuldres treow* (tree of glory, the Cross). Almost certainly it is a matter of chance that no such expression for 'ship' happens to have survived.

3. See Shippey (1972), 85–98. Examples of recurring alliterating phrases are given in Oakden (1935), 199–210.

4. The 'oral-formulaic theory' (of which more in Chapter 5) has a bearing on this issue. Some aspects of this theory have been better received than others.

5 OLD ENGLISH VERSE: STRUCTURE AND ORGANISATION

1. A possible reference to a poet's use of variation occurs in *Beowulf* 871–4:

> Secg eft ongan
> sið Beowulfes snyttrum styrian,
> ond on sped wrecan spel gerade,
> wordum wrixlan.
> (*Afterwards a man recited Beowulf's exploit and skilfully related an aptly-made tale, varying [?] words.*)

166

A difficulty with this interpretation is that the expression *wordum wrixlan* occurs elsewhere in Old English poetry with the meaning 'to exchange words, to converse formally', but since the poet in *Beowulf* is not involved in an exchange of speech the more technical sense 'to use poetical variation' is possible. The most useful and accessible accounts of variation are in Brodeur (1959), 39–70, 272–83 and Robinson 1985.

2. *Chiasmus:* A term used in rhetoric to describe a construction involving repetition of words or elements in reverse order (ab:ba).

3. The example is from Shippey (1972), 85–6, who also gives examples from religious verse, pp. 86–7.

4. For more on the subject of varying line-units see Malone (1943).

5. Cf. *Beowulf* 1392–4, 1762–7, 2262–5; *Christ* 590–8, 664–81; *Christ and Satan* 163–71; *Elene* 131–7; *Judgment Day II* 254–67; *Juliana* 472–94. Other poems which use the catalogue in their overall structure are *Deor, Fates of the Apostles* and the two collections of *Maxims*. See further Stanley (1955), 446–7.

6. Klaeber's edition has *Eotena* (of the Jutes), but a good case for *eotena* (of enemies) is made in Kaske (1967).

6   MIDDLE ENGLISH POETIC DICTION

1. The linguistic differences between the Caligula and Otho versions have often been attributed to differences in the dates of the manuscripts, with Otho being placed as much as 75 years later. However, palaeographical and bibliographical evidence suggests that they are likely to be of approximately the same date. Cannon argues (Cannon 1993) that the differences are largely stylistic, reflecting the Otho reviser's wish to eliminate many of the archaisms associated with the English tradition in favour of newer words associated with the romance genre.

2. These and other examples in this section are taken from Turville-Petre (1977), 69–92.

3. For a sensitive analysis see Gray (1972), 101–6.

7   MIDDLE ENGLISH VERSE: STRUCTURE AND ORGANISATION

1. This 13-line stanza has hitherto been regarded as a unique 9-line stanza with internal rhyme in the first quatrain. The case in favour of the longer form is in Stevens and Cawley (1994), xxix–xxxi.

2. Such periphrases are particularly characteristic of the *Gawain* poet. For further examples see Menner (1920), xvii–xviii.

3. For detailed statistics on alliterating patterns in Middle English poems, and on the absence of alliteration, see Oakden (1930), 181–200.

4. Most of the work done on the pronunciation of final -*e* relates to Chaucer. Kökeritz, for example, gives the rule of thumb that it should be pronounced (1) at the end of a line; (2) within a line 'whenever the scansion so requires' (Kökeritz

1961, 18). While so liberal a recommendation partly reflects our inability to devise firm rules, it is also likely to reflect some inconsistency of practice by Chaucer himself. For a lively appraisal and summary of views see Robinson (1971), 82–108. Burnley (1989), 13 notes of inflexional -*e* in Chaucer that 'its use is remarkably stable in good, early manuscripts', but that there are exceptions. Much of what is true of Chaucer is also true of his contemporaries.

5.   See pp. 74–7 above. The whole concept of formula in Middle English has been called into question by Turville-Petre (1977), 89–92, who objects to the imprecision of this definition. Most scholars, however, seem to find the term, and the concept, useful.

6.   There are useful classified lists in Oakden (1935), 195–379. For an interesting appraisal see Turville-Petre (1977), 83–92.

7.   Numbers are based on Oakden's lists, which are generally reliable but not always complete.

8.   A treatise popular in the middle ages was the pseudo-Ciceronian *Rhetorica ad Herennium*. It lists 45 'figures of speech', which are explained and exemplified. Despite their technical names, some of them are extremely simple and common. Thus, *repetitio* is the use of the same word or phrase at the beginning of successive syntactic units, *contentio* the use of contrast, *circumitio* the use of circumlocution, and so on.

8   LINGUISTIC VARIETIES

1.   See further Sisam (1953) and Godden (1992), 496–8.
2.   See above, p. 77.
3.   For details of the parallels with Old Saxon see Timmer (1948), 27–39.
4.   Chaucer, for example, remarks upon the 'gret diversite in Englissh' (*Troilus and Criseyde*, V, 1793–4).

9   EXAMPLES OF ANALYSIS: *BEOWULF* AND *SIR GAWAIN*

1.   Digitised test images were made by the British Library in 1993 with a view to producing an electronic facsimile, eventually to be made available in a variety of formats, including CD-ROM. Each page of the manuscript was photographed at high resolution, in white light, ultra-violet light and with fibre-optic cable. Letters are now visible at the edges which were previously obscured by the paper frames, and some of the words erased during the writing of the manuscript can now be deciphered.

2.   The term is usually also applied to words which occur more than once but which are unique to a particular poem. *Wig-fruma*, for instance, occurs only in *Beowulf* 664 and 2261 (line 21 of this extract).

3.   It is also much used in *Andreas*, a poem which has many parallels with *Beowulf* and which may have been influenced by it.

4.   A table of scansion types in the whole of *Beowulf* is in Bliss (1958,) 135–57.

5.   The *ge-* prefix may give the perfective sense 'had seen the last of'.

6.   Davis notes that the 'bob' lines are written in the manuscript to the right of the long lines, often two or three lines up, and that, since the 'bob' lines seldom contribute anything essential to the meaning, and are often distinctly redundant, they may have been added by the author as an afterthought. However, they were not added in the surviving manuscript later than the poem as a whole, since they are in the same hand and ink as the rest. See Tolkien and Gordon (1967,) xi and 152.

7.   Davis calculates that there are approximately as many distinct individual words (about 2690) as there are lines in the poem (2530), and that there is thus an average of a new word for every line (Tolkien and Gordon 1967, vii).

8.   Most French words are, of course, ultimately Latin in origin. The name of Gawain's horse Gringolet, which has its source in French romance, and the word *cros* (50), which was borrowed into English from Scandinavian, both probably derive more remotely from Celtic forms.

9.   Other words in *Gawain* with a wide range of meanings are *breme, clene, clere, comly, cortays(ly), fayre, fre(ly), gentyle, goud(ly), hende(ly), lufly(ly), semly(ly)* and *worþy(ly)*.

Bibliography and List of Works Cited

Editions of Old English and Middle English Poems

The following editions have been used, but, in the interests of uniformity, small changes (such as the hyphenation of compound words, the expansion of the ampersand, and minor changes in punctuation) have been made in some of the quotations. Old English poems for which no separate edition is listed are cited from *The Anglo-Saxon Poetic Records*, ed. G. P. Krapp and E. V. K. Dobbie (New York and London: Columbia University Press, 1931–54), 6 vols.

Andreas and *The Fates of the Apostles*, ed. K. R. Brooks (Oxford: Clarendon, 1961)

The Battle of Maldon, ed. D. G. Scragg (Manchester: Manchester University Press, 1981)

Beowulf and the Fight at Finnsburg, ed. F. Klaeber, 3rd edn (Boston: Heath, 1950)

The Romance of Sir Beues of Hamtoun, ed. E. Köbling (London: EETS, extra series, 46, 48, 65, 1885–94)

The Riverside Chaucer, ed. L. D. Benson (Oxford: Oxford University Press, 1987)

The Chester Mystery Cycle, ed. R. M. Lumansky and D. Mills (London: EETS, supplementary series, 3, 9, 1974–86)

Two Coventry Corpus Christi Plays, ed. H. Craig (London, EETS, extra series, 87, 1957)

Cursor Mundi, ed. R. Morris (London: EETS, 57, 59, 62, 66, 68, 99, 101, 1874–93)

Cynewulf's 'Elene', ed. P. O. E. Gradon (London: Methuen, 1958)

The Dream of the Rood, ed. M. Swanton (Manchester: Manchester University Press, 1970)

The Poems of William Dunbar, ed. J. Kinsley (Oxford: Clarendon, 1979)

Everyman, ed. A. C. Cawley (Manchester: Manchester University Press, 1961)

Exodus, ed. P. J. Lucas (London: Methuen, 1977)

The Fox and the Wolf, in *Early Middle English Verse and Prose*, ed. J. A. W. Bennett and G. V. Smithers, 2nd edn (Oxford: Clarendon, 1968), pp. 65–76

Genesis A, ed. A. N. Doane (Madison: University of Wisconsin, 1978)

The Saxon Genesis, ed. A. N. Doane (Madison: University of Wisconsin, 1991) [*Genesis B*]

170

The Story of Genesis and Exodus, ed. R. Morris (London: EETS, 7, 1865)

John Gower: Confessio Amantis, in *The Complete Works of John Gower: Vols 2 and 3: The English Works*, ed. G. C. Macaulay (Oxford: Clarendon, 1901)

The Guthlac Poems of the Exeter Book, ed. J. Roberts (Oxford: Clarendon, 1979)

The Romance of Guy of Warwick [Auchinleck MS], ed. J. Zupitza (London: EETS, extra series, 42, 45, 59, 1883–91)

Havelok, ed. G. V. Smithers (Oxford: Clarendon, 1987)

Hoccleve's Works: The Regement of Princes (London: EETS, extra series, 72, 1897)

Interludium de Clerico et Puella, in *Early Middle English Verse and Prose*, ed. J. A. W. Bennett and G. V. Smithers, 2nd edn (Oxford: Clarendon, 1968), pp. 196–200

Judith, ed. B. J. Timmer, 2nd edn (London: Methuen, 1961)

Juliana, ed. R. Woolf (London: Methuen, 1965)

King Horn, ed. R. Allen (New York and London: Garland, 1984)

Kyng Alisaunder, ed. G. V. Smithers (London: EETS, 227, 237, 1952–7)

Laȝamon's Brut, ed. G. L. Brook and R. F. Leslie (London: EETS, 250, 277, 1963–78. [Quotations are from the Caligula text unless otherwise stated.]

William Langland: The Vision of Piers Plowman: A Critical Edition of the B-Text, ed. A.V.C. Schmidt (London: Dent, 1978) [Quotations are all from the B-Text.]

John Lydgate: Fall of Princes, ed. H. Bergen (London: EETS, extra series, 121–4, 1924–7)

Religious Lyrics of the XVth Century, ed. C. Brown (Oxford: Clarendon, 1939)

Mankind, in *The Macro Plays*, ed. M. Eccles (London: EETS, 262, 1969), pp.153–227

Morte Arthure, ed. M. Hamel (New York and London: Garland, 1984)

The N-Town Play, ed. S. Spector (London: EETS, supplementary series, 11, 12, 1991)

The Ormulum, ed. R. Holt (Oxford: Clarendon, 1878), 2 vols

The Owl and the Nightingale, ed. E. G. Stanley (Manchester: Manchester University Press, 1972)

The Parlement of the Thre Ages, ed. M. Y. Offord (London: EETS, 246, 1959)

Patience, ed. J. J. Anderson (Manchester: Manchester University Press, 1969)

Pearl, ed. E. V. Gordon (Oxford: Clarendon, 1953)

The Phoenix, ed. N. F. Blake (Exeter: Exeter University Press, 1990)

Purity, ed. A. J. Menner (New Haven: Yale University Press, 1920)

The Old English Riddles of the Exeter Book, ed. C. Williamson (Chapel Hill: University of North Carolina, 1977)

Robert of Brunne's 'Handlyng Synne', ed. F. J. Furnivall (London: EETS, 119, 123, 1901–3)

Robert of Gloucester: Metrical Chronicle, ed. W. A. Wright (London: Rolls Series, 86, 1887), 2 vols

The Seafarer, ed. I. L. Gordon (London: Methuen, 1960)

Sir Gawain and the Green Knight, ed. J. R. R. Tolkien and E. V. Gordon, 2nd edn, revised by N. Davis (Oxford: Clarendon, 1967)

Sir Orfeo, ed. A. J. Bliss, 2nd edn (Oxford: Clarendon, 1966). [Quotations are from the Auchinleck text unless otherwise stated.]

Sir Perceval of Gales, ed. J. Campion and F. Holthausen (Heidelberg: Winter, 1913)

Sir Tryamowre, ed. A. J. E. Schmidt (Utrecht: Broekhoff, 1937)

The Towneley Plays, ed. M. Stevens and A. C. Cawley (Oxford: EETS, supplementary series, 13–14, 1994)

Thomas Usk: The Testament of Love, in *Chaucerian and Other Pieces*, ed. W. W. Skeat (Oxford: Clarendon, 1897)

The Wanderer, ed. T. P. Dunning and A. J. Bliss (London: Methuen, 1969)

William of Nassington: Speculum Vitae, ed. J. Ullmann, *Englische Studien*, 7 (1884), 468–72 [lines 1–370 only]

William of Palerne, ed. G. H. V. Bunt (Groningen: Bouma, 1985)

The York Plays, ed. R. Beadle (London: Arnold, 1982)

Other Works

ANDREW, S. O., *Syntax and Style in Old English* (Cambridge: Cambridge University Press, 1940)

ANDREW, S. O., *Postscript on 'Beowulf'* (Cambridge: Cambridge University Press, 1948)

BARTLETT, A. C., *The Larger Rhetorical Patterns in Anglo-Saxon Poetry* (New York: Columbia University Press, 1935)

BAUGH, A. C., 'Improvisation in the Middle English Romance', *Proceedings of the American Philosophical Society*, 130 (1959), 418–54

BAUGH, A. C. and CABLE, T., A History of the English Language, 3rd edn (Englewood Cliffs, NJ: Prentice-Hall, 1978)

BENSON, L. D., *Art and Tradition in 'Sir Gawain and the Green Knight'* (New Brunswick: Rutgers University Press, 1965)

BENSON, L. D., 'The Literary Character of Anglo-Saxon Formulaic Poetry', *PMLA*, 81 (1966), 334–41

BESSINGER, J. B., Jr, *A Concordance to the Anglo-Saxon Poetic Records* (Ithaca and London: Cornell University Press, 1978)

BLAKE, N. F., *The English Language in Medieval Literature* (London: Dent, 1977)

BLAKE, N. F. (ed.), *The Cambridge History of the English Language: Vol. II: 1066–1476* (Cambridge: Cambridge University Press, 1992)

BLAKE, N. F., 'The Literary Language', in *The Cambridge History of the English Language: Vol. II: 1066–1476*, ed. N. F. Blake (Cambridge: Cambridge University Press, 1992), pp. 500–41

BLISS, A. J., *The Metre of 'Beowulf'* (Oxford: Blackwell, 1958)

BLISS, A. J., *An Introduction to Old English Metre* (Oxford: Blackwell, 1962)

BORROFF, M., 'Sir Gawain and the Green Knight': *A Stylistic and Metrical Study* (New Haven and London: Yale University Press, 1962)

BRACHER, F., 'Understatement in Old English Poetry', *PMLA*, 52 (1937), 915–34

BRADY, C., '"Weapons" in *Beowulf*: An Analysis of the Nominal Compounds and an Evaluation of the Poet's Use of them', *Anglo-Saxon England*, 8 (1979), 79–141

BRODEUR, A. G., *The Art of 'Beowulf'* (Berkeley and Los Angeles: University of California, 1959)

BURNLEY, [J.] D., *The Language of Chaucer* (London: Macmillan, 1989)

BURNLEY, [J.] D., 'Lexis and Semantics', in *The Cambridge History of the English Language:*
Vol. II: 1066–1476 , ed. N. F. Blake (Cambridge: Cambridge University Press, 1992),
pp. 409–99

BURROW, J. A., *Ricardian Poetry* (London: Routledge & Kegan Paul, 1971)

BURROW, J. A. and TURVILLE-PETRE, T., *A Book of Middle English* (Oxford: Blackwell, 1992)

CALDER, D. G., 'The Study of Style in Old English Poetry: A Historical Introduction', in *Old English Poetry: Essays on Style*, ed. D. G. Calder (Berkeley: University of California Press, 1979), pp. 1–65

CANNON, C., 'The Style and Authorship of the Otho Revision of Laȝamon's *Brut*', *Medium Ævum*, 62 (1993), 187–209

CICERO, M. T. [attributed to], *Ad C. Herennium De Ratione Dicendi [Rhetorica ad Herennium], with an English Translation by C. Caplan* (London: Heinemann, 1954)

CLARK, C., '*Sir Gawain and the Green Knight:* Characterisation by Syntax', *Essays in Criticism*, 16 (1966), 361–74

CONLEY, J., 'Aural Error in Everyman', *Notes & Queries*, new series, 22 (1975), 244–5

DEKEYSER, X., 'Romance Loans in Middle English: A Reassessment', in *Linguistics across Historical and Geographical Boundaries*, ed. D. Kastovsky and A. Szwedek (Berlin: de Gruyter, 1986), I, pp. 253–65

ELLIOTT, R. W. V., *The Gawain Country* (Leeds: University of Leeds, 1984)

FAKUNDINY, L., 'The Art of Old English Verse Composition', *Review of English Studies*, new series, 21 (1970), 257–66

FISCHER, O., 'Syntax', in *The Cambridge History of the English Language: Vol. II: 1066–1476*, ed. N. F. Blake (Cambridge: Cambridge University Press, 1992), pp. 207–408

FRANK, R., 'Some Uses of Paronomasia in Old English Scriptural Verse', *Speculum*, 47 (1972), 207–26

FRANKIS, [P.] J., 'Word-Formation by Blending in the Vocabulary of Middle English Alliterative Verse', in *Five Hundred Years of Words and Sounds* , ed. E.G. Stanley and D. Gray (Cambridge: Brewer, 1983), pp. 29–38

GODDEN, M. and LAPIDGE, M. (eds), *The Cambridge Companion to Old English Literature* (Cambridge: Cambridge University Press, 1991)

GODDEN, M., 'Literary Language', in *The Cambridge Companion to Old English Literature*, ed. M. Godden and M. Lapidge (Cambridge: Cambridge University Press, 1991), pp. 490–535

GRAY, D., Themes and Images in the Medieval English Religious Lyric (London: Routledge & Kegan Paul, 1972).

GREENFIELD, S. B., *The Interpretation of Old English Poems* (London: Routledge & Kegan Paul, 1972)

HAWORTH, P., ' "Warthe" in *Sir Gawain and the Green Knight*', *Notes & Queries*, new series, 14 (1967), 171–2

HOGG, R. M. (ed.), *The Cambridge History of the English Language: Vol. I: The Beginnings to 1066* (Cambridge: Cambridge University Press, 1992)

JESPERSEN, O., *Growth and Structure of the English Language*, 10th edn (Oxford: Blackwell, 1982)

174

KASKE, R. E., 'The *Eotenas* in *Beowulf*', in *Old English Poetry*, ed. R. P. Creed (Providence: Brown University Press, 1967), pp. 285–310

KEISER, A., *The Influence of Christianity on the Vocabulary of Old English Poetry* (Urbana: University of Illinois, 1919)

KÖKERITZ, H., *A Guide to Chaucer's Pronunciation* (Stockholm: Almqvist & Wiksell, 1961)

KRAPP, G. P., 'The Parenthetic Exclamation in Old English Poetry', *Modern Language Notes*, 20 (1905), 33–7

LEYERLE, J., 'The Interlace Structure of *Beowulf*', *University of Toronto Quarterly*, 37 (1967–8), 1–17

LORD, A. B., *The Singer of Tales* (Cambridge, Mass: Harvard University Press, 1960)

MAGOUN, F. P., JR, 'Oral-Formulaic Character of Anglo-Saxon Narrative Poetry', *Speculum*, 28 (1953), 446–67

MALONE, K., 'Plurilinear Units in Old English Poetry', *Review of English Studies*, 19 (1943), 201–4

MARCHAND, H., *The Categories and Types of Present-Day English Word-Formation*, 2nd edn (Munich: Beck, 1969)

MCINTOSH, A., et al., *A Linguistic Atlas of Late Mediaeval English* (Oxford: Aberdeen University Press, 1986), 4 vols

MENDENHALL, J. C., *Aureate Terms: A Study in the Literary Diction of the Fifteenth Century* (Lancaster, PA: University of Pennsylvania, 1919)

Middle English Dictionary [MED]

MITCHELL, B., 'The Dangers of Disguise: Old English Texts in Modern Punctuation', *Review of English Studies*, new series, 31 (1980), 385–413

MITCHELL, B., *Old English Syntax* (Oxford: Clarendon, 1985), 2 vols

MITCHELL, B. and ROBINSON, F. C., *A Guide to Old English*, 5th edn (Oxford: Blackwell, 1992)

MUSTANOJA, T. F., *A Middle English Syntax* (Helsinki: Société Néophilologique, 1960)

OAKDEN, J. P., *Alliterative Poetry in Middle English* (Manchester: Manchester University Press, 1930, 1935), 2 vols

Oxford English Dictionary [OED]

PEARSALL, D., *Old English and Middle English Poetry* (London: Routledge & Kegan Paul, 1977)

QUIRK, R., 'Poetic Language and Old English Metre', in *Early English and Norse Studies presented to Hugh Smith*, ed. A. Brown and P. Foote (London: Methuen, 1963), pp. 150–71

QUIRK, R. and GREENBAUM, S., *A University Grammar of English* (London: Longman, 1973)

RANKIN, J. W., 'A Study of the Kennings in Anglo-Saxon Poetry', *Journal of English and Germanic Philology*, 8 (1909), 357–422; 9 (1910), 49–84

RAW, B. C., *The Art and Background of Old English Poetry* (London: Arnold, 1978)

ROBINSON, F. C., 'Some Aspects of the *Maldon* Poet's Artistry', *Journal of English and Germanic Philology*, 75 (1976), 25–40

ROBINSON, F. C., *'Beowulf' and the Appositive Style* (Knoxville: University of Tennessee Press, 1985)

ROBINSON, I., *Chaucer's Prosody* (Cambridge: Cambridge University Press, 1971)

SAUER, H., 'Laȝamon's Compound Nouns and their Morphology', in *Historical Semantics: Historical Word-Formation*, ed. J. Fisiak (Berlin: Mouton, 1985), pp. 483–532

SAUER, H., 'Compounds and Compounding in Early Middle English: Problems, Patterns, Productivity', in *Historical English*, ed. M. Markus (Innsbruck: University of Innsbruck, 1988), pp. 186–209

SCRAGG, D. G., *A History of English Spelling* (Manchester: Manchester University Press, 1974)

SCRAGG, D. G., 'The Nature of Old English Verse', in *The Cambridge Companion to Old English Literature*, ed. M. Godden and M. Lapidge (Cambridge: Cambridge University Press, 1991), pp. 55–70

SERJEANTSON, M., *A History of Foreign Words in English* (London: Kegan Paul, 1935)

SHIPPEY, T. A., *Old English Verse* (London: Hutchinson, 1972)

SHIPPEY, T. A., *Beowulf* (London: Arnold, 1978)

SISAM, K., *Studies in the History of Old English Literature* (Oxford: Clarendon, 1953)

SMITHERS, G. V., 'The Style of *Hauelok*', *Medium Ævum*, 57 (1988), 190–218

SPEARING, A. C. *Criticism and Medieval Poetry*, 2nd edn (London: Arnold, 1972)

STANLEY, E. G., 'Old English Poetic Diction and the Interpretation of *The Wanderer, The Seafarer* and *The Penitent's Prayer*', *Anglia*, 73 (1955), 413–66

STANLEY, E. G., 'Rhymes in English Medieval Verse: From Old English to Middle English', in *Medieval English Studies Presented to George Kane*, ed. E.D. Kennedy et al. (Cambridge: Brewer, 1988), pp. 19–54

SWANTON, M. (trans.), *Anglo-Saxon Prose* (London: Dent, 1975)

TIMMER, B. J. (ed.), *The Later Genesis* (Oxford: Scrivener, 1948)

TURVILLE-PETRE, T., *The Alliterative Revival* (Cambridge: Brewer, 1977)

VENEZKY, R. L. and HEALEY, A. DI P., *A Microfiche Concordance to Old English* (Newark: University of Delaware, 1980)

VISSER, F. T., *An Historical Syntax of the English Language* (Leiden: Brill, 1963–73), 4 vols

VON LINDHEIM, B., 'Traces of Colloquial Speech in Old English', *Anglia*, 70 (1951), 22–42

WHITELOCK, D., *The Audience of 'Beowulf'* (Oxford: Clarendon, 1951)

WRENN, C. L., *A Study of Old English Literature* (London: Harrap, 1967)

WYLD, H. C., 'Diction and Imagery in Anglo-Saxon Poetry', *Essays and Studies*, 11 (1925), 49–91

WYLD, H. C., 'Studies in the Diction of Layamon's *Brut*', *Language*, 6 (1930), 1–24; 9 (1933), 47–71, 171–91; 10 (1934), 149–201; 13 (1937), 29–59

Index

accusative absolute, 139
Actes and Life of Robert Bruce, 42
adjective, absolute use of, 49, 92–3, 152
Ælfric, 36, 37, 42
affixation, 50–1, 89, 91–2, 163
Agincourt, Battle of, 19
alcoholic drinks, 62
Alcuin, 35
Aldhelm, 35
Alexander the Great, 43
Alfred, king, 2, 4–5, 6, 12, 16, 29, 36, 94, 134, 136
alliteration, 30–1, 36, 42, 47–8, 53, 64, 74, 78, 85, 89–90, 93, 102, 107–10, 111, 118, 121, 122, 123, 129, 150, 154, 160, 161, 164, 167; characteristically alliterative words, 102; high alliterative rank, 105
Alliterative Revival, 42, 93, 102–5, 111–12, 122, 127–9
alphabet, 27
analytic syntax, 112
anaphora, 84–5, 162
Ancrene Wisse, 42
Andreas, 76–7, 82, 168
Ane Ballat of Our Lady, 98–9
Anglian, 137, 164
Anglo-Norman, 5, 18, 37–8, 146–7
Anglo-Saxon Chronicle, 5, 16, 18, 36, 37, 41
Anglo-Saxon, meaning of, 2
Anglo-Saxons, origin of, 2, 11
antithesis, 85
apposition, *see* variation
archaeology, 11, 14, 17
Arthour and Merlin, 43
Arthur, king, 43
article, *see* definite article; indefinite article
Arts of Men, 35

assonance, 108–9
asyndetic parataxis, 124–5
Athelstan, king, 15, 33
Athelston, 43
Augustine, Saint, Archbishop of Canterbury, 13
Augustine of Hippo, Saint, 36
aureate terms, 97–9
authorship, 4
Ayenbite of Inwyt, 44

Barbour, John, 42
Bartholomaeus Anglicus, 45
Bartlett, A. C., 73–4
Battle of Brunanburh, 52
Battle of Maldon, 30–1, 50, 52, 69, 73, 75, 82, 108, 139–40
Bede, 11, 14, 33, 35, 36, 132, 133, 134
Bede's *Death Song*, 132, 133, 136
Benedictine reform of the monasteries, 14
Benty Grange, 151
Beowulf, 5, 8, 14, 25, 32–3, 47–9, 51, 52, 54, 57, 58, 60–1, 63, 65–6, 68, 69, 70–1, 72, 75, 76–7, 78, 79, 82, 84, 85, 86, 90, 92, 104, 108, 138, 148–57, 160, 166–7, 168
Bessinger, J. B., 154
Bestiary, 44
Beues of Hamtoun, 119, 127–8
blending, 93
Bliss, A. J., 168
Boethius, 36
Bologna, 23
borrowing, 27, 36–7, 51–2, 163–5; *see also* loan words
Bracher, F., 85
Breton Lays, 43

brevity formula, 162
British Museum, 133
Brodeur, A. G., 71, 167
Brunanburh, 15, 33
Brut (by Laȝamon), 42, 89, 92, 108, 143, 166;
    different versions of, 96–7
Brut (prose), 42
Burgundy, 19
Burnley, J. D., 167

Cædmon, 33–4, 68, 132, 134
Cædmon's *Hymn*, 34, 68, 132, 134
caesura, 30, 31, 64, 112, 113, 160
Cambridge, 23
Cannon, C., 167
Canterbury, 14
Canterbury Tales, 9
capitalisation, 9, 80, 160
Castle of Perseverance, 91
catalogues, 82–5, 156–7, 162, 167
Cawley, A. C., 167
Caxton, William, 4, 41, 43
Celtic, 51; *see also* loan words
Central French dialect, 37
Chancery Standard, 41, 141
Charlemagne, 43
charms, Anglo-Saxon, 13
Chaucer, Geoffrey, 9, 45, 97, 102, 117, 122, 141,
    167, 168
Chaucerians, English, 45; Scottish, 45
Chester mystery plays, 46, 99
chiasmus, 73–4; meaning of, 167
chivalry, 20
Christ, 57, 167
Christ and Satan, 76, 167
Christian missionaries, 27
Christianity, 12–13, 24, 35; conversion to,
    28, 29
Chronicle of Robert of Gloucester, 37, 42, 92, 109
Cicero, 168
circumitio, 168
clause elements, 161
Cloud of Unknowing, 44
Cnut, king, 17
collocation, 64–5, 74–5, 99
colloquialism, 124, 137–8, 145
comic effect, 141
compounding, 50–8, 89–91
compounds, 67, 68, 113, 152–3, 163
concord, 155–6
concordance of Old English poetry, 64–5
Confessio Amantis, 44, 116–17, 120, 122, 123, 146
Consolation of Philosophy, 36

consonance, 109
contentio, 168
conversion, 49–50, 89, 92–3, 163
corpus of Old English verse, 53
correlatives, 80, 155
cosmology, medieval, 24
Cotswolds, 21
courtly love, 106
Coventry mystery plays, 100
Crécy, Battle of, 19
crusades, 20
Cura Pastoralis, 36
Cursor Mundi, 45, 109, 117, 140
Cynewulf, 27, 108

Dame Sirith, 46
Danelaw, 16–17, 40
Daniel, 154
dates of medieval poems, 8, 78
Davis, N., 168
De Clerico et Puella, 7, 46
De Proprietatibus Rerum, 45
definite article, 115–16, 161
Deor's Lament, 34–5, 78–9, 167
Derbyshire, 103, 151
dialect, 6–7, 26, 40, 102, 103, 110, 114, 131,
    132–5, 140–1, 147, 163, 164
Dialogue of Salomon and Saturn, 35
diversite, 147, 168
do as an empty auxiliary, 120–1
Domesday Book, 17–18
doublet style, 99
Douglas, Gavin, 45
drama, 46
Dream of the Rood, 49, 70, 81, 86, 132–3, 134–5,
    155
Dunbar, William, 45, 97–9
Dutch, 147; *see also* loan words

East Anglia, 11, 16, 21
East Saxons, 139
*Ecclesiastical History, see Historia Ecclesiastica
    Gentis Anglorum*
economy, Anglo-Saxon, 14–15; later
    medieval, 21
editing, 8–9
Edward the Confessor, king, 17, 36
Edward III, king, 18, 19
Edward IV, king, 19
Edwin, king, 13
Elene, 76, 82, 167
Elkerlijc, 147
end-stopped lines, 77–8, 79, 112, 125, 167

English Chaucerians, 97–8
enjambement, 77–8; *see also* run-on lines
enumeration, 69
envelope pattern, 73–4
Ethelbert, king, 13, 35
Ethelred, king, 17
ethic dative, 120
etymology, 55
Everyman, 147
exclamatory clauses, 79
Exeter Book, 5, 80, 153
Exodus, 54, 76, 82

Fall of Princes, 116
Fates of Men, 35
Fates of the Apostles, 69, 76, 167
festivals, 20
Fight at Finnsburg, 33
final -*e*, pronunciation of, 114–15, 167
finite verbs in Old English verse, 47–8
Flemish, 93
Floris and Blancheflur, 43
formula, definition of, 75, 76, 168
formulae, 75–7, 85, 108, 113, 127–9, 130, 134,
    138, 154, 162, 168; *see also* brevity formula
Fortunes of Men, 83
Fox and the Wolf, 44, 109, 124
France, 18, 19, 36, 38
Franks Casket, 133
French, 5–6, 37–8, 41, 45; Central dialect of,
    37; Norman dialect of, 37, 164; prestige of,
    39; *see also* Anglo-Norman; loan words

gan as auxiliary, 121
gender, grammatical, 155
Genesis, 63–4, 82, 138, 139, 154
Genesis and Exodus, 99
genitive, 116–17, 161, 166; group genitive, 117
genre, 101, 136
Gifts of Men, 83
Gloucestershire dialect, 103
gnomic *sceal*, 157
Godden, M., 168
Gordon, E. V., 168
Gower, John, 44–5, 90, 91, 115–17, 122, 123,
    146
Gray, D., 167
Great Vowel Shift, 1
Greenbaum, S., 131
Greenfield, S. B., 72
Grimsby, 94
group genitive, 117
gunpowder, 19

Guthlac, 80
Guy of Warwick, 43, 127–8

Hali Meiðhad, 42
Handlyng Synne, 44, 114, 117
hapax legomena, 53–4, 139, 153
hard words, 142; *see also* inkhorn
    controversy
Harley Lyrics, 45
Harold Godwineson, 17
Hastings, Battle of, 17, 36
Havelok, 43, 94–5, 121, 127–9
Henry I, king, 18
Henry II, king, 18
Henry IV, king, 18
Henry V, king, 19
Henry VII, king, 18
Henryson, Robert, 45
Higden, Ranulf, 39, 41
high alliterative rank, 105
Hild, Abbess, 33
Historia Ecclesiastica Gentis Anglorum, 36,
    134
historic present tense, 121–3, 161
History of Paul Orosius, 36
Hoccleve, Thomas, 45, 97, 120
Holofernes, 142
homilies, 44
Hundred Years War, 19
hyperbole, 162
hypotaxis, 80–1, 125–6, 155, 162

I sing of a Maiden, 105–6
indefinite article, 115–16, 161
infinitive, 118, 161
inflexional endings, 38, 40, 41, 112; *see also*
    inflexional levelling
inflexional levelling, 38
inkhorn controversy, 98
interference variety, 132, 139–40, 146–7
interlace, 72–3
Iona, 13
Ireland, 27

James I of Scotland, king, 45
Jarrow, 14
Jespersen, O., 95
Joan of Arc, 19
John, king, 18
Judgment Day, 167
Judith, 48, 78
Julian of Norwich, 44
Juliana, 80–1, 82, 154, 167

Kaske, R. E., 167
Katherine Group, 42, 43
Kempe, Margery, 44
kennings, 55–9, 153
Kent, 11, 13
Kentish, 26, 40, 132
Kentish Hymn, 77
Kentish laws, 136
Kentish Psalm, 132, 139
King Horn, 43, 94–5, 120, 146
kingship, Anglo-Saxon, 15
Klaeber, F., 72, 167
knighthood, *see* chivalry
koiné, 6, 136–7
Kökeritz, H., 167
Kyng Alisaunder, 118

Laȝamon, 42, 89, 143
Lake District, 26
Lancashire, 103
Lancastrian kings, 18
Langland, William, 42, 92, 118
Latin, 5–6, 18, 28, 29, 30, 35, 36, 37, 41, 45, 77,
    108, 132, 133, 139; *see also* Latinate
    vocabulary; loan words
Latinate vocabulary, 142, 143–4; *see also*
    aureate terms
laws, Anglo-Saxon, 15–16, 35, 136; later
    medieval, 23
Leiden Riddle, 132, 133
lexis, 40, 47–66, 88–106, 132, 144, 155, 160–1,
    163–5; meaning of, 2
Leyerle, J., 72–3
Lincoln, 94
Lincolnshire, 26, 164
Lindisfarne, 14
Linguistic Atlas of Late Mediaeval English, 40,
    140
literacy, 6, 7, 12, 27
literary language, 6, 39–40
litotes, 157, 162; *see also* understatement
living conditions, Anglo-Saxon, 14
loan words, Celtic, 51, 169; Dutch, 93–4;
    Flemish, 93; French, 36–7, 41, 51,
    93, 95–7, 98, 99, 100, 100–1, 103, 111,
    163–4, 169; Latin, 41, 52, 93, 97–9, 163–4,
    169; Scandinavian, 26–7, 38, 41, 44,
    51–2, 91, 93, 94–5, 96, 100–1, 103, 139–40,
    163
Lollards, 44
London, 1, 18, 22, 27, 41, 94, 102, 141
Lord, A., 75
Love, Nicholas, 44

Love's Labours Lost, 142
Lydgate, John, 45, 91, 98, 116
lyrics, 45, 90, 99, 101, 105–6

macaronic verse, 99
Magi, 133
Magna Carta, 18
Magoun, F. P., 75–7, 138, 154
Maldon, 33
Malone, K., 167
Malory, Sir Thomas, 43
Mankind, 142–5
Mannyng, Robert, 42, 44, 94
manuscripts, 3–4, 5–6, 7–8, 9, 27, 28, 88, 137,
    150–1, 160, 168; survival of, 5, 30, 40
Mary Magdalene, 46
Maxims, 35, 78, 167
medieval, meaning of, 1–2, 18
Menner, A. J., 167
Mercia, 12, 16
Mercian, 26, 40, 132
metaphor, 62–3
metathesis, 93
metonymy, 55, 60–1, 163
metre, 31–2, 47–8, 51, 53, 122, 154
Metres of Boethius, 77, 113, 139
Michael of Northgate, 44
middle class, 20
Middle English, meaning of, 1
Middlesex, 111
Modern English, meaning of, 1
monasteries, 6, 23, 28, 37
monasticism, 13–14
Monkwearmouth, 14
morality plays, 46, 97
morphology, 38, 40, 50, 132; meaning of,
    2, 67
Morte Arthur, 43
Morte Arthure, 43, 105, 113
Morte Darthur, 43
musical accompaniment to verse,
    32–3
Myrrour of the Blessed Lyf of Jesu Christ, 44
mystery plays, 21, 46, 97, 111; *see also*
    Chester mystery plays; Coventry
    mystery plays; N-Town mystery plays;
    Towneley mystery plays; York mystery
    plays

N-Town mystery plays, 46, 111
negation, 85–6, 119–20, 139, 156; multiple,
    120
nobility, Anglo-Saxon, 15

nominal phrase in Middle English verse, 113; in Old English verse, 47–8, 53, 54, 59; in variation, 68, 71
Norman Conquest, 1, 6, 27, 30, 88–9, 101, 108
Norman French, 37, 164
Norman kings, 18
Normandy, 36; loss of, 18–19, 38
Northumbria, 12, 13, 16, 27, 137
Northumbrian, 26, 40, 132, 133–5
Norwegian, 164
nursery rhymes, 31

Oakden, J. P., 166, 167, 168
Offa, king, 12
Old Danish, 26
Old English, earliest records in, 1
Old English, meaning of, 1
Old French, 146–7
Old Norse, 26, 95, 104, 140, 164
Old Saxon, 139, 168
oral tradition, 29, 80, 104–5, 110, 112, 130, 138
oral-formulae, *see* formulae
oral-formulaic theory, 166
Orm, 44, 92, 94, 95
Ormulum, 44, 94, 95, 117
Orosius, Paul, 36
orthography, 9, 40, 88–9, 132, 154, 160
Owl and the Nightingale, 42, 109, 120
Oxford, 23

paganism, 12–13, 17, 27, 35
pageants, 97
parataxis, 71, 79–81, 124–5, 155; definition of, 79; asyndetic, 79, 124–5, 162; syndetic, 79, 124–5
parenthesis, 81–2
Paris, 23
Paris Psalter, 77, 139
Parlement of the Thre Ages, 42, 112
parliament, 18
paronomasia, 63–4
Parry, M., 75
Paston family, 22
Patience, 43, 90–1, 113
pattern-welding, 60–1
Peak District, 103, 151
Pearl, 42, 91, 100–1, 102, 124
Pearsall, D., 130
peasantry, Anglo-Saxon, 15
Peasants' Revolt, 22
Pecock, Reginald, 41
perfective aspect, 123
periodic sentence, 126

personal pronouns as markers of attitude, 145–6
Peterborough Abbey, 41
Peterborough Chronicle, 94; *see also Anglo-Saxon Chronicle*
Phoenix, 77, 139
phonological change, 7
phonology, 40, 41, 88–9, 132, 167; meaning of, 2
Piers Plowman, 8, 25, 42, 92, 93, 113, 118, 146
place names, 11, 13, 26, 16–17
plague, 21–2
Plantagenet kings, 18
pleonastic expressions, 84, 119, 120
plurilinear units of syntax, 78; *see also* run-on lines
Polychronicon, 39, 41
prepositional phrases, 117–18, 128
prepositions, 161
Pricke of Conscience, 43–4
primogeniture, 20
printing, 1, 3
prosody, 30–3, 107–10, 160
Proverbs, 35
Proverbs of Alfred, 93–4
public duty, Anglo-Saxon, 16
publication, 3–4
punctuation, 9, 80–1, 125, 132, 155, 160, 166
puns, 63–4
Purity, 43, 113

Quirk, R., 131

Reeve's Tale, 141
reflexive pronouns, 120
Reformation, 5
Regement of Princes, 120
regional variety, *see* dialect
register, 54, 100, 101–2, 106, 131, 136, 137, 144,
religious orders, 6
religious prose, 6
repetitio, 168; *see also* anaphora
repetition, 84
Resignation, 58
rhetoric, 78, 80, 82–7, 98, 125, 130, 156, 162, 167
Rhetorica ad Herennium, 168
rhyme, 7, 8, 30, 42, 74, 102, 107–10, 111, 114, 117, 118, 121, 122, 143
Rhyming Chronicle, 42, 94
rhythm, 113
Richard Coer de Lyon, 43
Richard I, king, 18, 20, 43
Richard II, king, 18

Riddles, 9, 80, 133, 137–8, 155
Riming Poem, 86, 107
Robert of Gloucester, 92, 109
Robinson, F.C., 71, 139–40, 167
Robinson, I., 167
Rolle, Richard, 43
Roman Catholic Church, 22–3
romance, 19, 43, 109, 143, 167, 169
Romans, 2
rounding, 7
Ruin, 151
run-on lines, 78, 167
runes, 27
Runic Poem, 35, 57
Ruthwell Cross, 133, 134–5

saga tradition, 35
Saint Juliana, 42
Saint Katherine, 42
Saint Margaret, 42
Saint Paul, 46
Sawles Warde, 42
Scale of Perfection, 44
Scandinavian attacks, 36
Scandinavian languages, 26–7, 38, 41; *see also* loan words
Scandinavian settlement, 26–7, 38, 40, 41, 94
schools, 28–9, 39
Scottish Chaucerians, 97–8
Scottish dialect, 40, 45
scribes, 4, 6–7, 27, 40, 88–9, 137, 150–1
scriptoria, 4
Seafarer, 34–5, 49–50, 84–5, 151
semantics, 47, 50, 57, 71, 74, 105–6, 151–2, 153, 155, 164–5, 169; meaning of, 2
serfs, 15, 20
sermons, 44
Seven Cardinal Virtues, 24
Seven Deadly Sins, 24
Shakespeare, 142
Shippey, T.A., 62, 166, 167
Sievers, Eduard, 47; his 'five types', 31–2, 154
simplices, 52–3, 54, 55, 68, 152–3
singing, 32
Sir Gawain and the Green Knight, 25, 42, 43, 91, 92, 101, 103, 104, 105, 112, 113, 118, 121, 126, 130, 146, 157–63, 167
Sir Launfal, 109
Sir Orfeo, 7–8, 43, 110–11, 115, 117, 118, 119, 120, 121, 125–6, 146–7
Sir Perceval of Gales, 123

Sir Tryamowre, 122, 123
Sisam, K., 168
skalds, 56
society, Anglo-Saxon, 15
Soliloquies of St Augustine, 36
Song of Lewes, 109
songs, 45
Spearing, A. C., 127
Speculum Vitae, 39
spelling, *see* orthography
Staffordshire, 103
Standard English, 6, 27, 94, 104, 131, 133, 141; educated standard, 141–2; local standards, 41; *see also* Chancery Standard
standard language, concept of, 1, 6
Stanley, E.G., 58, 167
Statute of Labourers, 22
Stephen, king, 18
Stevens, M., 167
stress, 64, 164–5
Sturluson, Snorri, 56
Sulpitius Victor, 98
Sutton Hoo, 11–12, 13, 33, 58, 151–2
Swein, king, 17
swords, 60–1
syncopation, 137
syndetic parataxis, 124–5
synechdoche, 55, 60–1
synonyms, 53, 55, 68, 152, 163
syntax, 67–87, 107–30, 132, 160–2; French, 162; meaning of, 2, 67

tags, 112, 129–30, 161
tail-rhyme, 143
tail-rhyme stanza, 109
Testament of Love, 98
Thebes, 43
Thomas Becket, 18
Timmer, B. J., 168
titles, 8
Tolkien, J. R. R., 168
tournaments, 19–20
Towneley mystery plays, 46, 100, 109–10, 141, 145
traditional customs, 20
translation, 5, 6, 29, 36, 44, 45, 77, 139, 140, 146–7
Travels of Sir John Mandeville, 45
Trevisa, John, 39, 41, 45, 140
Troilus and Criseyde, 117
Troy, 43
Turville-Petre, T., 103, 167, 168

unassimilated loan words, 99
understatement, 85–7, 157, 162
universities, 23
Usk, Thomas, 98

variation, 67–74, 124, 156, 162, 166–7
varieties, linguistic, 131–47; Old English,
    131–40; Middle English, 140–7;
    according to attitude, 132, 138–9, 145–6;
    according to education and social
    standing, 131, 135–6, 141–3; according to
    medium, 132, 137–8, 144–5; according to
    subject matter, 131, 136–7, 143–4;
    meaning of, 147; *see also* dialect;
    interference variety; register
variety classes, 131–2
verbal phrase in Old English verse, 59–60;
    in variation, 68; syntax of, 118
Vercelli Book, 135
Vespasian Psalter, 132
Vikings, 12, 16, 69, 139

Wakefield Master, 109–10, 145
Wakefield mystery plays, *see* Towneley
    mystery plays
Waldere, 30, 34–5
Wanderer, 78, 82–5, 151
Wars of Alexander, 102
Wars of the Roses, 18, 22
Warwickshire dialect, 103

Wat Tyler, 22
Wayland, 63, 133
wergild, 16
Wessex, 6, 137
West Saxon, 6, 12, 26, 27, 40, 55, 88, 132, 133–
    6, 137
Westminster, 4, 18
Whitby, Synod of, 13
Whitelock, D., 10
Widsith, 78
William I, king, 17, 20, 36
William, Duke of Normandy, *see* William I,
    king
William of Nassington, 39
Wiltshire, 151
Winchester, 14, 18
word-formation, 89–93; *see also* affixation;
    blending; compounding; conversion
wordplay, 144; *see also* paronomasia
world view, medieval, 23–5
Wulf and Eadwacer, 138
Wulfstan, 36
Wyclif, John, 41, 44
Wynnere and Wastoure, 42, 102

y- prefix on verbs, 115
Yeavering, 13
York mystery plays, 46, 144
Yorkist kings, 18
Yorkshire Wolds, 151